THE GenX READER

Douglas Rushkoff

Ballantine Books • New York

All rights reserved under International and Pan-American
Copyright Conventions. Published in the United States by
Ballantine Books, a division of Random House, Inc., New
York, and simultaneously in Canada by Random House of
Canada Limited, Toronto.

Owing to limitations of space, permissions
acknowledgments appear on pages 305 and 306.

Library of Congress Catalog Card Number: 94-94109

ISBN: 0-345-39046-6

Cover design by Richard Hasselberger
Text design by Alex Jay/Studio J

Manufactured in the United States of America

First Edition: May 1994

10 9 8 7 6 5 4 3

For my baby,
Tricia.

CONTENTS

Introduction

Us, by Us

Generation X means a lot of things to a lot of people. We are a culture, a demographic, an outlook, a style, an economy, a scene, a political ideology, an aesthetic, an age, a decade, and a literature.

To some, belonging to GenX is a cop-out. To us, it is a declaration of independence. We exist.

As it is most commonly understood today, Generation X refers to what can be called a "lost" segment of America's youth too young to remember the assassination of President Kennedy and too old to have missed the end of disco. Having watched our immediate elders transform from hippies to Yuppies to New Agers to landowners, we get the feeling we are living in the wake of the postwar baby boom and bearing the economic and cultural burden of a society run on financial credit and social debit. Following the massive "boomer" population, a huge lump in the snake's digestive tract called American history, we, the self-named baby "busters" have learned to call this intestinal vacuum home.

We did not ask to be encumbered with this legacy, but we have chosen to make the best of it. Although sociologists may have cast us as the despondent "thirteenth" generation—the hopeless mutant children of a society temporarily gone awry—we sure as hell are going to enjoy what's left of the cultural playground before our unemployment checks, parents' support, or McJobs give out. But our willingness to accept our inheritance—to enjoy the wasteland bequeathed to us—has brought the members of Generation X under the critical scrutiny of those who created and now, ironically, reject us.

Most people from outside Generation X condemn the twentysomethings as illiterate, unmotivated, and apathetic couch potatoes: We appear, apparently, to have no career goals, no cultural pride, no political ideology, no family values, and no discernible ambitions. Even this nation's educators gave up on Generation X and simply waited for our age group to pass through the public school system so that they could concentrate instead on training the minds of younger, more traditionally oriented pupils. Meanwhile, boomers heading for retirement fear that their Social Security benefits will depend on the likes of us: the kids who live off the mall, McDonalds, and MTV.

Until now, Generation X has been explained to the public by the people who fear and detest us most. Unable to see through the guise of apathy and anger worn by twentysomethings and unable to understand what's beneath it if they could, the many chroniclers of Generation X have reduced us to, at best, a market segment and, at worst, the downfall of the Western world. They have called us everything from "whiners" (*Newsweek*, Nov. 1993) to "a bad generation" (*Atlantic*, Dec. 1992). But we, the members of Generation X, reject this categorization, and our own writings tell a story very different from those of our elders. A story that hasn't been told before. A story that deserves telling.

Here is a collection of some of Generation X's most revered voices. It is a reader which demonstrates—in the words of GenX members—that while twentysomethings may indeed have dropped out of American culture as traditionally defined, we also stand as a testament to American ingenuity, optimism, instinct, and brilliance.

Faced with a culture and media in which personalities, images, and ideologies were formulated solely to sell products, politicians, and lifestyles, kids growing up in the 1970s learned to appreciate this landscape of iconography as a postmodern playground. The cultural icons with which we resonate are not Quaker Oats, the Lincoln Memorial, or Spencer Tracy but Pop Tarts, Lincoln Logs, and Pee Wee Herman. GenXers, organically speaking, are as smart as or smarter than any generation that went before us. It is only our set of associations and, more important, the degree to which these associations are framed in irony that set our crowd apart. (Remember, most of Andy Warhol's soup cans were painted before we were alive. To us, that stuff is classical.)

For GenX is the nightmare of a postindustrial, postmodern age. We are a marketing experiment gone out of control. Like any youngsters, we learned the language we were taught when we were kids. It just happens that this is the language of advertising.

Exposed to consumerism and public relations strategies since we could open our eyes, we GenXers see through the clunky attempts to manipulate our opinions and assets, however shrinking. When we watch commercials, we ignore the products and instead deconstruct the marketing techniques. This is what we love about TV. We have learned that "content" means lies, and that in context lies brilliance.

This is because we were born into a world where symbols meant more than reality and where the lifestyles of families on the tube were presented as attainable goals. This world of images painfully contradicted the downwardly mobile divorcescape of 1970s and 1980s America. We had a choice: adopt a set of unrealistic, essentially impossible goals and fail miserably or opt out of the consumer culture altogether.

As the Who advised us on our older siblings' hand-me-down 1970s vinyl, we vow we "Won't Get Fooled Again." Our apparent and oft-condemned apathy is actually a carefully modulated distancing from the cues and signals of the boomers' consumer culture—an appraiser's sideways glance at the efforts of our elders to capture what's left of our hearts, minds, and wallets.

GenXers live in a world we feel is geared to people ten to thirty years older than ourselves. We watched as baby boomers went to college, got great jobs, crashed the economy, and left nothing but McJobs—low-wage menial employment or "temping"—for their vastly overqualified little brothers and sisters. We watched rock 'n' roll take over the nation and then dry up like Mick Jagger before we got to college. We watched a generation drop acid and turn on, only to find an atmosphere of "just say no" and mandatory prison sentences by the time we were old enough to care for a buzz now and again. We watched a sexual revolution evolve into forced celibacy as the many excesses of the 1970s and 1980s rotted into the sexually transmitted diseases of our 1990s.

But contrary to popular opinion, GenX refuses to mourn. We are not complaining, get it? Instead, we celebrate the recycled imagery of our media and take pride in our keen appreciation of the folds within the creases of our wrinkled popular culture. Accepting unemployment—or underemployment—as a way of life, GenX college grads settle for temp jobs to pay the rent or move back in with Mom and Dad, then spend our real time making community access shows and countercultural 'zines or just hanging out at the comics store talking about them. Better yet, we read articles by social theorists and marketing analysts trying to understand our intangible but fascinating segment of society. And we laugh.

Because, most of all, GenX is a life philosophy designed to help us cope with the increasingly and disorientingly rapid deflation of our society, both financially and culturally. It is based on a commitment to reject the traditional values and linear reasoning of the dominant culture and instead embrace the postmodern swirl of a Wayne's World Lost in Space, both Dazed and Confused. It is a conscious effort to avoid engaging in anything that requires descent into the rat race or consumerist angst, a neo-Buddhism where attachments of any kind break the awareness so valuable to surfers of a consumer culture. It is an ability to derive meaning from the random juxtaposition of TV commercials, candy wrappers, childhood memories, and breakfast treats. It is a willingness to deconstruct and delight in the Toys "Я" Us wasteland of cultural junk while warding off the meaningless distractions of two-party politics, falling interest rates, and phantom career opportunities.

We are neither ungrateful for the world into which we have been born, nor unthankful for the hard-won battles of our predecessors. To most of us, concepts like racial equality, women's rights, sexual freedom, and respect for basic humanity are givens. We realize that we are the first generation to enter a society where, at least on paper and in the classroom, the ideas that Boomers fought for are recoginized as indisputable facts. Without the Civil Rights, Environmental, and Women's movements, there would be no GenX now.

But consider, for a moment, what it would have been like to grow up this way: we are the first generation for whom rock and roll is not a rebellion. We did not have to fight in Vietnam. We did not have to fight against religious institutions, dress codes, or even the so-called patriarchy. The Boomers envisioned a life unfettered by the constraints of traditional morality and meaningless lineage. That we can take all this for granted is a testament to their success. Thanks, okay? But it is impossible and pointless for us to remain in idle appreciation of these political and cultural strides, and we aim instead to push the envelope a bit further ourselves. And sometimes that means taking a very different tack.

Herein lies perhaps the greatest but most elusive difference between

Busters and Boomers. To us, it appears that Boomers still operate out of a sense of guilt and obligation. Unable to trust their own inner natures, Boomers appear to take comfort in systems of thought—"isms" ranging from Freudianism and Marxism to Relativism and even New Age-ism. Any action or thought must be tested against some absolutist template. Boomers need to feel they are working to promote a positive system or to dismantle a negative one. They constantly evaluate their beliefs against the authority figures they either admire or detest. They live either in defiance toward their enemies—whom they perceive as in control—or in obligation to those they see as less fortunate, less powerful, and thus more worthy than themselves. Movies like *The Big Chill*, *Grand Canyon*, *Broadcast News*, and TV shows like *thirtysomething* accurately depict the painstakingly self-searching Boomer preoccupation with the moral correctness of every employment opportunity, human relationship, spoken statement, and product purchase.

Busters understand and appreciate this inclination for paralyzing moral self-examination, but we do not engage in it. Born into a society where traditional templates have proven themselves quaint at best, and mass-murderous at worst, Busters feel liberated from the constraints of ethical systems, but also somewhat cast adrift. It must be nice to have something external to believe in. Something that doesn't move. Something absolute. Having no such permanent icon (no God, no Country, no Superhero) we choose instead—by default, actually—to experience life as play, and trust that the closer we come to our own true intentions, the closer we will come to our own *best* intentions. We fight social injustice head-on—make no mistake about that—but these battles look different because we no longer fight for "causes." We don't need causes to rally behind. The real issuses—ones that "agendas" only mask—are quite plain to us already. Most Busters wouldn't even consider this a conscious moral strategy; the whole notion of morality is, in the best sense of the phrase, taken for granted. Or, in Buster terminology: whatever.

The flippancy with which we regard the very spine of the Boomer movement has, unfortunately, provoked outsiders to attack us, or, at the very least, to remain wary. Our general apathy, coupled with our occasional "us versus them" defiance toward our elders (we're not *perfect*), keeps our world of recycled, self-referential imagery and post-moral understanding out of the reach of anyone but children.

The following samples of GenX lit are characterized by more than the age group from which they were extracted (and at bargain basement prices, we assure you). They show tremendous insight into the root causes of our current state of affairs. They prove GenX's willingness to accept the inevitable aspects of our reality without the cushioning platitudes or political correctness of our boomer predecessors. What everyone else calls our nihilism, these texts reveal as an unprecedented moral and intellectual courage to confront issues rather than cower before them. Our writers are our cultural playmakers and demonstrate an almost Beckettian ability to find humor in the darkest despair, a Brechtian objectivity to bracket painful drama with ironic distance, and a Chekhovian instinct to find the human soul still lurking beneath its outmoded cultural facade.

It's easy to judge the following selections as angry, pessimistic, and dark. They are not. Even though the characters in our stories are often driven to insanity, they maintain a sense of humor and self-respect about their own sad plights. Even though our essays make harsh appraisals of the current political and cultural regime, we see the ways in which it can be corrected through grass roots cultural hacking. Even though we admit ignorance about the workings of much of the dominant generation's power brokering and cash harvesting, we see our increasing apathy as a strength and make a conscious effort to teach our compatriots how to remain liberated from the mind-numbing Muzak-intoned hypnotic demagoguery perpetrated so successfully on everybody else. You have been trained—entrained, actually—your whole lives to see our clarity of vision as malicious subversion and our ironic distance as cultural poison. Maybe this anthology will change your mind.

Whether you like it or not, we are the thing that will replace you.

CHAPTER 1

HERE WE ARE

Here We Are

"What is the sound of one hand clapping?" poses Lisa Simpson to her brother, Bart, in a Zen koan she hopes will bring him the inner peace he needs to prepare for a miniature golf tournament. Bart flaps the fingers of one hand against the same palm, making a soft thwacking sound. "That's an easy one!" he answers.

No, this isn't the Tao of Bart.

GenX existed the moment it announced itself, in its own voice, to itself. Nirvana's "Smells Like Teen Spirit" said it with greater volume than a single hand clapping: "Here we are, now," exclaimed the grunge band. Apparently others agreed and put not only the band but the city of Seattle on the map of the cultural Zeitgeist.

The first references to GenX were self-references. A generation saw itself in the mirror for the first time and realized that its own reflection was unique. What characterized its uniqueness—and this is where even Zen falls short—is this very quality of self-reflexiveness.

One way to define GenX is as a framing device: GenX is merely a kind of self-conscious irony, the ability to step back from direct experience and watch oneself experiencing life. The moment GenX began was the moment when the first buster "bracketed" his own experience, the minute someone stepped back and, in a wink-wink-say-no-more fashion, related the ironic distance he felt from his own existence.

This chapter contains the seminal works of Generation X self-consciousness from the moment in literary, journalistics and film history when the first Busters said, "Look at me looking at me!"

Douglas Coupland

Interview in

Elle Magazine

While Douglas Coupland did not invent the term "Generation X" (it was the name of a 1980s punkish Billy Idol band), his now-famous novel was the first to use it as a way of categorizing the post-boomer milieu. Coupland had no idea his book would become the definitive volume for a generation. It was meant as fiction, after all.

Today, it is hard to tell whether Coupland is the greatest beneficiary or saddest casualty of the GenX phenomenon. Boomer media attempts to classify him as Buster first, and a writer second. Anyone who has read Coupland's work knows that his insights transcend generational boundaries. Still, what makes this recent interview by Elle's Kim France so fascinating are the verbal techniques Coupland employs to resist being pigeonholed: his responses are frought with ironic distance, bemused self-consiousness, and suspicion towards the mainstream media.

Douglas Coupland, created a monster, and its name is Generation X. Simply utter the catch-phrase popularized by his book of the same title and the thirty-two-year-old author will flinch, as though it physically pains him to think about it. "A kid from Chicago wanted my permission to print up Generation X T-shirts," he says, "and I told him there is nothing less Generation X than a Generation X T-shirt. I get a lot of offers to speak to liquor distillers, or whatever, for ridiculous amounts of money. It's just so horrible. That's not why I do this. Maybe in a few years, when I'm broke and derelict, I'll regret not having done it. But I just can't."

Though it can be tiresome to hear people bemoan the means by which

11

they became famous, Coupland's angst has a ring of sincerity. After all, *Generation X: Tales for an Accelerated Culture* was being sold as a cult novel of twentysomething despair and ennui before it went on to actually become just that. The timing was a marketing executive's dream: Just as the sun set on the media's decade-long fascination with baby boomers, Coupland came along to provide a breezy, ironic examination of a generation that grew up with *The Brady Bunch* reruns, Watergate, and downward mobility. The book was originally supposed to be a sort of *Preppy Handbook* for twentysomethings but turned into a novel when Coupland decided he couldn't write such a thing. Still, it was full of pithy expressions, like "McJob," that caught on in a way that might seem predictable to some but took Coupland, a former art student who had never planned to be a writer, totally by surprise. He was broke and living in Montreal at the time, he says, with little access to the English-language press, and had no idea how conveniently his book had dovetailed with the emergence of a new and potentially lucrative demographic in the States.

Since then, he's had an odd ascent, agreeing to precious few interviews on the topic of his generation but becoming a mouthpiece for it nonetheless. "I can understand why he bristles at being seen as a symbol," says Jacob Weisberg, one of Coupland's editors at *The New Republic*, where he writes occasional humor pieces. "No writer aspires to speak for a generation; they aspire to write good books." Others are less sympathetic. "Doug tries to say, 'I'm not a spokesperson,'" says Jason Cohen, who, with Michael Krugman, has written the parody *Generation Ecch!* "But he's allowed himself to become one, which keeps him from being taken seriously as an artist."

It's revealing that Coupland and the authors of *Generation Ecch!* share a publishing house (Simon & Schuster), because there's easily as much money to be made bashing Coupland as there is promoting him. For every twentysomething who enthusiastically shares his vision, there is one who dismisses him as a poser who has profited by perpetuating a generation's self-loathing. It doesn't help him that in photos a certain smugness comes across, as though Coupland can't quite get over just how devastatingly clever he is. Or that his editor is Judith Regan, known less for quiet literary successes than highly accessible best-sellers by Rush Limbaugh and Howard Stern.

Nobody is more painfully aware of this image problem than Coupland himself, and his solution has been to become deeply worrisome and a bit controlling when it comes to publicity. Though he's got a new book, *Life After God*, to promote, it takes several prolonged phone calls to get him to agree to an interview at all. First off, he won't talk to anyone who hasn't read all three of his books. Furthermore, he only agrees to a photo shoot after wresting control of every aspect of it, right down to choosing the flower he's holding in his hand.

Having said all of this, it seems worth noting that in person Coupland comes off as charming and genuine. "Why don't you come up to my room? You must be exhausted after being in public spaces all day," he offers when I call from the lobby of his midtown Manhattan hotel. It's not a come-on: He's used to the relatively slower pace of Vancouver, where he lives, and simply can't imagine anyone functioning for eight hours straight in New York's relentless maelstrom. Upstairs, Coupland is staring out the window at the sun setting on the Chrysler Building. Though it's late afternoon, the day is just starting for him. He stays up late most nights reading, sleeps until noon, and has the perpetually groggy demeanor of someone who's not quite on the rest of the world's schedule. He says he chose this particular hotel because he heard it had fifty-two floors, and he knew if he stayed at or near the top, it would be very quiet.

Quiet is such an important commodity to Coupland, in fact, that he expresses alarm when he learns that I read the last twenty pages of *Life After God* in a noisy coffee shop. The book—Coupland's attempt to leave the irony and cynicism of his earlier work behind—is a compilation of very short stories that detail characters who are trying to get some spirituality back into their lives. "It's too easy to be flip. It's too easy to be ironic," he says. "It's really enormous fun to sit around and riff about, you know, the Van Patten family or Kristy McNichol's career ups and downs, but there's nothing really nutritious or substantive about it."

Nonetheless, Coupland has fed on popular culture his entire life. "I remember seeing the *World Book Encyclopedia* in third grade," he says, "looking under 'P' for 'Pop Art,' and seeing the Warhol Marilyns, the Lichtenstein *Whaam!*, and it was like, *boom*, that's it. And to find out that was actually a real sensibility, that you could actually think of yourself as being pop . . . I immediately latched on to it." Since then, he says, he's realized that "a lot of it is detestable and silly and dumb. But at least it allows me to be able to communicate with relative ease to someone who grew up thousands of miles away. It's a common bank of experience."

Coupland's gift—and, as it sometimes strikes him, his curse—is the ability to tap into this common bank and distill it into bite-size, digestible morsels. Last summer, for instance, he invented a glossary of words inspired by information-age politics for the Op-Ed page of *The New York Times* ("nanotune" is "a brief zap over to MTV during a televised political debate"; "flag bait" is "a voter easily swayed by patriotic imagery"). He continues to write these wordplay-driven pieces for the *Times* and *The New Republic*— "They've become sort of the official outlet for that part of my brain," he says. And despite his efforts to drop the irony, the agility with which he riffs on popular culture makes it difficult for him to stop. "It makes you sort of like those doors at the beginning of *Get Smart* that open sideways and upside down, and there are just more doors to the core inside of you. You tend to buffer yourself more and protect what you know in yourself because you know how easily it can be trivialized or *Hard Copy*'d," he says. Adds Jacob Weisberg: "Doug is a very good phrasemaker, and these concepts of his catch on. In fact, they catch on to the extent that they become overworked clichés within a few months."

Like Andy Warhol, one of his idols, Coupland has a childlike fascination with the world. He stares in store windows for so long he has to be dragged away. He calls friends from airplanes just to say hi. And, most Warholian of all, he appears to enjoy the access to celebrity that his celebrity has afforded him. His "virtual community"—Coupland's nickname for the group of friends he keeps up with via phone, plane, and fax, sounds like a *Who's Who* of babybust movers and shakers. He wrote the introduction for the book version of director Richard Linklater's first feature, *Slacker*, and recently attended a party at Joel Schumacher's house, where he spent the entire evening bonding with director Quentin Tarantino over bad '70s TV trivia. He and REM lead singer Michael Stipe have become such close friends (though Coupland is quick to point out that "it's not like we're on each other's speed dials, or anything") that a section of *Life After God* is dedicated to Stipe. "Because REM was one of the few things that didn't suck about the '80s," he explains.

And for all his grousing about being in the public eye, he did agree to star in a number of short spots on MTV in conjunction with the publication of *Life After God*. "I'm creating and giving vent to different personas, or sort of sub-Dougs that live inside of me," he says, adding that because he doesn't have cable, he'll never see the spots and is confident that they won't turn him into any more of a public figure than he already is. "It's sort of like Mel Gibson doing toothpaste commercials in Japan," he says.

Coupland's friends insist the MTV thing has nothing to do with advancing his fame. "Doug is an incredibly creative guy," Weisberg explains. "He is overflowing with creativity in 300 directions, and he will seize any opportunity to try something new, whether it's painting or movies, film or writing." His good friend Jane Pratt, editor-in-chief of *Sassy* magazine, agrees. "He has the energy level of a twelve-year-old boy," she says, "and he's constantly looking for outlets. I don't think he even realizes before he does these things how people will perceive them."

And clearly, Coupland wasn't thinking about his role as mantle bearer of the jaded when he wrote *Life After God*. At the time, he was in a deep depression that came on the heels of mediocre reviews for his second novel, *Shampoo Planet*. Coupland found himself in the unfortunate position of agreeing with his critics. "I guess it was just too much of a contrivance," he explains. "Or there wasn't enough . . . honesty in it. You do a book and it's like a protracted trance you're in, and of course you can't see the forest for the trees. And I think a lot of reviewers picked up on that." Like *Generation X, Shampoo Planet* dripped with ironic references to fast-food culture; Coupland says that when he sat down to write his third novel, "it was somehow going along that same old road—all the razzle-dazzle. And finally I just threw it out."

The book he found himself writing instead, he says, "was an exercise in reduction, in just trying to get rid of the pyrotechnics." He found himself drawn to the concept that his was the first generation raised without religion. "If you are raised without any concept of an afterlife," he says, "what does your picture [of life] become? How could I have gone so far without asking such an obvious question?"

Life After God is the story of a young man named Scout (for all practical purposes, Coupland) who is beginning to ask these questions. Along the way, he encounters countless others who've numbed themselves—via drugs, stupid jobs, empty sex—and are searching, awkwardly, for meaning. Scout and his friends are also dealing with leaving their twenties at a point in time when the blueprint for thirty—kids, a house, stability—has been discarded but nothing really workable has appeared in its place.

Coupland tells these stories in a series of fablelike vignettes. In one of the more poignant stories, an old friend tells Scout, "I'm trying to escape from ironic hell: Cynicism into faith; randomness into clarity; worry into devotion. But it's hard because I try to be sincere about life, and then I turn on the TV and see a game show host and have to throw up my hands and give up. Too many easy pickin's! Clarity would be so much easier if there weren't so many cheesy celebrities around." At one point, Scout concludes: "I think there was a trade-off somewhere along the line. I think the price we paid for our golden life was an inability to fully believe in love; instead, we gained an irony that scorched everything it touched. And I wonder if this irony is the price we paid for the loss of God."

At moments like these, when *Life After God* hits the mark between irony and sentimentality, it works beautifully. But certain passages in which Coupland urges the reader to get in touch with nature and learn from the animals are so sincere they border on corniness. "Don't you think it comes off really hokey?" asks Jason Cohen. "Like, since this is a generation without spirituality, Doug's little fables will help us get in touch with our spiritual side. It's like a modern-day version of *The Prophet*." This is a harsh, but not necessarily inaccurate, criticism. At times, *Life After God* reads like '70s feel-good bestseller *Jonathan Livingston Seagull*, or any number of L. Ron Hubbard books. Then there's the self-important sound of the title. Even people predisposed to like Coupland and his work worry that he's setting himself up for the most savage critical response yet.

Coupland is aware of what a vulnerable position he's put himself in—"I hope it's not embarrassingly sincere," he says of the book—but he's trying not to care what people think. "I'm vulnerable. So what?" he says. "I've decided, So be it. I was invulnerable for so long, and it got me to a certain point, and then I realized something had to change." And ultimately, after the condescending reviews and professional snipes, what matters is that Coupland is—at the very least and perhaps not totally successfully—trying to provide hope for a generation that never had any to lose.

Shampoo Planet

Douglas Coupland

In decades to come, it will be interesting to find out which will be regarded as Douglas Coupland's most significant cultural contribution: the fact that he heralded Generation X, or that he wrote a body of literature. Most Busters would guess the latter.

Coupland has taken a stylistic leap forward for ("American") literature. Though, on the surface, only subtly different from standard, first-person narrative, his writing style is the first to evoke such deep emotional resonance using a landscape devoid of traditionally archetypal imagery. No lighthouses, Oxford's or eighth-generational lineages here. Just the stuff of real life in the 1990s and the courage to share it, moment by moment, as it is experienced on the inside.

This excerpt, from Coupland's second novel, Shampoo Planet, reveals some of the author's own visions for the future of the human tribe—the world as it unfolds beneath his tires on the highway or his pen on the writing tablet.

We are yet again prisoners of the Lariat Motor Lodge, Mount Shasta, California—the Comfortmobile won't be discharged from the clinic until 5:30. Stephanie and I are allowed to keep our motel room until 5:00 and we are both sen*sat*ionally bored—so bored we feel stoned, like we've drunk a bottle of cough syrup each. Travel restlessness fills us; we want to *move*.

Stephanie's juggling lace hankies and firing her cap gun at the ceiling. Lunch kills 3,600 seconds. I post last night's letter to Frank E. Miller in Seattle, addressed to "Biff" Miller, his college nickname, thus boosting the letter's chances of being read by Frank E. Miller himself.

On the way back from the post office, I stop at a Bank of America ATM and withdraw from my rapidly disappearing savings. I then convert my withdrawal into a wad of low-denomination bills. I feel like a crack dealer. I have an idea.

YOUR INABILITY TO ACHIEVE SOLITUDE MAKES YOU
SETTLE FOR SUBSTANDARD RELATIONSHIPS

YOU DON'T BELIEVE MAGIC IS POSSIBLE
IN LIVES LIVED WITHIN TRADITIONAL BOUNDARIES

I am writing a list of tragic character flaws on my dollar bills with a felt pen. I am thinking of the people in my universe and distilling for each of these people the *one* flaw in their character that will lead to their downfall— the flaw that will be their undoing.

Jasmine, Anna-Louise, Daisy, Mark, Dan, Stephanie, Monique, Kiwi, Harmony, Skye, Gaïa, Mei-Lin, Davidson, Pony, Grandma and Grandpa, Eddie Woodman, Jim and Lorraine Jarvis—everybody's here. Even me. And more.

What I write are not sins; I write *tragedies*. And I am writing these tragedies in a manner that the recipients can easily absorb. And I won't say whose flaw is whose. I continue. In no particular order:

YOU DISGUISE YOUR LAZINESS AS PRIDE

YOU ARE PARALYZED BY THE FACT
THAT CRUELTY IS OFTEN AMUSING

YOU PRETEND TO BE MORE ECCENTRIC
THAN YOU ACTUALLY ARE BECAUSE YOU
WORRY YOU ARE AN INTERCHANGEABLE COG

YOU MISTAKE MOTION FOR GROWTH
AND ARE LURED INTO VEXING SITUATIONS

YOU DEFEND OTHER PEOPLE'S IDEAS
AT THE EXPENSE OF YOUR OWN

YOU STILL DON'T KNOW WHAT YOU DO WELL

YOU ARE UNABLE TO VISUALIZE
YOURSELF IN A FUTURE

YOUR INABILITY TO SUSTAIN SEXUAL INTEREST
IN JUST ONE OTHER PERSON DRAINS YOUR
LIFE OF THE POSSIBILITY OF INTIMACY

YOUR OWN ABILITY TO RATIONALIZE YOUR BAD DEEDS
MAKES YOU BELIEVE THE ENTIRE UNIVERSE
IS AS AMORAL AS YOURSELF

YOU WILLFULLY IGNORE THE SMALL, GENTLE
OBSERVATIONS IN LIFE WHICH YOU KNOW
ARE THE MOST IMPORTANT

Stephanie is mutilating cash, too, garnishing my mottoes with messy red lipstick kisses as we bring into the foreground the secret language of money—biting the invisible hand that feeds us.

YOUR FEAR OF CHANGE IS TOO
CLEARLY VISIBLE IN YOUR EYES

YOU ARE WASTING YOUR YOUTH,
YOUR TIME, AND YOUR MONEY
BECAUSE YOU WON'T ACKNOWLEDGE
YOUR SHORTCOMINGS

YOUR REFUSAL TO ACKNOWLEDGE
THE DARK SIDE OF HUMANITY
MAKES YOU PREY TO THAT DARK SIDE

YOU WORRY THAT IF YOU LOWER YOUR GUARD,
EVEN FOR ONE SECOND,
YOUR WHOLE WORLD WILL
DISINTEGRATE INTO CHAOS

YOU WAIT FOR FATE TO BRING ABOUT
THE CHANGES IN LIFE WHICH YOU
SHOULD BE BRINGING ABOUT YOURSELF

YOU ARE DAZED BY THE EASE
WITH WHICH OBLITERATION CAN BE OBTAINED

YOU FEEL YOU HAVE MORE MEMORIES
THAN YOU HAVE ENERGY
TO PROCESS THOSE MEMORIES

YOU ARE UNABLE TO DIFFERENTIATE BETWEEN FACADE
AND SUBSTANCE

Hours later we pay the Comfortmobile's hospital bill with some of our "tragic cash." The mechanic, after reading his money, can't herd us out of his garage fast enough.

Stephanie and I are eager to flee Mount Shasta. Our plan is to drive at warp speed down Interstate 5, then branch over Route 299 onto Highway 101 toward Humboldt County and my dad's house. We could have spent the night in Mount Shasta, but we felt the unfightable urge to move. Hopefully tonight we'll drive through Trinity and Siskiyou Counties before we OD on driving and need to crash in a cheap motel.

Our drive into the night is chatless and tunage-free. The scenery is flat, dry, and Lancasterish. Stephanie falls asleep beside me and I think about the family and friends I've left behind me back at home. I pull into a Circle-K grocery to buy a nostalgic bag of Cheezie Nuggies and a ginger ale, feeling a twinge of pride in belonging to a society that can maintain a beacon of light and technology like this Circle-K out in the middle of nowhere. Convenience stores: the economic engine of the New Order.

The store inside is a spacious warehouse of potato chips, chocolate bars, pop, and car magazines—and little else. Dwindling numbers of species outside; dwindling selection of products inside. It's the new balance of Nature.

The store is also lit to the point of painfulness by a ceiling loaded with more fluorescent bulbs than a landing mothership. Shielding my headachey eyes, I make my consumer choices, then head to the counter, where the clerk is wearing sunglasses. I pay the clerk with a five-dollar bill on which I have felt-penned the words:

I AM AFRAID OF THE DARK AGES

* * *

Have you ever researched your family tree? Have you ever tried to meet an unknown relative merely because you shared blood? Telephoned a stranger out of the blue? Knocked on the door of this stranger's house because you knew shared chromosomes pulsed behind it?

Maybe you have and maybe you were pleasantly surprised. But then, maybe you regretted doing so. Maybe you realized some folks are best left a name and a date on a piece of yellowing three-ring notepaper in the back of a kitchen drawer, your sister's hot date's phone number scribbled in one corner (MURRAY IS A GOD: 684-1975) and a half-finished game of hangman doodled on the other corner (H_ATH_RJ_L_CKH_D).

Maybe you saw these strangers and you said to yourself, "You are not me"—but you were wrong. They *are* you; you are them. You are all one forest.

My biological father, Neil, lives in a cedar-shingled Hobbit-type house trimmed with purple, deep inside the redwoods. On the thatched roof above the Plexiglas light bubble and long-dead solar panels is a rainbow wind sock; a sky-blue 1940s truck muralled with latex paint clouds is parked out front amid a patch of lupins, Shasta daisies, Scotch broom, and California poppies. Stephanie and I have had to unlock two gates and pass three DO NOT ENTER signs to access this house, aided by an iffy map sketched by Jasmine years ago which had the two gate keys taped to the bottom. What a treasure hunt.

For today's big surprise meeting I'm wearing a shirt and tie. A decade had passed since I've seen Neil, so I want to look mature. I am expecting much insight into why I am the way I am as a result of this trip, and my knees go limp upon seeing the house.

Neil's children, maybe ten of them, blond with pale blue wolf eyes, are strapping each other with frizzes of redwood bark as Stephanie and I drive up. Two girls hold Barbie dolls with third eyes painted on their foreheads. All of these children fall silent when they see the Comfortmobile, then fall to the ground, like in a 1950s nuclear alert.

"Jesus."

"*Sacré bleu.*"

The kids start wailing and screaming, crawling to the side of the house. Two women in white prairie dresses run onto the porch, each wiping her hands off on an apron. One of the women shrieks inside, and Neil, white-bearded like God, clad only in bib overalls and cowboy boots, runs down the house's porch aiming a 12-gauge shotgun as Stephanie and I stop our walk toward the house, frozen—petrified.

"What do you want?" he barks.

"Neil?"

"What of it?"

"I'm Tyler."

Neil knits his brows, cocks his head, then says, "I don't know any Tyler. Tyler—oh—*Tyler.* Tyler?" He lowers his gun, whistles an all clear. He lumbers down the steps to hug me, his snowy beard clinging to my crispy gelled hair as to Velcro. The past minute of fear is erased. "And this—" he says, turning to Stephanie—"Is . . . uh . . . *Daisy.*" He goes to hug her and Stephanie flinches.

"No, Neil. This is Stephanie. A good friend. Daisy is in Lancaster."

Neil hugs her, regardless.

The children are swarming about us, touching my tie and reaching for Stephanie's hoop earrings. In their faces I see snatches of my own face—I didn't realize I had so many half-siblings, and I experience an odd pleasure while meeting them—like eating a pear you know was harvested from a twig grafted onto an apple tree. The kids are wearing T-shirts with molecules printed on them: LSD, chocolate, testosterone, valium, THC, and other mood-altering chemicals.

"Come inside," Neil says. "Have lunch. Be with us. Let us gather."

"Pa sells these shirts at festivals," one of the kids offers. Her shirt is filthy.

"My decoy business," Neil says, then whispers into my ear: "*The Feds.*"

"Does MTV have a molecule?" I ask.

"What's MTV?" Neil replies. "I don't like designer drugs."

The scariest aspect of the kitchen is that there are no boxes or cans or other tokens of this nation's mighty food-distribution system—no recognizable brand names. No processed foods. No microwaves. No electricity. Nothing. Jars are filled with bits of plants and grains that I don't recognize, even with Jasmine's training. Crystals are nudged into all corners of the ceilings. Incense reek permeates all porous surfaces. Knickknacks are smooth and carved from redwood: hippie accessories to Eden. This kitchen makes the kitchen in Lancaster seem like the Space Shuttle.

And these two women, Laurel and Jolene—spacey-eyed and barefooted—don't talk. Nada. They *do* smile a lot, but their smiles are creepy hippie smiles, like the smiles friendly folk give you in a small town when your car breaks down and they feed you and feed you and you think it's great, only to discover in the end you're going to be their Thanksgiving dinner. Nonetheless, Laurel and Jolene have fixed a no-doubt nutritious lunch, a flavorless legume casserole.

During the meal, as we sit around a large redwood dinner table, Neil is wholly uncurious about my visit. He doesn't ask me even one question. Not even, say, *"How long are your here?"* or, *"Why are you here?"* He is also bleary-eyed. Stoned. I think the women are tripping, too. The kids aren't high, though. They're bestial, alternating between being mean as a sack of cats, or as dull as a sack full of sacks. Boy, they need discipline.

"Jasmine is in good spirits," I offer. Neil nods, saying this is great, but Laurel and Jolene don't respond to a mention of their once-rival. When this lunch isn't scary, it's boring. I give a few sundry details about life in Lancaster.

Stephanie keeps squinting, trying to see hints of my face under Neil's beard. "Oh lady, you've got to stop looking like that," Neil says. "I'm freaking out."

"Zut! My apologies," says Stephanie.

I give up on conversation with these deadheads, and talk to Stephanie as though only the two of us are present. This strategy seems to work well, relieving the elders of taxing thought processes. "Jasmine met Neil at a Rainbow festival in Redwood City. Neil was a guide."

"A guide?"

"He guided people through acid trips. Sweated it out with them in bathtubs. Talked them down. He and Jasmine lived in the middle of a total scene: bikers, speed freaks, suicides—casualties lying all over the place. Neil guided Jasmine through a bad dose of microdot. They lived for a while in the woods outside of Mount Shasta, then moved to the new commune in B.C. together."

"Freaks." Neil chuckles trollishly to himself.

"Jasmine says that because of both acid and Neil, she's well aware of the infinitely rich possibilities of life. She says acid opened doors she never knew existed. But she also said that once she began to fear acid, she could never drop it again."

"The Fear," Neil says with authority, then brusquely adds: "Coyote, take Norman his lunch."

"Yes, Pa," says one of my half-brothers—Coyote, I suppose—grabbing a plate of casserole and heading out a rear door.

"Who's Norman?"

"Jasmine not told you?"

"No."

"Norman is your godfather."

"Wild!" This is just the sort of exciting fun fact I was hoping to find by visiting Neil. "Really?" Imagine—being able to meet the human specifically chosen to provide me with religious instruction.

"But Norman's kind of out of things. He's not much to talk to," Neil adds.

Silence. I know what *this* means. "Casualty?" I ask.

Neil, Laurel, and Jolene nod.

* * *

After lunch Neil shepherds me into a tepee sweat lodge in an alder grove behind the house. Stephanie, daggers in her eyes, has been delegated by Neil to stay behind in the kitchen to help clean up. "We have male energies and lore to exchange."

As Neil and I walk out back, naked except for yellowed, frayed guest towels wrapped round our waists—towels stolen two decades back from the Fairmont Hotel in San Francisco—I see Stephanie's face through an oval kitchen window, her hands washing dishes in the sink. She's angry as a buzzing hornet at having been abandoned in the 13th century.

The children swarm about us, their directionless motions and fluttering long white hair mimicking the imbecilic liquid world of fish under the sea. In their hands are strings of plastic and clay beads, which they trade with each other like strands of genetic material. These children are not allowed to enter the sweat lodge with us.

Smoke streams out a hole in the roof. Inside the air is chewy and salty and hot. The gel in my hair is an odor magnet and I'm going to emerge from this experience smelling like lox. Redwood planks burn my thighs while Neil lights a joint and offers me a toke. "No thanks. I have to drive."

He arches his eyes in surprise. "Young people have no memories. You're unable to mourn the past."

"Huh?" These hippies.

We sit and get mellow while Neil smokes his "Dr. Jay."

"Did Jasmine tell you the story of Norman and the bicycle?" Neil asks.

"Never."

"After Norman flipped out in Santa Cruz we had to baby-sit him. We smuggled him up to British Columbia with us, up to Galiano Island."

"I was just up there. Up at Galiano."

Neil ponders this. "Yeah? See anything?"

"Zero. No traces left of the commune. Except a file of chimney stones—and there are condominiums half a mile away."

"The disappearing act. Is the blackberry path still there?"

"Barely."

Neil tokes the joint, holds his breath, then blurts out a cloud of muck. "The path used to be more like a road—it's where Jasmine was riding when the bicycle story happened. She was pregnant. With you. She was riding to the general store to phone Vancouver. Norman was running the other way screaming at an invisible attacker—the Pope or a bank regulator from the Channel Islands. I think he was yelling about deutschemarks—and he plowed smack into Jasmine. The two went flying."

Another long, windy toke. My hair feels like it's dissolving. "They were both lying on the ground, stunned, collecting their breaths—staring into each other's eyes like they'd just made love. Then Norman reached over and placed his hand on Jasmine's stomach—*you*—smiled, trembled, then calmly walked away. He stopped being chased by bankers after the crash. He stopped being paranoid—even though he was still a casualty in other ways. But because of the transformation—the loss of paranoia—Jasmine thinks of you as being blessed. Special. She ever told you she thinks you have healing power?"

"No."

Neil finishes off what's left of the joint. "She does. She still sends Norman birthday presents. And pictures of you. That's how I recognized you." One final toke. "You're a photographer?"

"I'm hoping to be a professional. We're moving to Los Angeles right now."

"Snap a picture of Norman for Jasmine. We haven't had cameras here in years."

"Does Norman talk? Does ..." But Neil stops responding. He's fried. Meanwhile, the steam heat becomes too much for me. I sit for a few minutes with my catatonic biological father, then leave the sweat lodge and scurry back to the house, air freezing on my sweaty bare skin. Stephanie is standing out by the garden. Seeing me she pleads, "When can we *leave*? I want to *leave*."

"Hang on. I have to wash the smoke out of my hair. Is there a shower here, or do they just wait for rain? And I have to take a picture, too."

"Please, be sna-*pee*."

Around the front of the house, the children are clustered around the Comfortmobile's rear driver-side tire, hooting and hollering like skatebrats at the Ridgecrest Mall.

"What's up, Coyote?" I ask Coyote—the only demi-sibling I'm able to identify. Coyote points his thumb as a skinny man, dressed in rags with a hillbilly beard, sitting cross-legged beside the car, licking his reflection in the black paint.

"Meet Norman," says Coyote.

Get me out of here.

An hour later, at the Hitching Post Cafe in Ukiah, California, I am recovering from my father's house.

The cafe's shellacked Elvis burl clocks, its pie racks full of gooey, chemical-based lemon pies, and its edelweiss still lifes painted onto saw blades seem positively life-affirming after this morning's descent into madness.

We can't eat enough chemicals: *"Caffeine—caffeine—caffeine,"* I chant to the waitress.

"Nutrasweet!" adds Stephanie.

"Edible oil products!"

"White sugar!"

"Now!"

Stephanie and I spent the first three miles back on the open road screaming like banshees—like we'd just escaped being roasted alive—giddy with a sense of escape. It was enough simply to rinse my hair, change clothes, and peel out through the gates.

Now we just want to see the future. Any future.

* * *

Another day: San Francisco and wooden houses painted the color of children's thoughts. Stephanie and I are lost in rolling fog, sniffing the asbestos tinge of the Comfortmobile's taxed brake pads.

The fog disappears and so does our breath: "Check the view, Stephanie—talk about glamour—a real futurescape: Bank of America—Intel—TransAmerica—and across the bay, nuclear aircraft carriers in Oakland—all of this, *plus* the earthquake faults threatening to cum at any moment. What a city—it's so *modern*."

Later we break for a cappuccino near Cyclotron Road by the Lawrence nuclear facility on a street of freaks on the liberal nipple of Berkeley. Stephanie phones France—Monique's kitten, Minuit, is still on the verge of death.

Next stop: a pilgrimage to Apple headquarters in Cupertino, then into the Silicon Valley: Los Altos, Sunnyvale, Palo Alto—twelve lanes of traffic zooming past eucalyptus trees on fire. Hot hot *hot*.

Traversing the Bay Bridge, sun glimmers on fragments of abandoned earthquake-ravaged freeway held up to the sky by uncollapsed poles—like the sculpture garden at the Ridgecrest Mall. "Stephanie, all I need is air in the spare."

The traffic jams abruptly. Lolling here in this glorious West makes me think of photos of those dead factory towns in other parts of the world—those zones of long-dead, rusting technologies like ball-bearing and naphthalene factories—tetraethyl lead, PVC, and carbon black—powered by bituminous coal and ideas that aren't working anymore—cities so big and so dead as to have their own complete cosmologies of the afterworld. I feel sorry for these places. Examples? I envision screaming housewife mummies in pearls dog-paddling in the molten coke lakes of the anti-Pittsburgh. I picture eyeless ghost engineers huddled above the blueprints of iron machines that will eat the sky in slow motion. I imagine skeleton passengers on a BOAC prop flight that will never land, their bones clad in smart wool suits, lifting cocktails to grinning skull faces, rattling and chanting with rage at their eternal damnation, gleefully clacking their fibulas together and toasting the black-and-white industrial landscapes below—the anti-Bremen, the anti-Portsmouth, the anti-Hamilton, the anti-Yokohama, and the anti-Gdansk—the plane puncturing the fluffy clouds of smokestacks—billowing gray tufts of dioxides and burning time.

Now, contrast these visions with the shiny turquoise buildings of the West: blue-jeaned employees playing with hackeysacks during lunch hour; employee babies learning Japanese in corporate crèches, freeways brimming with the success stories of the New Order—software, jets, and submarines; white bond paper, vaccines, and slasher movies. With relief, I have found the antidote to my father's house.

"Stephanie," I say, "we are going to become rich in Los Angeles."

"I hope so, Tyler. Life is rich."

"You read my mind."

The Silicon Valley is a necklace of futuretowns. What is a futuretown? I shall explain.

Futuretowns are located on the outskirts of the city you live in, just far enough away to be out of reach of angry, torch-carrying mobs that might roam in from the downtown core.

You're not supposed to notice futuretowns—they're technically invisible: low flat buildings that look like they've just popped out of a laser printer; fetishistic landscaping; new-cars-only in the employee lots; small backlit Plexiglas totems out front quietly brandishing the strangely any-language names of the company housed inside: Cray. Hoechst. Dow. Unilever. Rand Pfizer. Sandoz. Ciba-Geigy. NEC. Futuretowns are the same in Europe as they are in California,. I figure they're the same the planet over. Futuretowns are like their own country superimposed onto other countries.

Stephanie and I drive through these futuretowns of the Silicon Valley with tunage cranked to eleven.

"What should we play next?" I ask.

"British industrial noise!" Stephanie wisely decides. We scavenge the tapes from the backseat, which has degenerated into a jambalaya of bicycle shorts, cassettes, maps, and turkey-jerky wrappers.

We then return our gaze to the mirror-boxed futuretowns circling us— the hard drives of our culture, where the human tribe is making flesh its deepest needs and fears: teaching machines to think; accelerating the pace of obsolescence; designing new animals to replace the animals we've erased; value adding; reconstructing the future.

We don't set our TV shows in futuretowns, and we don't sing songs about them. We don't discuss futuretowns in conversations and we don't even have a real word for them. Industrial parks? I think not. A contradiction in terms.

Futuretowns aren't places—they're documents. They are the foundries of our deepest desires as a species. To doubt them is to doubt *all*.

We stop for gas in Santa Clara. Stephanie goes to a Pacific Bell booth to phone France again. Alone in the car I see the digital numbers on the gas pump race forward like time; only 2,549 shopping days left until the year 2000. I felt-pen more words onto a stack of one-dollar bills:

LET'S JUST HOPE WE ACCIDENTALLY BUILD GOD.

Twentysomething

Jefferson Morley

This cover story for the Washington City Paper *predated even Coupland. While it makes no mention of the term "Generation X" or baby busters, it demonstrates early recognition of the fact that kids born after the baby boom had their own experience of American culture and politics, too. In this ironic reaction to* thirtysomething, *the television show that turned our tubes into boomer guiltcleansers, Morley captures the way a legacy of social issues, media events, and song lyrics can shape a generation's world view.*

I was born sometime after *Brown vs. Board of Education*, sometime before the Kennedy assassination. I graduated from high school after the Watergate break-in, before the Reagan tax cuts. After "Do your own thing" and before "Be All That You Can Be." After the bomb shelter and before the nuclear freeze. I'm old enough to remember being too young to know about 1968 when 1968 was happening. I've got what you might call a '70s sensibility.

I can't quite say what the '70s sensibility is. If I ask people they usually say something about the swine flu vaccine or Evel Knievel or Disco Duck or Jimmy Carter or the Symbionese Liberation Army. Then I hear a good '70s classic on the radio like "Backstabbers" and I get a sense of what the '70s sensibility is: *They smile in your face/all the time they want to take your place.*

And then I forget again, tell myself to live in the real world. But if I hear from somebody else with a '70s sensibility, I start thinking again that maybe I'm on to something. A friend of mine who teaches history in Northern California wrote me a letter quoting a historian who said: "Every generation must invent its own tradition." That's something the '70s generation has never done. We're overdue.

1. THE ME DECADE

There never—never!—was such a misnamed thing as the Me Decade. (Compared to the '80s, fr'instance?) The whole mythology of the Me Decade depends on ignoring a crucial fact about the '70s: It was our coming of age, our time. The Me Decade, whether celebrated or denounced, is a product of and for the '60s grown-ups. What's been completely forgotten is that the youth of the '70s had a certain something that informed that time, and maybe not only that time.

The '60s—as we are told with tedious regularity—were a decade that belonged to idealistic and courageous kids. But the "kids" of the '60s never let go. When the '70s came around, the real kids—e.g., me—weren't allowed to stake a claim to the decade. We were deposed from our own coming of age by the baby boomers who, to this day, control the media and hog the spotlight. You see, there were actually two different decades going on at once: the Me Decade for the older generation and something entirely different for the children of the '70s.

Not that I blame the '60s-types for getting almost religious about that Me shit. They'd grown up. They had jobs. They had cheap weed. They had easygoing rules about sex that meant they were free of the past. They had cars and houses. Some of them had hot tubs and some of them were getting into this thing cocaine. For them the Me Decade was more like the Meeeeeee Decade with that one syllable stretching well into the 21st century. Most of all, they were getting old! That was the joke. They were thirtysomething back then.

These comfy folk were always telling us 13-year-olds that we had missed out on the glories of the '60s. What they didn't know was that we had stumbled into a secret passage of our own. The great untold secret of our generation is that growing up in the '70s was much more interesting than growing up in the '60s: Hair was not An Issue. In fact, there were hardly any rules at all. Liberation was the given, not the goal. We weren't old enough to waste our time worrying about self-fulfillment. We had to devise our own rules as we went along.

So we were less idealistic but more realistic. Less wild and less authentic and less sincere, but also less melodramatic and less violent. Less courageous but also less foolish. Less moralistic but more ethical. We were a sweeter, sadder, sexier, funnier bunch than the kids of the '60s, and they've never forgiven us for it.

2. PICK UP THE PIECES

The sensibility of the '70s begins with the sound of the '70s. You could hear Hall and Oates singing *Everybody's high on consolation/everybody's telling me what is right for me.* Growing up in Minneapolis, I had a radio by my bed and I'd let it play quietly all night. You'd hear "Midnight Train to Georgia" hanging out at the park and "Rocket Man" as you were going to sleep and "Rock the Boat" when you were at your part-time job at the ice cream store. You might get lucky and hear Stevie Wonder telling somebody "You Haven't Done Nothin' " (I thought he was talking to the '60s types and I liked that). You'd be on the freeway and you'd hear "Reeling In the Years." And there wasn't anything finer than hearing "Moondance" late on a summer night.

You could hear the sound of the '70s anywhere, you just didn't know when. The hockey players tended to get into Foghat and David Bowie and BTO and Zeppelin and Deep Purple and Black Oak Arkansas ("Jim Dandy"). Your basic earache. But then about five guys would cruise by in a Camaro five-speed and they'd have enough pot smoke coming out for you to get a contact high right then and there. (I liked those guys better when they smoked pot than when they drank.) They'd have something like "Suffragette City" blasting on the eight-track. Rednecks? Probably but not necessarily. Some of them were just punk rockers ahead of their time.

One of those guys had an older brother in Vietnam. I didn't know him but I said I did. A few kids were into a guy named Bruce Springsteen but I didn't know anything about him except they played him on the one "progressive" rock station and I couldn't really get it on my cheap bedside radio. For me War was a band not a Vietnam thing. I went to a party and remember hearing "The World is a Ghetto" and "Southern Part of Texas." *She's from the southern part of Texas/yes, she was born in a hurricane.* They were still playing War when I left and crossed the railroad tracks to go home.

Thinking back on it, maybe there was more going on than we really knew. Turn on the TV and there was the *Partridge Family* or *Family Affair.* Turn on the radio and you'd hear Sly Stone croaking *It's a family affair/it's a family affair* like he was getting sick to his stomach. And you'd go to a party and in a blacklight room the stereo would be blasting and everybody'd be zoning out on War: *Freedom is expensive/She couldn't post no bond or bail.*

3. INFLATION

For us everything seemed normal. I remember wondering why people were surprised that prices were going up. I thought, that's what prices did. Some people were dismayed that America was losing the war in Vietnam, but to me it seemed like America had always been losing the war. Some people were scared that George Wallace was running for president, but he ran every time, didn't he?

4. ARTHUR BREMER SHOOTS GEORGE WALLACE

The racist was paralyzed from the neck down. "The Jeffersons" was on TV and it was pretty stupid. We had busing at my high school. I don't know what happened in Boston but it wasn't so bad. I remember that Lisa W., a rather fine black girl, indicated to me that maybe she and I should go to the prom. I backed out for some reason I can't remember. But still. The '70s were a time when there was a truce in the race war.

5. THE LATE SAM ERVIN

Remember Harold Hughes? He was a senator from Iowa, an ex-alcoholic, who ran for president in 1972. He used to tell voters that he'd broken all Ten Commandments. Today they'd say he didn't have "character."

Remember Sam Ervin? A white Southern senator who had been opposed to civil rights his whole life. He stared down at some Nixon administration cockroach who was trying to make some excuses for the Watergate scandal and roared, "You may think you can live on the windy side of the law, mr. _____ (fill in the blank), but the Constitution says you can't!" Think what Sam Ervin would've done with an odious weasel like Ed Meese.

6. "THIS . . . IS HOW-WUHD COH-SELL"

I never noticed Howard's toupee. I didn't know what a toupee was. I never stopped to think, How did a fuddy-duddy liberal Jewish lawyer from New York get on TV in the first place, much less become a boxing announcer? He sucked up to Muhammad Ali and bugged the shit out of him, too. He made "Monday Night Football" worth watching. He used big words and used them improperly. He was a jerk but there he was. He certainly wasn't a Brent Gumbel or a Bryant Musberger.

7. DISCO BASKETBALL

We had the old American Basketball Association. They played with a red-white-and-blue ball but there wasn't anything Patriotic about it. They had the three-point shot, which offended the patriotic-types. Worse yet, basketball was getting taken over by a bunch of bad boys with names like Louie and Fly and Doctor J. It was flashy, acrobatic, immature, in-your-face fun, without corporate sponsorship. Plus you got to see all the dance moves to come later in the decade.

8. KC AND THE SUNSHINE BAND

There is nobody more despised by '60s retreads (and the '70s types who imitate them) than a guy named Harry Casey—as in KC and the Sunshine Band. Which is reason enough to like the guy. But Casey was also a prophet of the Top 10. *That's the way, uh-huh, uh-huh, I like it (uh-huh, uh-huh).* Remember KC hit the big time roundabout 1974–75, right when the Vietnam war was ending. KC was on the radio and in Vietnam the communists were storming the embassy trying to tear the roof off the sucker. On TV you could see those pictures of U.S. helicopters leaving the roof of the embassy in Vietnam with people hanging off the rudders. *That's the way, uh-huh, uh-huh, I like it.*

Think about that for a second: Jerry Ford's pissing his pants, the Viet Cong are in the embassy trying to tear the roof off the sucker, the helicopters are barely clearing the tree-tops—and the teeny boppers of Minneapolis are getting down in the homecoming assembly: *That's the way, uh-huh, uh-huh, I like it (uh-huh, uh-huh).* You weren't supposed to like these things and we did. A stupid catchy pop song was more important than whatever it was we were fighting for in Vietnam in 1975. We had our priorities straight.

It's no wonder people hate KC, especially these days. He was a white boy riding the black man's groove. He liked to dance and couldn't have been more different from tired-out sensitive souls like James Taylor and Dan Fogelberg. And where was KC from? He sure wasn't from Kansas City. He wasn't from Haight-Ashbury or El-Lay, or any such respectable '60s place.

He was from Miami, and a very first-person-singular place: My-Am-Me. City of the '80s, or so I've read. He sure didn't care about Vietnam. He knew where the future was—the sunshine of the white and powdery variety. So tell me he was not one prescient guy.

9. TRAVIS BICKLE

Taxi Driver came halfway between Arthur Bremer and John Hinckley Jr.—but he wasn't real. He was up on the screen. He tries to protect Jody Foster, who mouths some '60s cliches about how liberated she is. He blows away her pimp, the slob who runs the hooker hotel, the john. He blows away all this corrupt scum in a bloody disgusting frenzy—and wakes up to find he's a hero in the tabloids. But Travis Bickle knows he's a criminal. *Freedom is expensive/She couldn't post no bond or bail.* You had to find the moral inside of yourself and you had to live with it. What they say about you on the broadcast news is not just irrelevant. It's a soothing lie.

10. THE BICENTENNIAL

Nobody really got into the Bicentennial in 1976, at least not in the red-white-and-blue way that you were supposed to. Some people were disappointed because we did not go out and behave as people did during the 1984 Olympics or the 1986 Statue of Liberty party. The Bicentennial, thanks to us, was a dud.

11. EVEL LIVES

I was rooting for Evel Knievel. I figured if the guy wants to put himself in a homemade rocketship and go flying off to meet a certain death in some canyon in Idaho, well, he was trying to prove something. He couldn't have been doing it for the money. Evel survived and as soon as he did he must've started wondering why he had survived, a very '70s feeling. It's probably still bugging him, which is why you never hear about Evel Knievel anymore.

12. ELVIS DIES

Johnny Rotten said it should have been Mick Jagger. Then Sid Vicious up and died first which pissed me off because a lot of people moralized about it. But, hey, Mick Jagger is brain-dead and the hippies are long gone. But you still see punks hanging out in the high schools and the parks.

13. DISCO

I know, I know. I'm supposed to say Disco Sucked. It didn't. In fact, for one white-suited, platform-shoed white boy from Minneapolis, it was great. *New York City. Just like I pictured it. Skyscrapers and everything.* I knew the Hustle and the Latin Hustler (I took a class with a bunch of nice-looking girls). I was always into the pre-disco Earth, Wind and Fire-and-Boz Skaggs sound. So naturally, when Yvonne Elliman came along, I liked "If I Can't Have You (I Don't Want Nobody Baby)" and Evelyn "Champagne" King singing about "Shame" and somebody (I don't remember who) doing a fabulous remake of "Oh Lord, Please Don't Let Me Be Misunderstood."

Some people didn't like disco because it sounded black and they preferred the tedium of the Eagles. Some people didn't like it because it was associated with gays (which was their problem, not mine). Others didn't like it because it was easy to dance to—another way of saying they didn't want to dance. (Fine, so sit down and shut up.) In fact, most people liked disco. Girls especially, and not only because they liked to dance. I thrilled to "I Will Survive" and Donna Summer doing "Bad Girls." She had it right. *Bad girls/ talking about the sad girls.* That was the kind of girl I was looking for. (Toot Toot. Beep Beep.)

14. A GOLDEN AGE OF COMEDY

We *made* the '70s a golden age of Comedy. The very first "Saturday Night Live" show ever had George Carlin as guest Emcee. That '60s hippie-dippy shit was OK—but who was this guy named after a suburb making fun of the president? Gerald Ford wasn't president. Chevy Chase was. At college we used to line up to watch "Saturday Night Live." We had "All in the Family" and "MASH" and Monty Python on TV. There was Lily Tomlin ("Is this the party to whom I am speaking?") and Steve Martin ("Well, Excuuuuuuuuuuse Meeee!"). Back then Woody Allen was making movies that were funny. John Belushi was telling the world, "But noooooooooo!" Richard Pryor was busting loose. One of his earliest, funniest, and best movies was a forgotten '70s classic called *Blue Collar* where he plays an autoworker in Detroit who's having a good time trying to ignore bills he has to pay. The '70s were bad times but people have forgotten an elementary fact: Bad times are funny.

15. FROM AM TO FM

In the summer of 1977 the progressive radio station in Minneapolis changed over to a new "format": album-oriented rock. It was very tasteful. No disco allowed. No blacks allowed either, but nobody ever put it that impolitely. The truce in the race war broke down. But the race war did not resume; the antagonists were merely herded into different formats. Whites got their AOR-thing; blacks got their "urban contemporary" thing. Pretty soon, whites got "My Sharona," which started the New Wave (no punks allowed). That same summer blacks and whites alike got the rhythm: Chic had a big crossover hit with "Good Times." And the late '70s had its seductive, slight ironic beat: *These/Are/The/Good/Times.*

16. COCAINE

Cocaine got going in the '70s, I admit. But just before cocaine there was a brief moment when it no longer made a difference whether you got high. To call someone a narc—an undercover narcotics agent—was no insult. A "narc" was not some secret FBI infiltrator. "Narcs" were people who did the unexpected, who you didn't know quite where they were coming from.

People with a real '70s sensibility know when to get high and when not to. They know that "Turn on, tune in, drop out" is bullshit in the same way that "Just Say No" is bullshit. They also know that both are good advice. Cocaine made all that very easy to forget and it screwed up a lot of people. But remember this, most people who did it didn't let it ruin their lives. Most of them just had a good time and had a very complicated '70s sensibility about it: The white powder was a motherfucker but it wasn't the real problem. The problem was, Why did everybody in the late '70s all of a sudden want to do it so badly?

17. MUHAMMAD ALI

The Greatest was no longer the greatest. He won his title back once, twice, three times. Cosell defended Ali to the bitter end, but when Ali was beat so was Cosell.

18. THE VIETNAM MEMORIAL

As cocaine and inflation and formats elevated everything above what it was really worth, something got forgotten—a certain sensibility that didn't fit into any format. This sensibility lived on, underneath the formats. Springsteen found it in the darkness on the edge of town. *You had to find the moral inside of yourself and you had to live with it.* You can find it in the reflection on the black panels that make up the most popular monument in Ronald Reagan's Washington. Maya Lin, who designed the Vietnam Memorial, is my age. When the memorial was first built, people thought it was odd that she was so young. What did she know about Vietnam, a girl who grew up in the '70s?

19. BRIGHT LIGHTS, BIG CHILL

I was in New York a couple of months ago and I was talking to a friend of mine. We were talking about clubs and music and women and he said something about the "Bright Lights, Big City era." Just like that: the Bright Lights, Big City era. Kind of like the postwar era. It's over. The postwar era is over and the Bright Lights, Big City era is over. *These/are/the/good/times.* And all I could think was, damn!, I didn't do coke (well, not that much), I never picked up a girl with razor blade earrings in a nightclub. I hadn't even read the book and now it's over.

And that got me thinking again about the Sound of the '70s. Why is it that there's never been a '70s revival? A '70s TV show? How come no one has tried a new Ollie North-version of "Backstabbers"? *They smile in your face.* Why are no movies set in the '70s? Maybe it's because what was best and worst, most fun and most scary about the '70s took place outside of the Bright Lights, Big Chill format. The real life of the '70s—then as now—is almost entirely unnoticed. That is our secret, our tradition.

20. EPILOGUE

A change in the weather/is known to be extreme

I was a cub reporter in Minneapolis in the summer of 1979. Some guy out in the suburbs had wigged out. He was a young guy with an older brother in Vietnam if I remember correctly. He had a gripe about the local cops. They had beaten him up or something. So he climbed up the local water tower, fixed himself up with some food and blankets about 100 feet off the ground, and refused to come down until somebody addressed his grievances. I was sent out to cover the story.

It wasn't much of a story. He sat up there. A lot of people gathered down below and cheered him on while some psychologically sensitive policemen tried to persuade him to come down. They said they'd make sure everything got taken care of—which was bullshit but they sounded sincere. The only way this thing was going to end was if the man up on the tower bought the bullshit—or jumped. I was on hand to observe either possibility.

So I spent a brilliant warm July afternoon and evening sitting in my car looking at the water tower and listening to "What a Fool Believes" on the radio. *The wise man has the power/to reason away/what seems to be.* As the sun began to set President Jimmy Carter came on the radio. He started giving his speech about our national malaise and he told a whole nation to come down off its water tower. I was thinking, Do I have a malaise? when, right in the middle of Carter's speech, the guy on the water tower decided to come down. The police hustled him to an ambulance and drove off into the '80s.

Slacker

Richard Linklater

This movie moved like nothing else we had seen before, except maybe some foreign film with subtitles. Instead of having a plot or a protagonist, the story just wandered aimlessly from person to person in a vastly under-employed and overeducated Austin, Texas. In this scene, a guy who leads a penniless rock band is trying to get a date with the recent psychiatric ward discharge, when he is interrupted by a girl attempting to make an interesting sale. Linklater's movie demonstrated, in both form and content, the meandering, painful, but always ironic and amusing slacker lifestyle.

EXT: DOWNTOWN STREET—DAY

Walking down the street, he passes a woman he seems to recognize.

ULTIMATE LOSER

Stephanie?

STEPHANIE

Oh, hi . . .

ULTIMATE LOSER

Wow, I haven't seen you around in a long time.

STEPHANIE

Yeah, I just got back about a week ago . . .

ULTIMATE LOSER

Yeah? From where?

STEPHANIE

Dallas.

ULTIMATE LOSER

Dallas? What were you doing up there?

STEPHANIE

Hanging out . . . resting. I was in the hospital for a while. It was really awful.

ULTIMATE LOSER

Your parents, probably . . . ?

STEPHANIE

Yeah, you could say they put me there. So what are you up to?

ULTIMATE LOSER

Same old same old . . . just lollygagging around. Still unemployed. I'm in this band . . . well, the one I was in before but we've changed our name. We're the Ultimate Losers now. And, ah, the singer's still a jerk. We're playing this Friday . . . if you want to come I can put you on the list. I'm sleeping a lot . . .

Just then they're approached by a ranting girl (Pap Smear Pusher) *who had walked around the corner at a brisk pace and seems to know them.*

PAP SMEAR PUSHER

Yo, hey dude . . . Man, I am freaking out so severely. Did you hear what happened on the freeway? You didn't see the local news today? Oh, it was beautiful. This old man driving into town from San Antonio . . . this old man about forty or fifty years old, going about a hundred miles per hour down the freeway, waving a gun at people . . . laughing. Like doing fucking chicken squawks at people out the window and showing them his gun and going like ahhahahaha, ahhahahaha, hahahaha. Things like that—people were freaked—they didn't know if he was just a lunatic with a squirt gun or what. And then, check it out, the guy started firing. On the freeway, randomly through his windows. He shot one bullet up at the roof of his car and it just ricocheted around and around inside with him for a while. He was like out of his mind. Everybody tried to get off the freeway. Some chick who had a bullet lodged in her ponytail called the pigs in San Marcos and they had six or seven pig cars chasing him into the south side of town. He was still swinging the gun around and laughing . . . fuckin' laughed all the way. Finally his car spun out and slammed into the grassy knoll, you know the median. As soon as his car came to a halt, man, he just put the gun to his head and blammo! Offed himself, man, blew himself away right there . . . it's like, I don't know, he had had enough . . . enough.

ULTIMATE LOSER

Do you know Stephanie?

PAP SMEAR PUSHER

Oh yeah, I thought I heard you were in "Timberlawn"?

STEPHANIE

I got back about a week ago.

PAP SMEAR PUSHER

All right, cool. Oh yea, I know what I gotta show you guys . . . this will blow your gourd. I have this friend, all right, she's a gynecologist in Hollywood, and she scored this for me from the lab where she works. It's a Madonna pap smear. I know it's kind of cloudy, but it's a Madonna pap smear. It's got Ciccone on the top—that's like a medical label, Ciccone. Check it out, I know it's kind of disgusting, but it's like, sort of getting down to the real Madonna. I don't know if you can see it now but I freaked out when it came in the mail it had two pubic hairs in it and I showed it to this one asshole and he stole one of them. But if you look real close you can see it's still in there . . . it's about as black as they come. Do you think maybe you'd be interested in buying something like this . . . it's like a high-dollar item, it's one of a kind, chance of a lifetime.

ULTIMATE LOSER

I'm sure . . . But I'm pretty broke right now.

PAP SMEAR PUSHER

What about you? Do you think you know anyone who might be . . . I mean, it's a little bit getting closer to the rock God herself than just a poster. No? All right, your guys' loss. Thought I could swing a bargain. Can't blame you—I tried. It's a material world and I'm a material girl. I better cruise, man, I gotta check this guy Chico on the East Side—he's real interested in this. Hey, how's your band going anyway? What is it, Beautiful Loser?

She leaves before hearing his answer.

Richard Linklater

Following the success of Slacker, *Linklater's ultra–low budget debut, Holly-wood realized that there might be some money in marketing the GenX sensibility back to itself and funded Linklater's next effort,* Dazed and Con-fused, *a movie about what it was like to go to high school in the 1970s. After watching their local film student become an international star, this tiny but popular 'zine's Austin correspondents took advantage of an opportunity to interview one of their own.*

JON: Tell me your take on *Dazed and Confused.*

RICK: It's what I set out to do. *Dazed* was made more in the editing room than *Slacker.* The way it was shot, it was so obvious what it was going to be. Dazed has a big cast, 24 main characters, and a lot of cross-cutting. It's a lot more of a rock & roll movie, a lot of music and cutting to music and trying to get its energy. That was the most fun thing, the music. We used all period music, from May 28, '76 and before. So it's ZZ Top, Aerosmith, Ted Nugent . . . We couldn't get the rights to "Dazed and Confused," so we got another Zeppelin song.

CARLA: I love the first scene showing a Camaro packed with teenagers driving in slow motion to "Sweet Emotion."

R: That came to me when I was under the influence of nitrous oxide getting my root canal, and that image came to mind.

C: [laughs] It's something my sister and I would have put in the movie. I had a Camaro, so it was perfect. One thing Mark and I noticed was there weren't any kids wearing braces. Did you overlook braces?

44

R: Actually there were some extras with braces. Most of the actors were professionals, and they didn't wear braces.

C: I just remember that in the '70s it seemed like everybody wore braces.

R: Yeah, it's like 1 out of 5. I never had braces, just a retainer.

C: Oh, retainers were fun! Were you able to click yours on and off your teeth with your tongue?

R: Oh yeah, I'd pop it off with my tongue, and at lunch you'd just set it right on the side of your tray by your food.

C: Yeah, and nobody would care because they all had one next to their trays too.

J: When we talked before, you compared *Dazed and Confused* to *American Graffitti*, as everything that *Graffiti* was not. In *Dazed*, as in *Graffiti*, you have people moving through the night—one night, isn't it?

R: Yeah, one night. I call it *Slacker* with about four or five laps. You keep coming back to the same characters. All of them have their own story . . . not all of them, but the main ones. I think they're younger than the people in *Graffitti*. *Graffitti* was a whole other time and place, and they all seem so much older. They were making big life decisions. The oldest kids in *Dazed and Confused* are juniors in high school becoming seniors, so it's not like they can go out in the world and start changing things or be different people. They're stuck for at least another year.

J: That's a weird twilight zone, actually.

R: Yeah, the future's on the horizon, so there's a little angst about that, but they know they have one more year to kind of fuck around, so that's what they're doing. More than anything, it's about being stuck where you are and being frustrated. The thing about small towns is how creative people can be with their own space and how humans create a liveable system, no matter how bad things are. You create your own world that you can survive in, or that you can get by in, psychically, through the day. That's what you see happening in the movie. There's always talk about how being a teenager is such an oppressive situation, domestically and institutionally, so riding around is a statement of freedom.

J: Drinking beer . . .

R: Drinking beer. Smoking a lot of pot, too. It's being hailed as a pro-pot movie. *High Times* had a half page on it . . . "hot movie for the 90s!" There is a shitload of pot, but I just had to be honest, because for teenagers, smoking pot symbolized rebellion and freedom from those oppressive circumstances. I don't have a real attitude one way or another about it, but kids have been brought up with this "Just Say No" stuff, and it seems sort of Orwellian that it's been pumped into their heads without much thought. It seems so dangerous. We're all self-medicating in some way or another constantly. I guess that's how I view drug use. It brings it out in a real matter-of-fact way and doesn't have an attitude about it, one way or another. It's not saying it's good or bad.

J: The people are just smoking dope as a cool thing to do.

R: Yeah, as teenagers do. And smoking a lot of it. The party really cranks up, and they're all hitting on bongs, driving around, smoking . . . it's so weird. I feel like I've gotten away with a lot of stuff.

C: What was in those joints they were smoking?

R: Well, it tasted real bad, but it smelled like real pot. It helped the atmosphere. But I don't know what it was. We had fake beer too, "near beer," and it tasted horrible too.

C: How come you decided to do a movie about slackers and '70s teenagers? Do you consider yourself to be in the slacker category?

R: Uh, yeah, it was the culture I lived in, I would say.

C: Do you think the two groups are related?

R: Yeah, you could say *Dazed* is like a prequel to *Slacker*. You could pick people out of *Dazed* that would be smart enough to go to grad school but disenchanted, knowing what they definitely didn't want to do. So for me it's kind of autobiographical, you know, a freshman in high school in '76. I'm interested in the teenage mindset, and the energy of being a teenager.

C: Do you miss being a teenager?

R: Oh, God no! [laughs] I'm very glad to be out of it!

J: We talked once before about *Dazed and Confused,* and I've thought since then about the condition of the teenager at that time, the postmodern teenager who's living in a world that's completely changed without anybody really acknowledging the changes, which result from the communications revolution and so forth. Do you get into that very much in *Dazed?*

R: I think you feel that as an atmosphere. These kids have been through it, they grew up with TV, and they refer to that every now and then. They kill time . . . a lot of them are pretty cynical. Our parents had their ears glued to the radio listening to FDR, a good man who was there to protect us . . . but by the time we were teenagers, it was like, "What crook is in office now?" There wasn't any of that belief in the institutions. But I see that as very healthy, a healthy cynicism, which is realistic ... for the first time, I think the people who were coming of age were not in some dream about the world they were living in. They'd been slapped around, and they'd grown up realizing cold hard facts about life.

J: Before, you couldn't really scrutinize the world you were living in the way we've been able to, actually since the '50s but more so since the '60s and '70s ...

R: The information age. Megainformation. That amazes me, that there are kids who are so plugged in, whereas back then you were reliant on mass media.

J: I meet a lot of kids online, and I'm shocked when I learn how young some of them are. They're really bright, and they've figured things out that I hadn't figured out when I was 30 or 35 ... I was still working on these puzzles, and they know. I used to be impressed that we knew so much more than the college grads 50 years ago by the time we had a high school education ... but now, by the time you're out of middle school, not only do you have the facts, but you have some of the understanding. You don't really have the maturity to handle the understanding, sometimes, and I think that really bowls 'em over. Hackers are a good example of that. A little knowledge is dangerous.

R: Yeah, some of these kids are living hooked up to a computer and a modem. Wiley Wiggins was telling me about a friend of his who's not in school anymore. He's young, about Wiley's age ... quit school, and he's online all the time.

C: I heard you guys just spotted Wiley coming out of a drug store.

R: Coffee shop. It's kind of a slacker location, a happening place called Quackenbush. It has a big espresso bar.

C: Oh, I was there with Jon and the rest of the *bOING! bOING!* crew!

R: That's where Wiley was discovered. I like to say he's a fifteen-year-old with all the bad habits of a grad student. Smokes cigarettes and drinks espresso all day.

C: He seems like a natural talent.

R: Yeah, he was the one we picked out of several hundred people we met.

C: Did you pick anyone else off the street?

R: Kind of. We recruited some kids from high school hallways.

C: Those lucky kids!

R: For fucking up their lives? [laughs]

C: Toward the beginning of the movie, the kids are at someone's house, and they're drinking out of these wax paper cups with bright yellow and orange swirls, and it was so nostalgic to see those again! They used to be so popular. How'd you remember those?

R: There are companies who give you that kind of period stuff. Or people in the art department find you stuff. Trying to keep the period accurate was fun.

J: How about violence in the film?

R: Yeah, it's a big part of it, actually. It's a real abuse of power; the seniors have initiation rituals into high school. I see it as a social critique of the abuse of inherited power. It's pretty abusive; some people think it goes too far. The girls get initiated more formally. The pick 'em up from school, the eighth graders, and lay 'em all out, dump stuff on 'em. It's this big party, run 'em through a car wash, and that's it. The guys, however, are running for their lives, and the seniors have these paddles, and when they catch 'em, they beat 'em.

J: Sounds pretty realistic.

R: Yeah, and when they catch them, it's harsh. I put music behind and it's kind of ironic. Wiley [Wiggins] gets the hell beat out of him. They catch him after a baseball game. They bend him over a car and they all wear him out, to Alice Cooper's "No More Mr. Nice Guy." It's one of my favorite sequences in the movie, just the way it works, the cutting, and what I had in mind there . . . to pull it off felt good. It's harsh, but those are really cruel times.

J: Wiley said you had some realistic fight scenes.

R: Yeah, at the beer bust itself we had a very realistic fight scene. You get the whole pack mentality. There's going to be guys who, if they don't pick up a girl, will get into a fight. Every one of those parties I went to, inevitably somewhere in the evening there was some kind of fight or disturbance. Human design flaw, I would call it.

C: So what kind of projects do you have lined up?

R: A couple of different things. One's about two construction workers.

C: Why construction workers?

R: I've worked in construction. For now I'm still learning a lot. I feel more comfortable doing things I know really well. I wouldn't be any good at doing a *Die Hard 5*. I wouldn't be the right guy. But I can do things I know really well. I know what being a teenager in the 70s is like. It's weird. Some people look at *Dazed* as an indictment of teenagehood. Teenagehood has a lot of energy, and there's a certain fun and exuberance there, but at the same time it's pretty fucked up too. So I think *Dazed* has both. One thing I refuse to do with the movie is pass judgement. Some people look at it and say "cool!" And other people look at it and say, "God, look at all these people wasting their lives! How depressing." So it really comes down to where you're coming from.

C: Yeah, it just depends on how you interpret it. It's probably just an extension of the person who's watching it.

R: Yeah, absolutely.

J: There seems to be a pagan revival now, people who want to know their bodies, get back to their essential nature without acknowledging any distinction of spirit versus body.

R: That's healthy. That comes back to drug use. It seems that most people have a need to transcend, to find a spiritual quality. It's just how that gets answered. You can be a Bible thumper answering that need, or a new ager. We all find our own rituals and our own methods of answering that spiritual need.

J: It's important to have something you can focus on that will take you away from your egocentric concerns.

R: Right.

J: Where you can actually get beyond yourself. Christianity does that for some, but people who reject Christianity because it's been so dominant in our culture are having trouble finding where to plug in so that they can get outside themselves. A lot of them are doing twelve-step programs.

R: Yeah! And you kind of need to . . . plug into some other kind of ideology. It could be any kind of dogmatic thing.

J: Cinema!

[laughter]

R: Cinema, yeah, that's what I'm plugged into. It became my view of the whole world, I think. That's my twelve-step program.

Whatever

Mark

Saltveit

Harvard graduate Mark Saltveit has held over forty jobs—some fun, and some not so fun. Among the better ones were masterminding "Real People for Real Change," a Political Action Committee dedicated to preventing George Bush's re-election. He succeeded. Currently, he runs a small computer training company and writes palindromes for an upcoming collection.

In this anti-manifesto, that first appeared on a computer bulletin board, Saltveit proposes that any attempts to categorize GenX are doomed to failure. The only thing that can classify this bunch, according to Saltveit, is a world view that goes beyond such market-directed oversimplification.

What is GenX? Who are these "slackers"? Just about every newspaper and magazine in America has been discussing this. But the real question is: Who's asking? And you know who—baby boomers looking for another trend, and the boomer press that caters to them.

You can't define this generation in a paragraph or an article. The best you can do, I think, is give examples. Here's what my friends did in one town (Portland, Oregon) during one period (the late 1980s) before anyone thought about GenX, or what defined it.

We worked hard at low-paying jobs (some arty, some just bad); lived in shared houses; drove old American muscle cars; and shopped at thrift stores. Our hang-outs were brew pubs and bars with cheap, strong drinks and funky, dated furnishings, such as the Satellite Room or an old Chinese restaurant called—and I'm serious—Hung Far Low. Or we went to rock clubs where good live bands played alternative rock for a three-dollar cover or less.

Later, GenXers started a couple of great places with fun, cluttered, ironic decor and good music. The X-Ray Cafe had Twister parties after the last band on Saturday nights. Dot's had a school library rack full of trashy paperbacks, like *The Partridge Family* and anti-drug books.

My friends played a lot of basketball outdoors (sometimes at night, drinking) and rafted rivers. We bought a $150 raft, made a frame from one-by-six planks and wing nuts, and ran the many rivers close to Portland. There were lots of low-stakes poker games, and pot luck dinners where we'd pick a country and cook its food.

We passed around lots of alternative publications like *Factsheet 5*, Archie McPhee's catalog, the *Clinton Street Quarterly*, and *Seattle's Rocket*. The TV was on a lot, but almost never the networks. We watched old reruns, bad movies, New Wave Theater, then Nick at Nite, and later, The Comedy Channel. My sister and I made a public access TV show of alternative and punk rock, called Wasted Talent.

And everyone reminisced a lot about the "Banana Splits", space food sticks, Wheel-Os, "Nanny and the Professor", Goober Grape, "Room 222", etc. On the other hand, few besides punkers went for tattoos and piercings, and Ren and Stimpy were not especially popular.

That was my crowd, but there aren't too many generalizations you can pull from that. Fun but cagey? I don't know. Anyway, who would think that one article or essay could sum up something as big as a generation? No slackers that I've met. And yet, that seems to be the basic idea behind the reigning trend, journalism, written, of course, by boomers for boomers.

One thing is, almost everything we did was cheap or free, because no one had any money. We explored all of the low cost alternatives and spent time on the good ones. If people did have money, they usually travelled overseas or bought music gear and started a band.

It's easier to say what GenX isn't. Mostly, slackers avoid the stupid excesses of baby boomers (baboos) that have filled the media all of our lives. GenXers are almost never shallowly earnest, smugly triumphant, materialist, or conformist. Liberal boomer guys often pretend to be sensitive, but few GenXers would be caught dead drumming in the woods at a New-Age workshop. You might find some Deadheads in a drum circle, but they're baboo fakers anyway.

Slogans, gurus, phony caring and sharing, demonstrations, movements, pop psychology books that tell you how to live your life—these are rarely found in the younger crowd.

There aren't going to be any silly, defining slacker clothes—no white go-go boots, granny glasses, or bell bottoms. (Maybe long shorts). The grunge look was a desperate attempt to define GenX clothes, and fashion houses lost a fortune on it.

Besides, wearing flannel, jeans, and boots is no trend. Lots of men wear them for casual or work clothes in the Northwest, because they're warm, durable and cheap. My great-uncle Ben, a carpenter who died in his eighties, was grunge most of his life, but he kept clean and might've hit you if you called him that.

But it's the nature of that older generation to turn everything into a trend. (They've certainly made plenty of money doing it.) All my life I've listened to baboos bragging to the media that they're going to make peace and love, then revolution, go back to the land, create a disco inferno, and—in the 1980s—dress for success and wealth. You know what, boomers? You blew it every time, and you looked like idiots trying. Ha!

And talk about conformism—look at their dances. They started with the sixteen named dances (Twist, Hully Gully, etc.) that everyone had to know, then graduated to line dances (from the disco Hustle to today's country Boot Scootin' Boogie, where everyone marches together like army troops. Aerobics are even worse—they include the drill sergeant.)

Now, baby boomers are not monolithic. Journalists always forget the right wing baboos who supported (and volunteered for) the Vietnam War, fill fundamentalist churches, and ran this country (so badly) in the 1980s. But whether they are fundamentalists, Rush Limbaugh dittoheads, or PC liberals, boomers always look to their peer group for identity and direction.

When faced with a trend, slackers are more likely to shrug and dismiss it with one word: Whatever.

The apex of boomer conformism is mass media news, which, of course, created the whole GenX issue. Baboo writers, editors, and viewers are constantly looking for trends and movements, making them up if necessary. Today's press corps is largely worthless—a pack of shallow conformists so easily manipulated that it's a joke.

Part of this is the historical coincidence of this huge generation and the mass media themselves: not only the TV networks, but the nationwide chains of bland, corporate newspapers that have sucked all life out of the daily press. Maybe the Pepsi Generation is doomed to shallow group thought and trend-mongering through years of training by MCA, CBS and

Time. New technology for cable TV, desktop publishing, and cheap recording studios arrived just in time for slackers.

So—what is GenX? There's no answer, because that's an ignorant boomer question. Who knows? Who cares? Whatever.

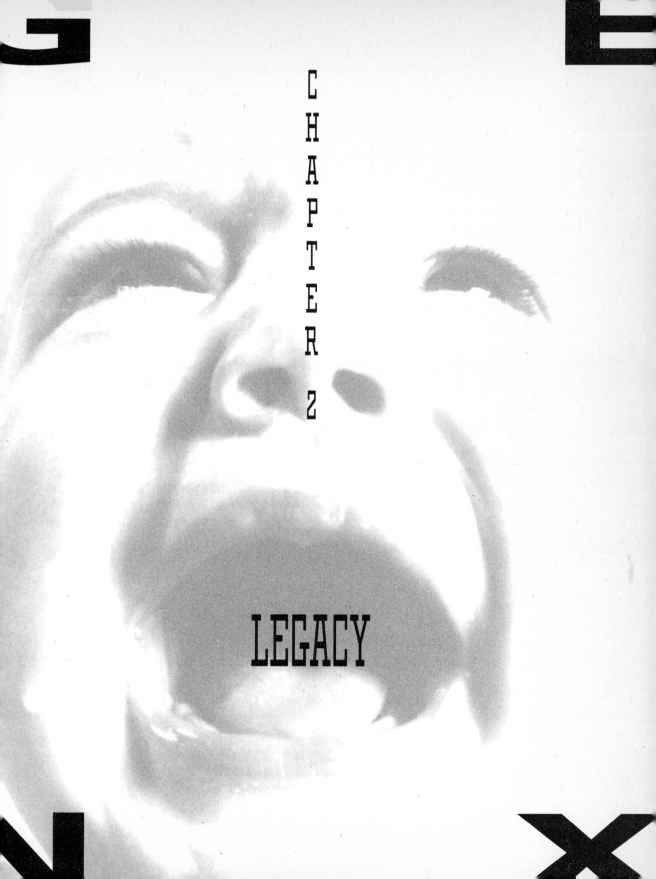

CHAPTER 2

LEGACY

Legacy

Every group has its forefathers. Its heroes. Generation X is no exception, even if its progenitors are seemingly unlikely ones. These are the stewards of recycled imagery.

Busters inherited junk culture. It's not our fault if we loved it—well, aspects of it. The imagery of our childhood was television from the tail end of the boomer era. The innocent world view espoused in series like "The Brady Bunch" stood in sharp contrast to what we saw in the world around us in the early 1970s. But there were hints, even in the midst of Bradymania, that theirs was not a kosher home. It was left to us busters to dissect the corpse of boomer media and uncover the hidden lies and moral inconsistencies.

What irks us, though, is that we get criticized for loving the Bradyesque imagery of our childhood, criticized again for exposing it as a naive boomer fantasy, and criticized yet again for reveling in postmodern deconstructional analysis of these images. To understand the busters' love–hate relationship with our cultural legacy, you have to grant us one simple fact: We were thinking while we were watching the tube.

The buster cultural legacy has two main tributaries: boomer tube and beatnik literature. We are the ideological love children of Jan Brady with Bart Simpson or Kate Jackson with William Burroughs. We have inherited both the simplistic innocence of our mass-mediated social engineering and the postmodern, psychedelic ability to reframe reality as if from the outside. These two genetic threads—the joy of unselfconscious participation and the irony of metaparticipation—are the GenX birthright.

Bradymania!

Elizabeth Moran in

Teenage Gang Debs

Elizabeth Moran's book Bradymania! *is a testament to the Brady phenomenon. Her ongoing analysis of this cultural institution explores just how this fictional patchwork bunch became the foster family for a generation of children from broken homes and disjointed upbringings. In this reportage for a GenX 'zine from Robert Reed's funeral, Moran pays tribute to all-American architect-dad Mike Brady and the gay Royal Academy of Dramatic Arts actor who played him.*

SATURDAY, 7:30 A.M., SOMETIME IN 1990

Riing! "Hello?" "Ms. Moran?" "Yes." "This is Bob Reed." Bob Reed? Robert Reed? Mike Brady! (I'm really awake now, set to fly out of bed to grab my interview questions.) "I want no participation in this book. Any book written on "The Brady Bunch" is a bunch of crap. Why should *you* make money off of something *I* did?" Click. End of discussion. Was I dreaming? Was this a practical joke? Did this really happen? Oh no, Mike Brady's a jerk!

If you've read my book, *Bradymania*, you'll notice that I've selected a quote I particularly liked for each Brady bio. The above was the quote I particularly liked (well, actually, it was the *only* direct quote) from Bob Reed, but my editor made me change it to one less severe. After all, "Elizabeth, the man just died!"

MONDAY, JUNE 8, 1992: BOB REED'S MEMORIAL SERVICE AT THE PASADENA EPISCOPAL CHURCH

Frankly, I went to the funeral to see who else was going to be there. And, quite frankly, most everyone else was there to see who else was going to be there or because they *had* to be there. The church was huge, and I mean really, really big, made especially big since only about 50 people total were there. As usual, I'm early. And as I'm hanging out, the first thing I notice is this gorgeous flower arrangement in the foyer from Barry Williams and his wife, Diane Martin (former Miss Arizona whom Barry met on a blind date). Later I found out Barry organized this whole deal.

Next I saw Florence Henderson and her husband walking around the church gardens. As usual, Florence looked great, but I didn't talk to her because I never really felt comfortable around her. Bottom line, I think she was fed up with the whole Brady thang and just barely tolerated me.

Mike Lookinland, his mom Karen, and Joe Seiter (Brady Bunch tour manager and choreographer) arrived next! These are three cool people. No attitude. Down to Earth. Normal. Joe and Karen provided most of the behind-the-scenes photos for my book, and I'm forever grateful. And Mike is my favorite real-life Brady. After we exchanged "Hi"s, this usher escorted us into the private Brady room adjacent to the church.

To tell you the truth, we were only there a few minutes and I didn't have time to see who was there, but I did have a nice chat with Barry's mom and Mrs. Whitfield, the Brady's longtime school teacher. And Barry and Flo were polite. As for the other Bradys, Chris Knight was a no-show (but his parents were there), and Maureen McCormick, Eve Plumb and Susan Olsen weren't there at that point. Ann B. couldn't make it from Pennsylvania.

Next, we were all ushered into the left front pew of the church. The Brady Box. Susan sat behind me . . . another cool Brady. Upon seeing me, she says to her parents (practically so the whole church can hear "She's the one who did the trivia book!" Could you say that a little louder, Susan? *Not* in the Brady Box were Maureen and Eve. They were across the aisle, and when Flo motioned for them to come over, one of them, I forget exactly who, shook her head no. This was the first sign of dischord among the Bradys.

There's nothing much to say about the eulogy. Barry said something nice, and this lady, Bob's only friend, said something nice, and this minister who didn't know Bob said something nice. We were in and out of there in 20 minutes and back into the private Brady room. And let me tell you, it wasn't a pretty sight. Barry and Maureen immediately got into an argument when Barry asked Mo what she thought of his book. All ears were strained on this one, but Barry dragged her off to the other side of the room. It was quite obvious she didn't like it. The temperature in the room was quickly going up, and to appease everyone Karen, Mike's mom, tried to get everyone together for a group photo. Eve and Maureen wouldn't have any part of it and one of them said something to the effect, "No, because you'll turn around and sell it for someone's book!" I wonder who that could be? This was about the time I left. Believe me, I would have loved to stick around, but it was kinda obvious I had NO business in that room. Upon leaving I was accosted by a wall of photographers. Can you believe it? I actually had to find a back route to my car.

Looking back at my initial conversation, or non-conversation, with Bob Reed, I can now understand why he was so bitter. He was a man dying of AIDS complications, so who wouldn't be bitter? He was a theatre actor, a man who studied Shakespeare in London at the Royal Academy; a man who won Emmy awards, but was best known as Mike Brady: father extraordinaire. Well, so what? He had a long and successful career, and to be known as Mr. Brady shouldn't have been an embarassment.

I do know that he truly cared for his Brady kids. He took them on trips, gave them gifts, and stayed in touch. Well, Bob, you'll be our dad forever, too. And we're not embarrassed.

Pagan Kennedy

My Religious Energy Crisis

Pagan Kennedy, the Boston author of Platforms: A Microwaved Cultural Chronicle of the 1970s, *is one of a crop of young writers making a name for themselves by drawing on their experience of that era. Irreverent yet authoritative, Kennedy has produced her own 'zines, published several volumes of short stories, and received an NEA grant for fiction. The following personal reminiscence of her transfer from a touchy-feely boomer–era Christian school to a raucous public school during the energy crisis of 1973 captures what it felt like to step out of McDonaldland and into the real world.*

Up until the sixth grade, I went to one of those earnest religious day schools, the kind of place that had been unduly influenced by early-seventies sentimental Christianity of the *Godspell* variety. They taught us how to weave God's eyes out of Day-Glo–colored yarn. Also to say "I love you as a Christian"—which we girls used as ammunition against the boys. You'd go up to a boy and say, "I love you," wait to see his look of panic, then quickly add, "as a Christian" and burst out laughing.

I was, like, queen of this school. For one thing, when it came to the SRA reading cards, I got up to the aqua ones while most of the other kids were still struggling with the brown ones. Best of all, when the Christmas play came around, I got to be Mary because I had the perfect hippie-style scraggly blond hair. The kid who played Joseph was black (for that multicultural effect). Jesus was a flashlight swaddled in toilet paper and lying in a doll's crib. I had a total crush on my stage husband, who was commonly acknowledged as the cutest boy in our class. When he and I stood there with our flashlight baby Jesus—while all the kids who had to play donkeys and sheep and cows groveled at our feet—I felt that everything in my life had clicked into place. I was popular.

Then tragedy struck. My parents began to realize that the school was turning me into a mini Jesus freak. I had started gazing at people with this glazed look and saying, "I prayed for you today. Jesus is going to come wash out your heart with soap and water." So the next year, 1973, I found myself at a new school. It was like going from *The Living Bible* to *Lord of the Flies*. My classmates never said "I love you as a Christian." Instead, whenever the teacher made one of his frequent disappearances, they slammed each other to the ground or kicked each other with their hard little athletic legs. The first week of school, I came home with a red welt on my face where someone had thrown a shoe at me. After that, I took to hiding between the door and the wall, trying to remain invisible in the midst of this progressive-education hell.

I was not alone in my misery. Watergate was in full swing—the adults were glued to the TV, watching men in suits argue. And suddenly there was this scary feeling that even as the government toppled, America was no longer the land of plenty. Inflation soared and the energy crisis hit. Gas had become as regulated a substance as liquor: you couldn't buy it on Sundays. The worst part was, even though everyone knew Nixon was evil, he still retained his supernatural powers, like some kind of crazy wizard locked in that White House, casting curses on this blighted land. It wasn't just speed limits he was tampering with, either. It was the very nature of time. In November, he decreed that America wouldn't "fall back" an hour for winter—we'd stay with the summer's daylight savings time in order to save energy.

So the winter of the energy crisis, kids went to school in mornings that were like nighttime. When I woke up at 6:30, it was really 5:30 in the morning (non–1973 time). And when my family sat around the table for breakfast, it seemed more like we were eating a midnight snack. All of the lights in the kitchen blazed and the windows, like black mirrors, reflected us as ghostly shapes. I used to imagine that the world outside had turned to tar, like some "Twilight Zone" episode where we were the last ones left on Earth, only we didn't know it yet. I cannot exactly express it, the horror of those black-windowed breakfasts. Here my parents were—my mother telling us to finish our oatmeal and my father reading the paper—as if they were trying to trick my sister and me into thinking everything was normal, that the sun was out instead of the stars.

At 7:30 (really 6:30—I was always subtracting an hour in my head), I walked the two blocks to my bus stop. When my mother hugged me good-bye, I could feel by the tightness of her grip how afraid she was to have me stand under the stars, alone, waiting for the bus. She made me carry a flash-light, which I clicked off as soon as she closed the door. I'd walk along be-tween the pools of light cast by the streetlamps, which made the pavement scintillate with each of my steps. It was magical and scary. My mother had told me not to talk to any strangers in the dark, and I half expected some man to follow me or watch me from the shadows, but no one ever did.

When the bus came, it bore down on me with its headlights, groaned, and then swung open its hinged door to let me in. It would carry me to my day of hiding in the corner of the classroom. It would carry me to this sense-less new school that existed inside this senseless world of oil rations, Water-gate, and Vietnam.

I kept having the same nightmare that year. I dreamed that I stood at my bus stop in the crisp, frosty air of night, my breath coming out like cigarette smoke. Just standing there, I felt a thread of terror. When the bus came, it moved the way things do in dreams—appearing soundlessly from nowhere. It rolled up like a hearse and came to a stop in front of me, but the driver seemed not to see me. I pounded on the bus, I yelled, but he wouldn't open the door, for the night had turned to tar, muffling my voice. And then the bus started up again and pulled away. That was all—so ordinary and yet so terrible. Nineteen seventy-three—so ordinary and yet so terrible.

Life in Hell

Matt

Groening

Though a late boomer himself, Matt Groening was still young enough in the 1970s to get a strong dose of nihilistic passion. His originally underground Life in Hell *comic strips surfaced in the mainstream by the early 1980s, just as the busters were coming of age and looking for alternatives to the rosy media that had been foisted upon them throughout their childhoods. The comic strips, even more than his megasuccessful TV series,* The Simpsons, *deftly captured the essence of the buster realization: Life is hell, no matter how U.S. consumer culture tries to convince you otherwise.*

LIFE IN
HELL

©1984 BY
MATT
GROENING

From *Work is Hell* © by Matt Groening. All Rights Reserved. Reprinted by permission of Pantheon Books, a division of Random, Inc., N.Y.

Classic Rock

Julian Dibbell

in Details

Perhaps the most truly felt legacy left to the buster generation is the sense that something truly great happened during the 1960s and that we missed it. We try not to be jealous and have come up with many rationalizations for why Joplin and Hendrix and Morrison were not as monumental or irreplacable as our teachers told us they were. But deep down, it hurts when we are told that someone else has "BT, DT" (been there, done that) and done it a whole lot better than we can ever hope to. To the rescue comes Julian Dibbell, a rock critic for the Village Voice, *who here forcefully expresses why a generation as truly revolutionary as our own just doesn't need another hero.*

Silence hangs over the former headquarters of the White Panther Party, an unassuming pair of houses wedged in among the giant University of Michigan frats and sororities along Ann Arbor's Hill Street. Up and down the street, noisy pledge-week parties are spilling out into front yards, and I am shuffling hotel-ward from the biggest of them, Fiji House's "Purple Haze," a floorful of people five to ten years younger than me dancing respectfully to live covers of Jimi Hendrix and Led Zeppelin, music that was already history by the time any of us were old enough to recognize it. And now I can't help stopping to peer into the darkness of the onetime White Panther commune—where a rock band called the MC5 and their pothead Svengali, John Sinclair, gathered in 1968 to plot "total assault on the culture by any means necessary, including rock and roll, dope, and fucking in the streets" (point two of the Panthers' ten-point program)—and wonder, a touch beer-bleary, what the hell I'm doing here.

Waiting for history to fork over a clue, I suppose. As the site of the White Panther phenomenon, Ann Arbor seemed a fitting vantage point from which to ponder the problem at hand: the persistent popularity of rock music from the '60s and '70s among "my generation." Long before Woodstock, Sinclair's weed-steeped rhetoric and the MC5's proto-metal crunge crystallized the caricature of '60s counterculture that would be sold to us come-latelies down through the decades—a nearsighted, sub-revolutionary politics of youth as a class defined, above all, by the music it listened to. Perhaps some residue of that moment would give me insight into the twisted mysteries of culture, generation, and rock 'n' roll.

And if it didn't, at least the visit to a college town would give me a closer look at musical attitudes among the flower of my more-or-less contemporaries—a demographic I felt professionally disqualified from speaking for, especially on this subject. Everyone knows, after all, that we rock critics (and anyone else who gets free records in the mail every day) have an abnormal relationship to pop-music consumption. And when it comes to rock's "classic" era, my generation of critics has a particularly fraught agenda, laced with Oedipal complications. We owe the very existence of our profession, you see, to the same crucible that forged the Woodstock Nation and other fantasies of an entire generation's absurd but invigorating self-aggrandizement. Unable to replicate that generation's faith in rock as the center of the cultural universe, we strive at best for an honest professionalism, at worst for a toy-block reenactment of their revolution, in an endless setting up and knocking down of fashions.

But it soon became clear, as I checked in with young folks at Michigan and around the country, that it would be pretentious of me to claim uniqueness for the psychodrama of the contemporary American rock critic. Everywhere I heard echoes of the same melancholy sense of having missed out on greater times. So far-flung was this sentiment that I even heard it from a right-wing, fundamentalist-Christian ROTC cadet. "I really would have liked to have been there and seen it," he told me. "You see those TV specials, they just amaze me, just what people thought, how they felt, their philosophies. You don't really see that as much today as you did back then." The corollary that the music was better then, too, was familiar enough to me by now that he hardly needed to add it. But he did: "I don't think today's rock will ever be considered classic by the next generation," he pronounced solemnly. "Some of it might be—Def Leppard, Van Halen. But I just really think rock hit its peak back then."

"Back then," of course, abbreviates a standard litany: Clapton, Hendrix, Zeppelin, the Beatles, the Stones, Simon and Garfunkel, Steve Miller, the Eagles, Dylan, the Dead, the Doors, James Taylor, the Allman Brothers, Pink Floyd, Bad Company, CSNY. Any college student could recite it, and much more readily than a list of favorite '50s rock 'n' roll artists or '70s punk bands (never mind disco greats). But not all of them would recite it reverently. Some see in its ubiquitousness not the endurance of great art but the crippling hegemony of the baby boomers. Or, as one student railed: "It's a fundamental reason why my generation has a sense of powerlessness. You feel like you don't even have control over your own culture." Nor does this fact let the victims off the hook, he was quick to add: "It really sort of stuns me how little interest in relativism and blasphemy college students have. You'd think they'd get a bigger kick out of, you know, not taking the Beatles as seriously as they're supposed to."

And yet, if the classic-rock phenomenon is at bottom an intergenerational struggle for control of pop culture, then surely the kids have deeper and subtler weapons at their disposal than merely not taking the Beatles seriously. Taking them out of context, for instance, is one rather more profound blasphemy that comes to mind. And, interestingly enough, it's the very one we commit on a daily basis. Because if it's a sure bet that any random twentysomething you select suffers from an alien nostalgia for the golden age of counterculture, it's equally likely (unless, perhaps, he's a Deadhead) that he'll explain his attraction to that age's music without any reference to the social or political values that informed it. *Sgt. Pepper*'s may once have been a lightning rod for the solidarity of a Western culture that was out to change the course of civilization, but for most young people today it's just one of many good, solid, classic-rock records. The music's onetime world-historical meanings have been stripped and replaced by fundamentally aesthetic ones.

This may seem like a small victory. But as the premise of a newly published, 292-page jeremiad called *Rock and the Pop Narcotic*, by one Joe Carducci, it starts to sound something like salvation. The main thrust of this creed is that rock's mass popularity at the high point of youth-as-revolutionary-vanguard euphoria was a historical accident of disastrous proportions. Ever since, he rants, "a middle brow sociologist mafia [has been] holding the history and meaning of rock music hostage to puerile left wing control freak fantasy." Raging against practically the entire history of rock journalism, he insists that there are really only two relevant questions to ask of a rock band: (a) is it a band (i.e., does it center around the live interaction of guitar, bass, and drums)? and (b)—the tricky part—does it rock? It is Carducci's relentless, almost nihilistic pursuit of this second question, of an elusive musical essence of rock, that makes his book not only the most provocative fan testament since Lester Bangs's salad days but also the first nearly convincing defense of rock as an aesthetic, rather than sociopolitical, experience.

But Carducci, ultimately, is too much of a rock puritan to become a prophet of today's youth, because if anything defines "my generation" culturally, it is a kind of pragmatic eclecticism with little use for grand, unifying obsessions. The fact that this approach has yet to be acknowledged (even, sometimes, by ourselves) as modern and revolutionary in itself says much about the self-centered, self-serving cultural hegemony that the baby boomers have imposed on their offspring. Classic rock may be this generation's musical common denominator, but outside of a few reactionary diehards, it's consumed as part of a rich, ever expanding collage of styles. Take a walk through any dorm in the country and you will hear a working compromise between a canonical past and a diverse present, classic rock mingling with college rock, hip-hop, and Top 40. Even at Purple Haze night down on Ann Arbor's fraternity row, the D.J. spins the likes of Snap! and Technotronic between sets of live retro-rock, while down the street the white boys of Delta Sigma Delta dance on the porch to the Black Muslim rap group Poor Righteous Teachers. This is the fallout of the big bang that first fused rock and youth culture: within today's fluid, fragmented musical environment, classic rock is just the hissing background radiation that tells us we're all still living in the same universe.

Because, after all, we're still living in the age of rock. Deep Purple makes more sense to us than, say, Glenn Miller made to the hippies. And for good reason: in making a clean break from their parentage, those hippies built the cultural arena in which *we* still live. Their perverse insistence that we both occupy that arena and tear it down fuels the dilemma of our generation. And it also fuels our elders' blindness to the ways we have transcended that dilemma. Where the other arts—and fashion, too—have been energized by resplicing fragments of their history into a kaleidoscopic present, rock's high priests continue to shackle the form to an exhausted ideology of permanent revolution. We know better. It's not that we're still waiting for history to give us our cues and clues. We've just decided it's more liberating to live with the past than to live in it.

CHAPTER 3

TRUTH, JUSTICE, AND THE AMERICAN WAY

Truth, Justice, and the American Way

In most American cities today it is not uncommon to find a doctor of philosophy tending bar or a physics master rolling burritos at Del Taco. Although many baby busters got the education our parents so wanted for us, we found ourselves on graduation day with little more than a diploma to be framed and education loans to be paid back.

There appear to have been two responses to this dilemma. For one group, whom we'll dub the slackers, the answer has been an apolitical distaste for social causes, especially those championed by liberal boomers. Rather than battling for scarce jobs in their "chosen" fields or stepping onto a competitive professional track, slackers opt out of "gainful employment" altogether. Whether they are victims of the post-Reagan economic fallout or willing participants in a social experiment called apathy, slackers are characterized by intelligence, cynicism, and a new bohemian irreverence for authority.

The members of the other group, the "next progressives," have taken an equally irreverent but much more active role in shaping what they hope will be the nation's future ideological and political agendas. In an unprecedentedly straightforward manner, these young activists dissect the failed policies and institutions of America's past in the hopes of reclaiming the promise of an open society with equal opportunity for all its citizens.

The End of Progress?

Eric Liu

Eric Lui, founding editor of The Next Progressive, *calls his publication, "a journal of opinion produced by men and women in their twenties." Informative, rational, well-thought-out, and, most of all, progressive, the magazine presents alternatives to the outmoded ideological duality of "liberal" versus "conservative" policy making. Naive as it may first appear to hardened cynics, Liu's editorial makes the point that it is incumbent on us to eradicate ideologies that threaten a sustainable future. This is GenX's call for America to accept a new paradigm.*

They tell us things have come to a close.

In our political culture today, the watchwords are "decline" and "end." Apocalyptic visions and dark millennial predictions abound. The end of history. The end of progress. The end of equality. Even something as ostensibly positive as the end of the Cold War has a bittersweet tinge, because for the life of us, no one in America today can get a handle on the big question, "What next?"

We are post-ideological, even post-postmodern. But we are not yet "pre-" anything.

For my generation, this cult of endism is particularly enervating. The twenties are supposed to be a time of widening horizons, of bright possibilities. Instead, America seems to have entered an era of limits—or at least convinced itself of that.

Whether it is the difficulty of finding jobs from someplace other than a temp agency, whether it is the incremental acceptance of "sacrifice" as a national modus operandi—the message seems to be: our time has come and gone, let's manage this with dignity and some sense of responsibility.

Even would-be optimists betray the underlying fatalism of our thinking.

To illustrate: a friend recently gave me a new book called *The Evolution of Progress*. The title sounded hopeful enough. But the book's thesis was depressing: that capitalism has played itself out, and that we should content ourselves with "human progress"—genetic engineering for a more perfect physical species.

Was this chilling, soulless notion of progress what America's founders had envisioned?

Maybe these pervasive cultural messages about endism are emanating from Baby Boomers entering menopause and midlife crises.

But this is not the time to cast generational blame. This is the time to ask ourselves: Can we redefine progress? Can we remake the American Dream?

I should confess up front that I'm prone to frequent use of phrases like "the American Dream."

Being the child of immigrants, as I am, can make a person intensely perceptive of the hypocrisy that lingers over many of our national myths and values. The gap between ideals and institutions, between high rhetoric and base reality, is especially striking to those who are expected to be the first "real" Americans in their family. But despite that—or perhaps, because of that—it can make a person intensely, fiercely, counter-intuitively proud to be an American.

So I want America to succeed. I want to help carve out a future that is not only slightly better than what I inherited, but astronomically better. I yearn for a leader who can wake Americans from our CD-listening, cable-watching, Taco Bell–eating slumber. I want to measure progress not by the monthly economic indicators, but by my sense of satisfaction with—by my sense of a stake in—American life.

To me the search for fellow progressives is very personal. My identity—my own sense of growth—is tied subtly to my perception of America's performance. Are we living up to our promise? Do we still believe that America has a unique destiny? I need to know.

Many first-time readers of this journal quickly reveal their bias when they see the title. The word "progressive" seems to provoke one of two reactions: "ah good, another generation of leftists"; or "oh no, another generation of leftists."

I am amazed by the extent to which progress, as an idea, has been appropriated by the left for the better part of this century.

From the first Progressive Era to the New Deal to the Great Society, America has been remade by people committed to the idea of a more active state. Progress meant a clean civil service instead of a boss-run patronage system. Progress meant a WPA instead of unemployment lines. Progress meant Medicaid instead of poverty and sickness. These were awesome achievements.

But today, it seems, the left has lost its claim to the progressive mantle. Too often, the left is now reactionary, defending an establishment—in politics and in academia—that is at once bureaucratically overweight and intellectually undernourished.

Conservatives are not faring much better. With an opportunity to kick the legs out from under the liberal tradition, most conservatives today are happy just to nibble, like gnats, at the knees. Too often, especially in national politics, conservatism is discernible merely as "not-liberalism."

The problem, from a twentysomething point of view, is that we are looking at the world all wrong. Progress is not about left or right. "Progressive" does not mean socialist. It does not even mean the Democratic Party platform of 1984 or 1988. It is about what works. Jack Kemp is as entitled to vie for the progressive label as Jesse Jackson. Progress is about fixing broken social service systems, untwisting crooked behavioral incentives, separating political means from public ends.

In this day and age, progress should—must—be about questioning fundamental assumptions. In one sense, progress is the leap from telegram to telephone, from mail to fax, from typewriter to computer. In politics, we need now to make the moral equivalent of such a leap.

The search for a new independent-minded approach to politics has given rise to "communitarianism" and a "New Paradigm." Both models reject the left-right way of looking at the world: communitarians stress responsibilities over rights, NPers favor individual choice over bureaucracy.

But do enough people relate to these terms? Probably not.

Still, while none of these new "ideologies," if we can call them that, has captured our political imagination, these forays into the murky waters of the post-post era are encouraging.

For the challenge today is to put all this change in terms that people—and especially young people—can feel and taste.

I ask our readers to help keep this conversation going. Is progress possible? Are Americans simply spent? Does the rising pragmatism of our politics represent an ascent to wisdom or a lull between storms? I ask you to be radical in your thinking—radical, as Erwin Knoll has said, in the sense of returning to roots.

Perhaps this generation will have to look not only to our peers and elders here in America, but to Prague, to Moscow, to Beijing, to Pretoria, where flux is king.

But even as we do, let us recognize that aspiring democrats around the globe have not invented anything new. The dusty documents of independence, freedom, and social justice that they read are ours. They've seen the light, and the light is us.

So today, in the midst of a technological revolution, from the chaos of post-partisan politics, a very conservative notion emerges. Progressives of the twenty-first century, no matter where we are in the world, will be those who have the singular and single-minded capacity to go back to basics: work, family, markets, responsibility, community, democracy.

It falls to this generation to peel back the accumulated layers of day-to-day, commercialized, materialistic American life, and to find that core of idealism. It falls to us to shake the country out of its deepening end-of-century blues. It falls to us, walking through our sterile suburbs or pacing our gritty inner cities, not only to say "This sucks," but to say, "This is how we are going to make it better."

It falls to us to take America back to progress.

Lead
or Leave

Invest in the Future

Boasting almost one million numbers, a network of over two hundred universities and chapters in all fifty states, this grass-roots GenX political campaign is aimed at forcing legislators to take responsibility for the current social, environmental, and economic crises before they become irreversible. Based on the premise that no generation should be asked to suffer the burden of the excesses of another, the "Lead or Leave" manifesto demands an end to generationally inequitable policies and seeks to replace them with a national commitment to protect the rights of all citizens without age discrimination and foster growth into a sustainable future.

WE NEED MORE JOBS AND MORE EDUCATION

"... Years of neglect have left America's economy suffering from stagnant growth and declining incomes ... They have left a mountain of debt and a Federal Government that must borrow to pay more than a fifth of its current bills. Perhaps most sadly, they have left the great majority of people no longer dreaming the American dream. ***Our children's generation may be the first to do worse than their parents.***"
—President Bill Clinton

RUNNING OUT OF GAS

Our economy is the engine that drives American life—no engine, no progress. And today, America is slowly running out of gas.

At the rate our economy has been growing, it will take twelve generations to double our standard of living. Before 1973—it would have taken only one and a half. And unless we get a rocket boost of productivity soon, interest on our debt is going to *reduce* future living standards by another 2.5 to 3 percent.

- The largest private employer in the U.S. today is not General Motors but Manpower Inc.—a temporary employment agency. And two-thirds of all new jobs created in 1992 were temp jobs with hourly wages that have no benefits, that could not lift a family out of poverty, that have no security.
- Minimum wage today has 26 percent less purchasing power than it had in 1970. People are working harder but paid less. At the same time, Social Security has grown at twice that rate of wages over the last decade.
- In the '80s, 20 million U.S. workers lost their jobs because their employers either went out of business or laid them off. And today, over half of all workers younger than 25 are paid hourly wages—which means no health benefits—and earn less than poverty level wages. That's over twice as many as in 1979.

YOU GET WHAT YOU PAY FOR

- *In spending on elementary and secondary public school education, the U.S. ranks **17th** among the industrialized countries, behind Italy, France and Australia.*

The Result:

> 5 million adults and almost 15 percent of all 17-year-olds in America are functionally illiterate—placing them on the outer bounds of American life.

> 12.5 percent of all 16- to 24-year-olds in America are high school dropouts. And every year, another half million kids walk away from high school—forever. The cost to the nation in lost earnings and foregone taxes—$240 billion a year.

- *Net spending on new factories and machinery has slumped for more than two decades, from roughly 17 percent of GNP in the late '60s to about 5 percent now.*

The Result:

> According to banking experts, the U.S. will slip to the world's number 2 manufacturing power for the first time this century. And by 2004, Japan's overall economy will be larger than ours—even though we have twice as many citizens.

- *According to the Economic Policy Institute, the federal government is running a $125.8 billion annual deficit in the investments critical to our nation's future, including education and training, children, physical capital, and civilian R&D.*

The Result:

> A quarter of our homeless population in the USA is children—meaning conservatively there are over 100,000 homeless children living on the streets of America.

> The U.S. ranks 20th among industrialized nations in infant mortality rates. Both Hong Kong and Singapore have us licked. And we lead the world in deaths of kids under age five due to preventable causes.

INVESTING IN THE FUTURE . . .

America's economic pie is shrinking, and it won't start growing again until we begin to close the "investment gap" that has left our workforce underproductive, our children undereducated, and our cities crumbling.

It's time to shift spending from current consumption towards long-term investments in people, education, health care, child nutrition, civilian R&D and infrastructure.

GENERATIONAL EQUITY

WHAT DOES "GENERATIONAL EQUITY" MEAN?

It means fairness and equality in the way the government asks each generation to pay for the benefits they receive. No single generation should be asked to suffer at the expense of another.

A GENERATIONAL WAR CAN BE AVOIDED . . .

"Lead or Leave" is not advocating a generational war—we're simply warning that one will occur unless we change course soon. **Generational inequities** are creating major problems and must be addressed.

"Lead or Leave" is actively mobilizing younger generations—but it is an organization for Americans of all ages. Only an alliance across generations can save our nation's economic future.

. . . IF WE ACT NOW

America is dangerously shortchanging younger generations. The federal government spends twelve times more on the elderly than on children, yet, 7 percent of the elderly are poor while almost a quarter of all younger Americans live in poverty.

- 20 percent of our children are living under the poverty line. By the year 2005, it is projected that one in three children in America will live in poverty—with the greatest increase among white children.
- Young people today pay twenty times more Social Security taxes (even after inflation) than their grandparents did fifty years ago.
- Rising health care costs are making basic care a luxury item. While every person over 65 is covered, one in eight children are without any protection at all.
- When benefits are subtracted from tax payments—a process called Generational Accounting—younger Americans have the highest tax burden of any generation and the lowest level of benefits.

WHAT ARE "ENTITLEMENTS"?

Entitlements are the largest piece of our national budget pie. Entitlements are all government programs for which we automatically pay out benefits like Social Security, Medicare, farm subsidies, some student loans, and veterans assistance.

The three largest entitlement programs (consuming over 40 percent of the total budget) are Social Security, Medicare and Medicaid. The fastest growing entitlement is Medicaid—almost doubling in the last three years.

WHAT IS THE PROBLEM?

Entitlements were first established primarily as a means to help people out of poverty. Today, however, the largest chunk of entitlement spending goes to those who live above the poverty line. And with the budget pie shrinking, there's growing debate over who deserves government benefits—and how much.

THE TRUTH ABOUT SOCIAL SECURITY

America's Social Security system is in trouble. It has become an unfair, unsound program—relying on younger, less affluent and less numerous workers to support an older, more affluent and larger segment of the population.

Despite years of warnings, The Social Security Board of Trustees projects Social Security will go bankrupt as soon as 2020, even sooner (2000) for Medicare. And although Social Security is the largest single expense in our national budget, it has become a political "untouchable" for reformers who fear angering older voters.

MYTH: *Any Reduction in Social Security benefits will hurt poor Americans.*

FACT: Social Security and Medicare pay $75 billion a year to households with cash incomes over $50,000.

MYTH: *Social Security is a pension program. The money that comes out of your paycheck is saved safely in a bank for when you retire.*

FACT: Today's retirees get their benefits directly from the paychecks of working Americans. The so-called "trust fund" to be put away for the baby-boomer retirement has been robbed to finance current overspending.

MYTH: *People put into the system their entire lives and deserve every check.*

FACT: People **should** get back what they put in, plus compounded interest. Yet, many of today's retirees get three times what they contributed, regardless of need.

WHAT CAN WE DO TO ENSURE GENERATIONAL EQUITY?

America must adopt generationally equitable policies—**using need, not age, as the guideline.** We must commit to protect the poor—whatever their age, and we must begin to invest more in the future, and less on current consumption. This should be our national commitment.

THEN, NOW & IN THE FUTURE

1935
FDR launches Social Security to help elderly poor. Workers pay 1% FICA payroll tax. Baby Boomers born. National Debt: $250 billion.

1965
Pres. Johnson adds Medicare/ Medicaid to cover health costs; "safety net" for poor. Baby Busters born. National Debt: $1 trillion.

1993
Living in poverty: 7% of elderly, 20% of children. FICA rate is 15%. 1943 workers receive 300% of what they put in. 54% of federal entitlement spending goes to elderly. National Debt: $4.3 trillion.

2020
Social Security near insolvency. FICA rate: 40%; 1993 workers get 76% of what they put in, if any. Benefits for poor cut drastically. 70 million Boomers retire. National Debt: $13 trillion.

LIVING WITHIN OUR MEANS
AMERICA'S DEBT AND DEFICITS

What rises $1 billion a day, $40 million an hour, $11,000 a second? There's only one thing that grows that fast ... *the national debt.*

HOW BAD IS BAD?

America's national debt is $4.4 trillion dollars—enough to pay Michael Jordan's salary for 1.5 million years. And it's growing $11,000 dollars a second, $40 million an hour—a billion dollars a day.

WHAT IS THE NATIONAL DEBT?

The national debt is all the money the United States has borrowed since 1976, and hasn't yet paid back. It's so big that even if every sesame seed on every Big Mac ever sold was worth one dollar, it wouldn't come close to paying off the $4.4 trillion debt.

Think of it like a giant credit card with your name on it. You, and everyone else in America, owe a share of the national debt: $16,000. Over the course of your life, you can expect to pay $100,000 in taxes just for interest on the national debt.

The national debt and our rising annual budget deficits will have a huge impact on your economic future—how much you'll pay in taxes, your chances of getting a good job, owning your own home, or receiving good health care.

Everyone pays a steep price for our runaway deficits—particularly the poorest Americans who rely on government programs and steady economic growth, both of which are crippled by big deficits. Everything is hurt: jobs, homes, student loans, and the chance to invest in a stronger future.

HOW DID THE DEBT GET SO BIG?

For most of our two hundred years, we've borrowed responsibly, running deficits only in times of national emergency, such as a war or a great depression. But that ended in 1969, the last year America ran a budget surplus. Since the 1970's, our debt has grown steadily, skyrocketing from under $1 trillion in 1980 to $4.4 trillion today—and the debt is expected to top $6 trillion by the year 2000.

And a massive debt means massive interest payments—$300 billion a year to be exact—eating up twenty-five cents of every tax dollar, or twice the earnings of all the Fortune 500 companies combined. Money spent to pay off interest on our debt is totally wasted: it's money we don't have to invest in cleaning up our environment, rebuilding our cities or investing in education.

DEALING WITH THE DEBT AND DEFICIT

In 1992, the Presidential candidates hotly debated who had the best deficit reduction plan. President Clinton won office promising to tackle this national issue. After a tough political battle, Clinton passed his budget plan. According to economists, the plan will help reduce the deficit but will also add over $1 trillion to the national debt in the next five years.

America can no longer wait for serious deficit reduction. The government predicts *"economic and fiscal catastrophe"* if we don't get the problem under control in the next few years. Without dramatic change, we will have hyper inflation, Wall Street panic, or a debt crisis like a Third World country.

This is not a Republican or a Democratic issue. Both parties share equal responsibility for causing America's fiscal crisis—and for the solution. Everything except programs that protect the poor and disadvantaged must be on the table. No more sacred cows.

There are only two ways to reduce the deficit—cut spending or raise taxes, or both. Here are a few key steps to deficit reduction: deeper cuts in defense, limiting cost-of-living increases, means-testing entitlements, scaling back tax breaks like mortgage interest deductions, and cracking down on special-interest subsidies.

Katie Roiphe

The Morning After

*At twenty-four, Harvard graduate Roiphe, in characteristic GenX fashion,
blasted the feminist movement with a gentle but scathing appraisal of its
inability to comprehend the subtleties of sexuality in the 1990s.
Demystifying and even debunking the notion of a "rape crisis," Roiphe re-
stores common sense to an issue that has too long been debated by those
with agendas and ideologies at cross-purposes to the development of a
strong, healthy role for women in American society.*

Combating myths about rape is one of the central missions of the leaders of the rape-crisis movement. They spend money and energy trying to
break down myths like "She asked for it." But with all their noise about rape
myths, rape-crisis feminists are generating their own. If you look at the
scenes described in the plays, the poems, the pamphlets, the Take Back the
Night speak-outs, the stories told are loss-of-innocence stories. We all know
this plot: I trusted him—I thought people were good—then I realized—
afterward I knew. The rape, or sexual assault, is the moment of the fall. It
is the isolated instant when, in one victims's words, they "learn to hate."

* * *

People have asked me if I have ever been date-raped. And thinking back
on complicated nights, on too many glasses of wine, on strange and familiar
beds, I would have to say yes. With such a sweeping definition of rape, I
wonder how many people there are, male or female, who haven't been date-
raped at one point or another. People pressure and manipulate and cajole
each other into all sorts of things all the time. As Susan Sontag writes,
"Since Christianity upped the ante and concentrated on sexual behavior as
the root of virtue, everything pertaining to sex has been a 'special case' in
our culture, evoking peculiarly inconsistent attitudes."[1] No human interac-

tions are free from pressure, and the idea that sex is, or can be, makes it what Sontag calls a "special case," vulnerable to the inconsistent expectations of double standard.

With their expansive version of rape, rape-crisis feminists invent a kinder, gentler sexuality. Beneath the broad definition of rape, these feminists are endorsing their own utopian vision of sexual relations: sex without struggle, sex without power, sex without persuasion, sex without pursuit. If verbal coercion constitutes rape, then the word "rape" itself expands to include any kind of sex a woman experiences as negative.

When the novelist Martin Amis spoke at Princeton in 1992, he included a controversial joke: "As far as I'm concerned you can change your mind before, even during, but just not after sex." The reason this joke is funny, and the reason it's also too serious to be funny, is that in the current atmosphere you *can* change your mind afterward. Regret can signify rape. A night that was a blur, a night you wish hadn't happened, can be rape. Since verbal coercion and manipulation are ambiguous, it's easy to decide afterward that he manipulated you. You can realize it weeks or even years later. A psychiatrist at a West Coast campus told me that when he was on call, a patient called him at three in the morning to say that she had just realized she'd been raped two years earlier. This kind of belated revelation is not uncommon. A pamphlet warns that "a friend who has been raped may confide in you 10 minutes or 10 years after the attack."[2] This is a movement that deals in retrospective trauma.

"Rape" becomes a catchall expression, a word used to define everything that is unpleasant and disturbing about relations between the sexes. Students say things like "I realize that sexual harassment is a kind of rape."[3] If we refer to a spectrum of behavior from emotional pressure to sexual harassment as rape, then the idea itself gets diluted. It ceases to be powerful as either description or accusation. We threaten to confirm the vision of that eighteenth-century patriarch Henry Fielding when he writes, "These words of exclamation (murder! robbery! rape!) are used by ladies in a fright as fa la la da sa are in music only as vehicles of sound and without any fixed idea."[4]

On the not-so-distant edge of the spectrum, carrying this rhetoric to its logical conclusion, some feminists actually collapse the distinction between rape and sex. Catharine MacKinnon writes, "Compare victims' reports of rape with women's reports of sex. They look a lot alike. . . . In this light, the major distinction between intercourse (normal) and rape (abnormal) is that the normal happens so often that one cannot get anyone to see anything wrong with it."[5]

There are a few feminists involved in rape education who object to the current expanding definitions of sexual assault. Gillian Greensite, founder of the rape prevention education program at the University of Southern California at Santa Cruz, writes that the seriousness of the crime "is being undermined by the growing tendency of some feminists to label all heterosexual miscommunication and insensitivity as acquaintance rape."[6] From within the rape-crisis movement, Greensite's dissent makes an important point. If we are going to maintain an idea of rape, then we need to reserve it for instances of physical violence or the threat of physical violence. One woman, raped by a stranger at knife point, says that although she feels bad for women raped by their former boyfriends, she does not think their experience should be equated with hers.

Going against the current of much rape-crisis feminism, Majorie Metsch, Columbia's director of peer education, also distinguishes between rape and bad sex. "Most of the time when someone comes in and says 'I was really really drunk and I shouldn't have had sex last night,' it is not the same as saying 'I was raped.' My attitude is that you do not use language that the person herself is not using. It could be that it was just bad sex." Metsch reasons that the social and psychological weight of the word "rape" eclipses its descriptive value in cases of regretted sex. With this approach, she avoids injecting everyday college life with the melodrama of the rape crisis.

But some people want that melodrama. They want the absolute value placed on experience by absolute words. Words like "rape" and "verbal coercion" sculpt the confusing mass of experience into something easy to understand. The idea of date rape comes at us fast and coherent. It comes at us when we've just left home and haven't yet figured out where to put our new futon or how to organize our new social life. The rhetoric about date rape defines the terms, gives names to nameless confusions, and sorts through mixed feelings with a sort of insistent consistency. In the first rush of sexual experience, the fear of date rape offers a tangible framework in which to locate fears that are essentially abstract.

Notes

1. Susan Sontag, *Styles of Radical Will* (New York: Farrar, Straus and Giroux, 1976), 46.

2. "Acquaintance Rape." Rockville, Md.: ACHA, 1992.

3. Billie Wright Dziech and Linda Weiner, *The Lecherous Professor: Sexual Harassment on Campus* (Chicago: University of Illinois Press, 1990), 101.

4. Henry Fielding, *Tom Jones* (1749; reprint, London: Penguin, 1966), 471.

5. Catharine MacKinnon, *Toward a Femininst Theory of the State* (Cambridge: Harvard University Press, 1989), 146.

6. Neil Gilbert, "Realities and Mythologies of Rape," *Society* 29 (May–June 1992).

Ice Cube

Cheo H. Coker

for The Source

profile

Between a rock and a hard place, this once-angriest of rappers now balances a booming career, a wife and two children, a following of gangsta kids, membership in the Nation of Islam, and a personal sociopolitical agenda. Known for videos where typical scenes include a white man begging to be shot in the head by "Dr. Cube," this GenX rapper scares the shit out of most white adults—especially because their own kids buy his records and imitate his style. Something bizarre, even mutated, has risen out of the blackest ashes of urban decay, failed social programs, and oppressive racism. It has a variety of names—hip-hop, science, the 5 percent, gangsta rap—but it all boils down to an intolerance of the way things have been for too long. Ice Cube believes that white folks are responsible for the current mess but uses a typically GenX-style rationale and oblique media reference to the Menendez brothers: "The dollar has replaced all the bullshit morals they [whites] say they have—give 'em enough, they'll kill their parents."

At 2:30 AM, the abandoned L.A. Herald-Examiner complex swarms with activity. A small team of production assistants dampen the ground with water from a truck's tank while another group fogs the air with artificial smoke. For a simple tracking shot, the elaborate setup seems incredibly extravagant.

Gary Gray, the 23-year-old mastermind behind "It Was A Good Day," slouches in his high-backed director's chair. The quiet vigilance of his expression lets everyone know who the production's real HNIC deploying his minimum-wage pawns to ready the set for his power piece, a dark knight with a record deal and a belligerent attitude.

"PLAYBACK!"

Ice Cube, radiating nonchalance, emerges from the shadows with a gangsta stroll. Draped in black from the tip of his black power Afro-pick to the bottom of his spotless Chuck Taylors, the rap superstar is down for whatever. Lurching to a sudden halt, he slowly turns his head over his right shoulder and gives the telescopic lens The Stare: intense, fiery eyes, flared nostrils and bushy eyebrows pointing down like arrows. It's the trademark look that's graced album covers, St. Ides ads, his Street Knowledge tour jackets and virtually every picture he's ever taken—a visual "Fuck all y'all." It's the anchor of his hardcore image, the rubber stamp that seals every document he presents to his burgeoning mainstream audience.

"Cut," yells Gray. Adjusting the brim of his baseball cap, his eyes remain glued to the monitor. "Let's do it again from the top."

Cube retraces his steps and repeats the whole routine no less than ten times. The Stare never changes. It falls over his face like a mask at the first sign of a protruding lens or iridescent flash. It's Black rage on a platter, ready to come out at the twist of a knob or the push of a button, stylized and sanitized for mass consumption. Five years after *Straight Outta Compton*, this is what the game boils down to.

L.A.-based gangsta rap, once "disturbing" enough to merit the attention of the FBI and police groups, now dominates the radio and video waves. Snoop Doggy Dogg is suddenly cover material for every rag from *Rolling Stone* to *Newsweek*, cementing his place in history as the first artist to have a debut album to enter the chart at number one. "Let Me Ride" and "Check Yourself" dominated both radio and retail all summer long. Even Hammer protegés DRS weaseled their way into the hearts of millions with, of all things, "Gangsta Lean," a "Dead Homiez"–influenced ballad, compete with gospel inflections and prayers for dead players to "put down [their] dice."

FIRE & SNAKES

"I'm not selling Black rage to white kids, I'm selling truth."

Under the watchful eye of Brother Ron, Ice Cube's personal and religious assistant, the initial tension in the trailer is thick as the harder questions come up. A little after ten o'clock at night, cast and crew retire from the filming of "Really Doe" for a much-needed soul food dinner break complete with ribs (beef, of course), fried chicken, collard greens and macaroni and cheese. Cube passes on the food, offering terse answers to the barrage of questions set before him.

"I think once you compromise your integrity to sell records to a pop crowd, that's when you've gone pop. If you stay the same, and that pop crowd comes to you, you ain't moved a muscle. I'm on the pop charts , but I ain't poppin' shit! Popcorn! I ain't never compromised my integrity or eased up on what I was thinking, not like, 'Damn, I got white fans now.'

"Truth has no color," he continues, eyebrows slowly moving towards the cocked position. "I've gotten these fans without deviating, without holding back, without bullshitting, and if I always do the same way, I'll keep 'em. It ain't like they new to this. They know what Ice Cube was about when they bought my first record. The goal ain't to turn the other way and stop what I'm doing, it's to get more intense with it and see who's really down. Their people hide the truth from them, and maybe if it was shoved down their throats, they would respect us more."

Lethal Injection, his fourth album in as many years, opens with "The Shot." A generic white man waits impatiently in a hospital waiting room for an injection from "Dr. Cube," much like the way eager white fans line up at the cash register to purchase their annual hit of Ice Cube's funk-laden Black anger. He gives "Mr. White" his shot all right: to the side of his neck with a loaded pistol. *You want me to blow your head off you gullible muthafucka? And you're actually gonna pay me for it? Brace yo' self!*

"Call it however you see it," Cube continues, "but on the overall, that's a little segment. Hard law is the best law, brother. It's really about killing off the white way of thinking, that mentality. To put a bullet in somebody's brain—that's bullshit. I wanna put the truth into their kids, 'cause that's where the progress can be made. They need a generation of kids that turn to their forefathers and says, 'Fuck you. Y'all fucked up everything, you got us fighting each other, it's all your fault and I ain't with this bullshit.' From there on shit can happen."

Visions of his more than congenial relationship with the Red Hot Chili Peppers, with whom he toured the country on Lollopalooza two years ago and featured in his video "Wicked" immediately jump to mind. A shot with him and the band's bassist Flea arm-in-arm like little kids inspired the photographer to proclaim, "This is something Martin Luther King would have been proud of." Does he stand by his belief, as soon to be official member of the Nation of Islam, that all white people are devils?

"Yep," he replies gravely. "I do. Take a snake for instance, man. All snakes ain't poisonous, but they all snakes. You got some whites out there that are strictly devils and you got some that come out and they're harmless. But I think that if it comes to sides, I don't think no white person is going to come to our side to fight their people, I think it's going to be paired off. And that's the bottom line. We've been hurt man, we've been through some shit and we're still going through some shit. Most of the time, if you go back far enough and dig deep enough, you'll find a white person behind the shit we're going through now."

And Flea?

"We's cool."

But he's still a devil?

"He's not poisonous."

So why will a white audience continue to buy records from an artist who is doing his best to convince them they're evil?

"That ain't my problem, what they're getting out of it. I'm worried about what Black folks is getting out of it 'cause we need the medicine. I just do my records how I feel, and whoever don't like it don't have to pick it up. I can't think about what other people are going to think about my shit, I've got to come real."

"Enemy" and "Skin Is My Sin" are two records on the album that are produced by Solid Productions, a white remix team straight out of Denmark. Coming from a pro-Black radical stance, isn't it contradictory, like PRT's work with Tony D, to have a "devil" do the beats?

"Naw, man, you're getting it all wrong. I can work with anybody. I don't let that stop me from working with people or dealing with people. I treat people cool if they treat me cool. Are Solid Productions devils? Yes they are, but they cool so I treat them cool. Ain't no problem with that. I know some brothers that are devils, or should have the label cause they wicked and evil. If you cool with me, Black or white, I'm cool with you.

"It's white people that are stuck on that color thing. They the ones that told us, 'y'all's Black and we's white.' We just said we was people. We came out with open arms, and to this day, we come out with open arms. We do more harm to each other than we do white folks, so I ain't stuck on this color thing, youknowhutumsayin'? That don't keep me from being respectful with anybody who's respectful with me, because it should be about who you are and not what color you are, but white folks done set the standard, so they have to live by it. If you look at a lot of the evilness in the world, far enough down the line; white folks, in the middle of it. They don't give a fuck about nothing but the dollar. No human rights, no God, none of that. The dollar has replaced all the bullshit morals they say they have—give 'em enough, they'll kill their parents."

ROOTS & CULTURE

Even a complex, highly influential career like Ice Cube's has a simple beginning. Born O'Shea Jackson (he was named after his mother's favorite football player O.J. Simpson), he was the fourth child in the family, the second boy and the youngest by eight years. He grew up on the West Side of L.A., not far from Watts, and was into a lot of the things other kids from around his way were into: Girls, football, and basketball, in exactly that order. It wasn't until his 9th grade year, when challenged by a student named Kiddo to write a rap in typing class, did he realize he had a real gift with words.

"When I started writing, it was off-beat and *everything, but it rhymed*," he reminisces, the tension leaving his face. "I said my rap, Kiddo said his, but he had bitten all the songs he heard. Then. I kept going, and we tried to be like New York rappers, because that's who we admired. But, after a while I said fuck this, I'ma start doing some tapes about stuff that happened in my neighborhood about niggaz slanging, stuff like that . . ."

His interest in sports kept him from falling into a lot of the traps that caught his friends, like gangbangin' or getting really deep into selling drugs, but it didn't prevent him from keeping his eyes and ears open to his environment. He kept writing raps about the 'hood, at first with CIA, a group he formed with homies Sr Jinx and KD, and later with Jinx's cousin, Andre Young (later known worldwide as Dr. Dre). Around 1986, while he and Dre rocked the parties at Skateland by doing dirty parodies of songs like "Roxanne, Roxanne," he made his first connections with Eazy-E, a former drug dealer who decided to invest his money from the trade into his own record label, Ruthless. Soon after, Niggaz With Attitudes was born. After a year at the Phoenix Institute of Technology studying drafting (at the insistence of his parents), he came back and helped put together Eazy-E's *Easy Duz It* and *Straight Outta Compton*. The combination of Dre's production and Ice Cube's lyrical input pushed both records to the top of the charts without any airplay, simultaneously putting Compton on the map and making them all international superstars.

His Midas touch, however, didn't work when it came to his personal finances. After essentially writing two albums that sold a combined 3,000,000 copies, the only thing Cube saw for his services was $32,700. While their manager Jerry Holler took home over $130,000 from the $650,000 their tour made—allowing him to reside in a plush house in West Lake—Cube was still living in his mother's house, washing the dishes and taking out the garbage. He had no royalties, no merchandising, no publishing, and much to his chagrin, no contract.

Cube decided that he wasn't going out like Lonzo, Arabian Prince and other posse members who got lost in the sauce. If he could transform a talentless midget crack-slanger with a Napoleon complex and effeminate voice into a respected rapper just off the strength of his writing talents, he figured, then why not work the same magic on his own career?

"I talked to Dre before I left the group. He was thinking about some things too. I was like, 'Man, look Dre, you done did this, you done that . . . is your money right, for sure?' He was like, 'Nah man, my shit is kinda shaky too.' If I had one person to be down with me, we could have made a stand and they would have had to break us off. Tried to get Ren; he heard me but wasn't ready to do nothing. Dre, we talked for hours and I was like, 'I'm about to go to New York, man, to do my muthafuckin' record.' I was at my momma's house just pacin'. With the cordless phone, just pacin'. 'I'm about to leave the group, I just can't handle it.' 'You crazy,' he said. 'Don't do that.' 'Man, I got to go . . . Well, let's just have a meeting man, no Jerry Heller, just us five. Let's try to get this shit straight,' I told him. 'Awright,' he said, 'when you wanna have it?' 'Let's have it tomorrow, man, up at the studio,' I said. Eleven o'clock, I went to the studio, and nobody showed up. Fuck it."

A few months after leaving the group, jheri curl, khakis and Lench Mob in tow, he arrived in Greenwich Village to record *AmeriKKKa's Most Wanted* with the Bomb Squad. The game suddenly became more serious. "I found out I was more creative, and all I needed was room to breathe." He strokes his beard pensively. "A lot of ideas used to slip through the cracks because, around [N.W.A.] if you had a fucked-up idea they would never let you live it down. Arabian Prince once said that we should have named the first album *From Compton With Love* and they gave it to him from the time he said it till when he left the group. Now in this solo situation, I was quarterback.

Like with the song 'The Nigga You Love To Hate.' The original chorus was 'Love, Hate, Love Hate . . .' Shit was wack. So I said. 'Why don't we put "Fuck You Ice Cube!"' Jinx was like, 'Hell, naw, you don't want to dis yourself on your own record.' I'm like, 'That's exactly what I want to do. Yeah!' It fit together.

"Plus, hanging with Chuck D, man, he's a smart brother. I was out of L.A. for a month in strange New York away from the house with all these muthafuckas clownin' my Jheri curl. I was in a new environment, and brothers in New York are a little more on top of the knowledge than brothers out here. It was about me now. It wasn't about, 'I came to get my ticket to fly to the show' or 'What room am I in?' It was *you* buy the ticket, *you* find the room and *you* make sure the album is together. I was like, 'Damn!' Once I asked Chuck, 'How that sound?' and he was like, 'How you want it to sound?' Going to New York was the best move I ever made in my life."

It was also during this pivotal time that Cube was introduced to the Nation of Islam and the teachings of The Honorable Louis Farrakhan through Public Enemy's Brother Drew. He slowly killed off his "nigga" mentality, replacing it with a strongly Black nationalistic perspective that set the stage for *Death Certificate*. Only when he leaves the rap music game does he feel he can be true to the ideology that gives his life a sense of direction.

"When you got an X, brother, you fall under the spiritual laws of Islam and some of the language I use, I can't use it," he explains. "Some of it is getting to a 'dead' people, so I got to try to get a hold of them the best way I can. The Minister told me in exact words that I do more for him being outside the Nation than I do being with an 'X.' An 'X' is more surface. I'm in The Nation if you ask me, and if you ask him," he said as he nods his head towards Brother Ron to his right, "that's all that matters."

Perhaps it's his belief in the NOI principle of brotherhood among Black men that has allowed for him to resolve his conflicts with the other former members of N.W.A. Despite being hurt that he was "equalled up to a white man" like Benedict Arnold for leaving the group, he's back on amicable terms with MC Ren and Dr. Dre, and despite calling for his fiery death at the end of *No Vaseline* speaks to Eazy-E on some occasions. About Eazy he said, "We'll never do business, but we talk. They paid me my money, and that was my whole beef from the beginning, so I don't hold no grudges in there all right as long as they do me right even after all this."

His relationship with Ren, whom he just ran into for the first time in years very recently is "perfect," especially since, as Lorenzo X, he's joined the Nation. "Brother was just spiritually superior to the point where he was, when he was dead, but now he's straight," Cube says. His face radiates, albeit briefly, with a huge smile. "Me and that nigga talked for about an hour and a half and it was like old times. I was real happy about that."

He reserves most of his words for Dre, the member whom he was closest to before the breakup. "Dre is so creative, he's got to be at the top of the producers," he gushes. "He's just so damn good, you can't put his shit in a category with anybody else." As evidenced by his cameo in the latter's video, the two are on more than casual speaking terms.

"At first it was kind of timid," Cube says about their first meetings after the N.W.A. breakup, "but then we really started talking, man, like old times, going to his house and laughing about the ole shit Muthafucka was like, 'We ought to do a record together.' I was like, 'Shit, that's the bomb.' We had to finish our own projects, but now we're in the process of getting that chemistry started up again."

Helter Skelter, the name of their forthcoming collaboration, will drop sometime in the middle of 1994. An injection of chronicized funk matched with Ice Cube's distinctive flow should add some much needed variety to both their staid formulas, much the same way The Bomb Squad would be vastly improved with the re-introduction of Eric Sadler. The reunion of these pioneers with potential guest appearances by Ren and Snoop, could be the closest thing to the reformation of N.W.A.

"CAN'T WE ALL JUST GET ALONG?"

While most of the former members of N.W.A. are now at peace with each other, the rest of society has never been so divided. The gaps separating the races continues to widen, and even the most objective inquisitor can't help but admit that the ideal of integration has all but failed. Los Angeles, like most of America, is a racial timebomb. Therefore it makes sense to ask the one man, who despite his controversial views, has a captive audience on both sides of the fence: is complete separation the only solution to the race problem?

"Naw, that's not the only one," Cube replies. His attention is momentarily diverted by the image of the L.A.'s canyon fires as they flicker on the trailer's small television. The city is once again on fire. Ashes rain like snowflakes, instantly invoking memories of the recent rebellion.

"Re-education. Separation would just give us a fair playing field. I'm telling you, the muthafucka that won't *treat* you right won't *teach* you right. I don't need to learn nothing else about Europeans—I know enough about those muthafuckas. I need to know who *I* am," he emphasizes, "where I come from, my name. We're the only people on this Earth that carry other people's names—not God or his attributes."

His eyes lose their anger, and, for a brief moment, look sorrowful. "We was named after *wood*," he exclaims, rapping his knuckles across one of the trailer's cabinets to further stress his point. "Take a name like Eric Wood. It doesn't reflect nothing holy about your name—are you gonna see the Black Eric Wood or the white Eric Wood? When you hear the name Julio Chavez, you know what you're gonna see before you see the man: a history, a respect, a culture. A John Woo, the same thing. 'Darren Jones is coming,' shit, the Black one or the white one? No kind of respect, no kind of culture. They have no use for us anymore but to get us to play basketball, entertain them on sitcoms, think of new dance steps or new fuckin' fashion, so we end up becoming walking marketing tools 'cause we so open with our shit."

America's on the verge of exploding, and his revolutionary fervor is chomping at the bit, but Cube is no longer the naive young O'Shea without a job living under Hosea and Doris Jackson's roof. He has a beautiful wife and soon will have three kids. He talks about the streets of South Central, settings for his videos but no longer his home. "I can't live in South Central anymore," Cube explains. "It's like the jungle, man, and when somebody got a piece of meat, everybody wants it. I leave town too much, I got a wife and kids, and I don't want a hungry nigga running up in my house and snatching my kids talking about 'give us some money.' My family is more important than this business or saving face. I'm definitely still 'true to the game,' because it's not where you put your head, it's where you put your heart.

"If two of you muthafuckas is drowning in the water," Cube says, shifting a little, "you gonna get mad 'cause a muthafucka gets in a boat and try to help you up? Or you want him to drown with you? Nah, I'm jumping on the boat and throwing a life preserver in, saying 'Yo, let's all get on board.' I didn't get on and say, 'find your own way out.'"

Cube, however, has reached a critical turning point in his career. He realizes that the older he gets, the harder it is to lead the charge on a rap battlefield where the soldiers are often younger and deadlier.

"It's real easy to be hardcore when there's no situation around," he cautions. "But when one comes up, you see those hardcore muthafuckas skiddadle. I ain't gonna start no shit where there's none jumping off. I ain't hard as no bullet, so how hard can I be? Can't step through the earth, so how hardcore can you be? If I knock the shit out of you, you gonna bleed. Shit ain't about hardcore, you just got to be real."

Even the former king of hardcore, that man whose boasts used to strike fear in many a listener, has to admit that certain aspects of gangsta rap have simply gotten out of hand.

"It's out of control. I think a lot of people put out records that sound like comic books—a whole lot of shooting with nothing in it. And I don't want to do records like that, nor did I ever mean to. I wanted to do records that was real. I'd rather be real and kill one person than be fake and kill 40. It don't make no sense."

Every dog has his day. What will become of Ice Cube when he can't attract the spotlight anymore, when the club dates dry up and the records collect dust?

"Once muthafuckas say, 'Cube man, you ain't hitting no more,' then it's time for me to give it up. I don't plan on being in it forever any damn way. Maybe muthafuckas will remember me after I'm out of it, and they'll say, 'When he was down he was hot.' Maybe I'm producing that muthafucka that will knock me out the spot. They'll never say, 'Cube got in that position and just punked out or turned his back or went pop,' 'cause I'm true to myself and my audience. They'll say, 'Cube's shit wasn't hittin' no more and some new muthafuckas jumped in his spot.' And I'll humbly submit."

Strength Through Apathy

Douglas Rushkoff

As politics editor for a Los Angeles club-life fashion magazine, I quickly re-
alized that my audience and coworkers had little interest in the kinds of
news coming in on the AP wire service. My well-researched complaints
about politicians' pitiful explanations for their inconsistent behavior fell on
deaf ears: No one was watching the news, so no one heard the lies. Then
it hit me: A generation that has disconnected itself from the propaganda
machine can no longer be controlled by it. And just because GenX is ap-
athetic about mainstream news doesn't mean we don't care.

A recent *Times-Mirror* poll of Americans revealed that virtually no one
under 30 ever reads a newspaper or watches the news. This has led to a
resurgence of attacks on our nation's youth for being apathetic, lazy and
stupid. Why, these critics cry, don't young people care about anything?
Don't they understand the democratic process? Why don't they want to get
involved?

I went through a similar period of questioning last month, when an article I was editing made a passing reference to Willie Horton. No one around
seemed to know who he was. I decided to take a poll of my own. I asked
several dozen people on Melrose Avenue if they'd ever heard of Willie
Horton. Only one guy had.

And now, a reader quiz: Do *you* know who Willie Horton was?

Willie Horton was the murderer who Governor Dukakis let out of prison
on a furlough program. Horton went on to commit a rape during his time
out, and George Bush's team used the events as a main campaign issue. The

then Vice-President's campaign hinged on making Dukakis appear weak on criminals, and keeping the public distracted from Bush's own connections to the Iran-Contra affair. Willie Horton's picture seemed to appear in Bush's commercials more often than the president-to-be's.

It may be true that no one remembers Willie Horton, but why should they? He's just a sick murderer who committed rape. He has nothing to do with Presidential politics, the state of the nation, or your or my life. He was a cheap ploy, un-newsworthy, and ultimately irrelevant. It is not *really* sad that no one ever heard of Willie Horton—or that no one even cares.

Americans have stopped caring about the news because it is filled with Willie Hortons. The news exists more to distract us from issues than to inform us about them. In fact, it is our policy makers' intention to raise a generation that will remain apathetic, acquiescent and mute.

George Bush pretends that the most important issue in the United States today, the one worthy of a Constitutional Amendment, is flag burning. To him, this is supposedly the greatest threat to our nation.

If a kid bothers to watch the news, he or she gets to see George Bush, senators, and congressmen argue about flag burning. Now, honestly, how many times have you burned a flag, watched a flag being burned, or even thought about flag burning until Bush raised this issue? The only thing remotely close that I can remember is an episode of *Room 222*, when one of the students made a sculpture of a flag being flushed down a toilet. Some immigrant taking night school in classroom 222 was so upset that he hacked the sculpture to pieces, risking his own citizenship application in this act of vandalism. Heavy. (*Room 222* took place in the Sixties, so the young artist's right to free expression was, of course, vehemently defended.)

The least common denominator holding a country together is its sense of patriotism. If the American people have nothing to hold them together—no issue to agree on—it follows that a president seeking power needs to enforce patriotism. America as an idea, emblemized by the flag, is all that's left for Bush to rally behind. The youth of America, quite simply, don't give a shit about the flag. They don't particularly want to burn it, but they don't want to worry about defending the stars and stripes from wound-be arsonists either. Most kids would rather watch a good argument on *The People's Court* than read a Supreme Court decision about desecrating symbolic fabric.

The "uninvolved" status of our nation's young people is a direct result of our leadership's fear to do its real business in public. Take the Savings and Loan fiasco. We lost more than $150 billion so far to a Republican policy of financing shaky bankers. But the Democrats can't talk about it either, because they took cash bribes to look the other way. To keep public scrutiny away from these indiscretions, the public relations teams hired by our nation's policy makers think up ways to fill up our attention. They bore us away from involvement.

Reagan and Bush have avoided the kind of investigative journalism and public outcry that brought down Nixon—but not by keeping us *un*informed. It is by *over*-informing us. The White House currently churns out reams of statistics, reports and policies every day. Reporters are given more information about unimportant stories than they can possibly sift through. They don't have the time or the staff to go snooping around for more.

Meanwhile, in the real, unreported news, the world is in a food, health and environmental crisis. The AIDS epidemic is vastly underfunded. American tax dollars are still spent overthrowing non-hostile governments that don't trade with us the way we like. These are the issues young Americans might care about—and they do.

In fact, it has even become fashionable to care about these kinds of problems. When the United States evacuated the Philippines last month, more than 260 young Peace Corps volunteers were uprooted. Entrance into the Corps and other volunteer groups is more competitive than ever before. Rock & roll has become synonymous with the rain forest, and MTV has more coverage on hunger in Africa than network news.

I asked an FM radio news producer about his target audience. He told me, without a hint of sarcasm, that the typical listener—according to his marketing department—is a stoned adolescent male, masturbating in his bedroom. This producer, like incumbent lawmakers and their press representatives, underestimates our nation's youth. True, they don't read the paper or watch the news. Why should they? It's boring and useless. But they have started and will continue to turn elsewhere for the kind of information that matters.

Wiley Wiggins

Happy!

Seventeen-year-old high school dropout Wiley Wiggins is best known for playing Mitch in Richard Linklater's film Dazed and Confused. *His shoe-string Austin 'zine* Happy! *is a sarcastic slacker's-eye view of a world where the only thing anyone seems to want from a kid is his money. Wiggins's pet peeve, and one of the main reasons he dropped out of school, is the infamous Channel One, which, as he explains, "is a television program that students are forced to watch every morning in a large number of American public schools. The programming includes three minutes of paid advertisements for junk food and consumer culture crap. My magazine's original purpose was a mid-scale psychic terrorism campaign against Whittle Communications, the company that produced the garbage." He was also the mastermind behind a scam to distribute handheld remotes to students so that they could switch off the commercials from their desks.*

An explanation of the title:

Janet had come to the conclusion that modern life just plain sucked, and all her fantasies of escape had gone down in flames like crashing empty jets as she floated down on hot gusts of smoke with her parachute of idle thoughts.

In her nightmares masked men worked busily at shaving her pubic hair and painting over moles and blemishes with white paint that burned her skin and smelled like Nutrasweet. Then came the last touch, and she struggled in her bonds as the men presented her with her very own mask, a broad smiling happy face with no eyes.

"HAPPY"

Wiley's satire of a real school assembly where students posed questions to a reporter from Channel One.

STUDENT: Hello Mr. "Reporter." I was watching your insipid show at gunpoint today and saw a cute little politically correct segment about anorexia and how horrible it is that children will die for appearances. You then followed this up with a zit cream commercial featuring a rabid pack of teenagers ridiculing the outcast with pimples. How do you justify this?

REPORTER: Cool! We're glad you enjoyed the program! Be sure to attend class next week when we'll show you how to be cool on like, a date, dude. By the way, you use words that are totally uncool and like make my head hurt. So maybe you should just have yourself a Big Mac and chill out.

The teenage populace is the biggest spending group in America. We are the mindless base on which rests the towering pillar of capitalism. BE YOUNG, HAVE FUN, DRINK PEPSI.

"When you think of the power of television to educate, aren't you glad it doesn't?"—Alexander King

Of course it does, Alex. Sit back, click click, react.
Passive absorption versus active creation.
Eat or be eaten.

Wiley explains: "Happy has changed a lot since I finally dropped out of school and went out to find whatever fortune this country has left for people my age. School has become more of an inescapable metaphor than a real thing to be politically dealt with." So what began as a 'zine satirizing school soon developed into a forum for Wiley to experiment with prose:

Jeffrey ignored the elderly squeals, concentrating on the pad pad of his shoes against the wet asphalt. He slipped the filter off his smoke, careful not to rip the actual cigarette, and rummaged through his trench for a light. 14-year-old gutterpunk girls sat their little asses in the trash, embracing against the cold. Jeff thought he saw them playing with a rat or some shit, the creature's eyes distant from the toy affection being forced on it. He saw what it saw: food.

She sat in the restaurant with a green lizard glaze that passed badly for eyeballs covering her skull sockets. Her skin was smooth and crafted like soft beige clay. Her breasts were badly hidden in a gray T-shirt.

He walked in and sat across from her, thinking about maybe buying a sandwich. Thinking about the blinding blood white hate light that made its way through the windows collapsing the walls like wet paper. People had no time to scream as the Mini-mall Alien ship rooted its tendrils into the ground through the ashes of the city and the people it burnt dead and clean. It was eager to feed itself on the souls and the hearts of men fed to it via its symbiotic business relations with its parasite school districts bustling from its back like oozing boils.

Jeff surpressed a squeal. That was no way for a man or a city to die. The children were pumped silently from the school boils directly into the mall's digestive system. Never arguing, never speaking to one another, alone and dead. Jeff made his way over to the girl and offered her a cup of coffee. He was pleased to find out the green glaze wasn't blind. The mutants weren't dead just yet.

CHAPTER 4

THE DREGS

The Dregs

Maybe every generation is considered soft, weak, and whiny by the one preceding it. Maybe every generation feels it has been left with a junkyard of a culture and zero prospects for any future at all. And maybe every generation has its literary expression of the seeming futility of it all and the heroism required just to carry on.

From Huck Finn back to Oedipus, great literature appears to be about pariahs of one sort or another. What makes these guys and gals heroes is that they persevere no matter what. If the busters are truly generational outcasts, then it follows that GenX literature should be rich with such examples. While it's still too early in the decade to create a syllabus for GenX Lit 101, the following writers have already demonstrated an ability to find the heroic in the mundane and the glimmer of success in even the most disastrous of failures. After all, we've got less to work with here.

Rather than rafting down the Mississippi with an escaped slave or crashing the gates at Colonus after an eighty-year exile, the GenX hero escapes in Dad's Chrysler and crashes the gates at the Roxy by bribing the bouncer with a porno tape or a blow job. The central conflicts are the same; the cultural iconography is just a little updated.

But GenX writers are aware of their world's vapid nature. Their characters struggle for meaning and certainty in a landscape bereft of symbols with traditionally recognizable resonance. What characterizes these works, then, is their appropriation of the cultural dungheap for a new epic, scatological mythos. And above all else, these writers create characters who approach these dregs with joy, humor, and an odd combination of irony and naïveté. They are determined to make the best of things.

Walter Kirn

Can't Get Started

Despite his Princeton-Oxford education, editorial stints with Vanity Fair *and* Spy *magazines, and acceptance into the upper echelon of the New York Literary scene, novelist Walter Kirn remains, at his core, a small-town late-converted Mormon Minnesotan, amused and bewildered by his big-city success. His two books,* She Needed Me *and* My Hard Bargain, *have provoked reviewers to herald this thirty-year-old as the future voice of American literature. Still unconvinced of his ability or desire to climb to the top of this particular heap, Kirn maintains a safe distance from the boomer temptations laid before him. In this funny but frightening story, he makes it clear that—like most GenXers—he feels more comfortable thinking of himself as an outsider looking in.*

Last year, when I was still in college, still on track for a normal life, I had a big fight with my father and he stopped sending me money. I don't remember why we fought, only that I was back home for the weekend, washing my hair in the master bathroom with one of those tubes of coconut shampoo my father is always stealing from hotel rooms, when the bastard came in and sat down on the toilet and started chewing me out about something. I made some crack I thought he couldn't hear over the sound of the shower, and the next thing I knew, my father was yelling, lunging at me through the shower curtain. He pinned my shoulders against the wall and said it was either him or me, me or him. Then he slugged me. My father had attended Wisconsin State on a football scholarship—he set a team record for unassisted tackles—and I swear he thinks it gives him permission to blow up physically now and then. Anyway, I fell. I fell down onto the floor of the tub and was lying there naked, screaming at the guy, saying what a crazy fuck he was and that if he didn't lay off I'd kill him, when he lifted one of his size-eleven feet and stomped me in the chest.

"You know what you've cost me?" he said. "You know what you've cost me over the years? You think I'm some goddamned millionaire, don't you? Mister cash machine. Mister steak and lobster."

I tried to squirm away. I couldn't breathe.

"Seventy thousand bucks," my father said. "Seventy thousand a year, that's all I make. It used to be a lot, but now it's nothing. *God, I am disappointed in this country.*"

That's about as much as I remember.

Two weeks later my father cut me off. I didn't get the news from him but from an assistant dean at school. She called me to her office one morning and said my tuition was way overdue and that I should pay it immediately—by certified check if possible. I told her to call my father. "I already spoke to your father," she said. "He said you're independent now. He said you're supporting yourself."

"Like hell I am."

"Well, maybe there's a relative," she said. "Someone in the extended family who takes a special interest in your life."

"My family is not extended," I said. "Everyone's been divorced and remarried. Everyone's part of some other family now."

The dean shook her head and pushed the bill at me. "I hate to give ultimatums," she said, "but either you get another student loan or you can forget about classes next month."

I looked at the bill: $6,000. I had borrowed nine from the government already. I didn't want to go deeper into debt, but I knew that unless I got the extra six and managed to stay enrolled in school, I would have to start paying off the nine.

"Give me the loan application," I said.

I was one and a half semesters short of getting my degree in sociology. In high school, where they'd called it social studies, I'd earned mostly B's in the subject, along with one A and a C. With those grades, I wasn't exactly sure why the college had even accepted me. It was supposed to be such a prestigious institution, so incredibly ancient and selective. Maybe the admissions office had read my transcript wrong, or maybe they were just hard up that year. All I know is that most of these places everyone says are so tough to get into—all these schools and societies and clubs—are usually pretty easy to get into. If you're polite, that is, and can pay.

I thought I could pay. My father was a real-estate attorney who worked in the tallest building in St. Paul and lived in a paid-off three-story house whose two-car garage was always full. He said he would handle everything. "Education is priceless," he said. "You can't put a dollar amount on education."

But then we had that fight.

I was sharing an apartment at the time with a physics student from China named Peng. The rent was average: $400 a month. The utilities weren't bad either, except for the phone. Peng made lots of calls to China and stayed on for over an hour, not even talking, just listening. Some months, our phone bill was more than the rent.

Who was Peng calling? His family, he said. "Chinese families very close," he said.

Straightening out the phone bill each month—the account was in my name, so I had to pay the bill—was Peng's and my only activity together. His English was straight off a take-out menu; the only words he could pronounce so normal people could understand them were the names for all the elements, so there wasn't a lot we could talk about. Besides, I didn't know jack about physics and Peng didn't know any sociology. We could have talked about women, I suppose, but Peng didn't seem to care about women. He cared about his experiments. I asked him some questions to break the ice once, like what he thought of the Chinese government. He said, "Which government? Which China?" I didn't know there were two, so I dropped it.

After using a yellow marker to highlight all of Peng's calls, I would put the bill on the pillow in his closet. (I made Peng live in the closet because our apartment had only one bedroom and he could always sleep in the lab.) The bill was not a problem for Peng, since he never spent any money. Though he earned a modest illegal income from helping other foreign students troubleshoot their personal computers, he lived on broth and noodles and some kind of Chinese stew that looked like it was made from twigs and tar. He bought his clothes at the Salvation Army. I don't think he even carried a wallet.

The month my father stopped supporting me, Peng ran up a phone bill of more than 300 bucks. When I went to the bank to deposit the check he gave me, the teller sent me to someone at a desk who said my account was overdrawn by $107, plus $65 in penalties. I said that there had to be a mistake, but I knew there wasn't—I'd spent the money on car insurance and stereo repairs. The bank officer persuaded me to get a cash advance on my Visa and pay the bank back that way, but when he phoned Visa, the robot at the other end told him I'd reached my limit.

"But I sent them a check two weeks ago," I said, trying to remember if I had.

The officer shrugged. "That is not our concern," he said. "Our concern is replacing these funds. Our concern is . . ."

I tuned right out. The officer was my age, maybe a year or two older, and reminded me of those kids in grade school who volunteer to watch the class whenever the teacher goes to the bathroom. You expect those kids to succeed, and they do, and they never let the rest of us forget it. Finally, to make the guy shut up, I took out Peng's check and laid it on the desk.

"Were you hiding this?" the officer said.

"It isn't my money," I said. "It's my roommate's."

"Don't worry about it," he said, handing me a pen. The pen was on one of those weak little chains that make you want to steal whatever they're attached to. "As long as the check's made out to you, we'll be more than happy to accept it."

What I should have said then was "Yes, I'm sure you will," but instead I just endorsed the check. I think that's why old people talk to themselves: too many smart remarks in their heads they never had the guts to use.

Jessica DeWitt, my girlfriend, was big on anniversaries. We celebrated them constantly. I would be walking out of a lecture or eating pasta salad in the union, when she would come trotting up from out of nowhere and throw her arms around my neck and whisper "Guess what day it is?"

It could be almost anything: the anniversary of the day we met or of the first night we slept together or the first time I told her I loved her. It could be a month since then, ten weeks or nine lunar cycles—it didn't seem to matter. I asked her once if she knew her behavior wasn't entirely normal, and she said she knew it wasn't but that it was what her mom and dad did, and they had such an *amazing* marriage. This answer shut me up forever on the subject of our anniversaries. From what I had seen of her parents' marriage, it was nothing special, just a husband with lots of money and a wife who liked to spend it. But I did not want Jessica to know this—or, if she did know, to have to admit it.

Two weeks after my father cut me off and a day or two after Peng picked up the phone and found he couldn't call out anymore, let alone get through to China, Jessica made the surprise announcement that it had been a year to the day since we had seen our first movie together. She found me in a library carrel, where I had gone to recover from a meeting at which I had learned that student loans are not so automatic anymore. What's more, I had gotten a letter that morning from the Visa people, saying they'd put a stop on my card. My name was now on a list, they said, that would follow me everywhere, always. I sat in the carrel, eyes shut, reviewing my situation. Up until last month, I had thought of my life as a plan in my head, but now it felt more like a "situation." It felt like something around me, not inside me.

"We have a choice," said Jessica. "We can drive to the six-plex and see what's new there, or we can catch *The Bicycle Thief* at the Campus Film Club."

"Let's try *The Bicycle Thief*," I said. The truth was, I'd seen the movie before and hadn't enjoyed it particularly, but there was another consideration. The six-plex charged $6.50 a ticket and took a gallon of gas to get to, while the Film Club charged a buck and we could reach it on foot.

Jessica bent an index finger and stroked me under the chin. "But the screen at the Film Club's so small," she said. "Plus, if we go to the six-plex, we can get some dinner first."

After a boring five-minute argument, I decided that it would be pointless to try to make a cheap night of it. Better to go all out, I concluded, and have enough fun to last me for a while. Until my new loan came through—if it did—I might not get another chance. We drove to a Vietnamese café across the street from the theater.

"My parents discovered this place," said Jessica, settling in at the table and looking around at the crowded, red-lighted dining room. "It didn't have a review or anything. Now *everyone* comes here."

"Your folks are quite the trendsetters," I said. It was a nasty thing to say, but Jessica didn't seem to catch on.

The fact was, I didn't say it: I just thought I did. Lately, that had been happening a lot—beautiful comebacks sticking in my throat and then blaring out in my dreams at night.

Jessica mouthed the word "tea" and gave our waiter a cup-holding signal, closing her thumb and forefinger and tipping back her hand. Her diamond heart pendant bounced against her turtleneck. I'd paid $200 for the pendant and wondered if I could ask for it back. To do that, I'd have to break up with her, but $200 was $200, exactly twice what I had in the world.

Our waiter, who didn't look Asian at all, but more like he'd swum here from Mexico that morning, took his time delivering the tea. "This is just so typical," said Jessica, warming her hands on the cup. "It starts as a hungry-immigrant business and everyone's very attentive, but then things take off and they hire morons. I'll have to tell my folks."

"How are your parents, anyway?" I said, trying to conceal a darker thought. The pendant was sparkling outrageously; I wanted it.

"My parents," Jessica said, and she looked at me as though I might be hurt, "are facing some very difficult decisions."

"Decisions about their marriage?" I said, I could only hope.

"About their *lives*."

So it began. The rice came, the egg rolls, the candy-coated mounds of pork and duck that made me want to floss my teeth after every bite, but Jessica didn't let up for a second, just pouched the food in her cheek and kept talking. Her mother had had an asthma attack while scraping ice off the windshield of her Volvo—that was the first part. Her father was in Holland at the time because he was such a top man in his field that his company flew him all over the world to open new offices—that was also crucial to the story. This too: that Minnesota's income tax was just about the highest in the nation. Which would be fine, said Jessica, losing me for the dozenth time, if the winters weren't so cold and the summers so muggy. Asthmatics, she said, need warm, dry air—like in Arizona, where the state taxes were low. Then came some stuff about stock options—how Mr. DeWitt had loads of them—and something about the "rat race" and "stress" and how human beings "can only take so much." By this time our dessert had arrived—two dinky scoops of tea-flavored ice cream—and I was thinking I'd rather be home, watching Peng and his friends play Go.

"Anyway, that's his dilemma," said Jessica. "Cash in the stock and retire out West, or stay in Minnesota, keep working and jeopardize Mom's health."

This didn't sound like much of a dilemma to me, but I was not in a mood to speak up. The bright spot was that we had missed our movie, saving me $13.

Jessica leaned forward on her elbows. The pendant was within snatching range. "I'll tell you my one concern," she said. "My father is awfully young to retire. You think he'll be bored? I hope not."

The check came, and I turned it over. Fifty-one dollars, for nothing. "You think you could chip in a twenty?" I asked.

Jessica put her bag on the table and started fishing around for her wallet, acting like she hardly ever used it and didn't see why she had to now. "I don't know. Did you hear my question?"

That's when I lost it; I reached for the pendant. I don't think Jessica knew what I was doing. Neither did I—it happened that fast. She slapped away my hand, said, "Kirk, not *here*!" I opened my wallet, threw down some bills, then walked across the dining room, through the kitchen, out the door and across the street to a liquor store, where I bought a bottle of champagne that left me with only 86 cents, which I put in a charity jar on the counter.

Back at the Vietnamese place, I gave the champagne to Jessica.

"That's all there is," I said. "You've cleaned me out. Happy anniversary."

And this time I actually said it, too. Out loud.

Anyone can get a job at Burger King. You just walk in and ask—they have to hire you. Burger King is the safety net, the place you can't go lower than.

I thought.

The manager, a thin, young white guy whose mustache had separate, countable red hairs, led me into the kitchen and spread out my application on a counter. Grease spots came up through the paper, staining the paragraph at the top that talked about "opportunity for advancement." To avoid reading over the manager's shoulder, I looked around at the kitchen. Rust-colored shreds of iceberg lettuce rotted in a pile by the sink. Someone had stepped on a ketchup packet, making a bloody sunburst on the floor. A muscular black man with a gold hoop earring was sweeping up little squares of waxed paper. The air stirred up by his push broom blew the paper squares off to the side, and he didn't bother to follow them.

"Optimally," the manager said, "you would prefer to commence employment when?" One of those word-power guys.

"Immediately," I said. "I wrote on the form 'immediately.'"

The manager nodded. "Be frank," he said. "Is this some sort of emergency?"

The question ticked me off. Why else would someone serve Whoppers for a living except in an emergency? I didn't say this, though. I said, "Not really." If I told the story later, I decided, I could always claim I'd used the line.

The manager snapped his fingers at the black man, making a sharp, bony pop that echoed throughout the kitchen. "Julius, that's pathetic. This isn't some North Side chicken joint. This is Burger King."

Julius twisted his fists on the broom handle. I watched the tattoos on his forearms grow definite. "I'm covering for Sal," he said. "I don't even need to be here this shift. I'm a fry cook, not a broom boy. You hired me as a fry cook. Ask Claude there."

The manager looked at the ceiling, shut his eyes. He touched his hands to his temples. After a moment of silent self-massage, he let out a breath and turned to me. "I'm sorry. We're fully staffed at the moment. I don't foresee any openings."

"You're kidding."

The manager laid a hand on my shoulder and steered me back toward the registers. "Maybe you can understand," he said. "It's a delicate balance, running this place. Someone like you just wouldn't fit in." He lowered his voice and patted my shoulder, glancing back at Julius. "Trust me, you wouldn't *want* to fit in."

All I could say was " I have to fit in." My loan had been turned down the day before, and the dean had cut up my college ID card. My stereo, bought on time, had been loaded onto a van that morning by men who kept saying how sorry they were.

"Keep your pride," the manager said. "Our pride is all we have." He shook my hand, a solid double pump, and turned to one of the teenage cashiers. "Juanita, tie your hair up. This isn't your mom's apartment; this is Burger King."

Peng won a major science prize that week. According to a professor quoted in the St. Paul paper, one of Peng's experiments had shed new light on the barium atom. Peng was a genius. He was also rich. The prize—from the U.S. government—was worth over $10,000 in cash and scholarships.

Our phone, which Peng had had reconnected, rang off the hook with calls from Washington. Peng sat at the kitchen table, fielding them. A congressman called, a Du Pont engineer and someone from Immigration—I eavesdropped. They wanted Peng to stay in the country. They wanted to support him in his work. He started wearing a flap pin on his jacket and bought some country-music tapes. He was an American, that fast—a guy who had once asked me seriously if Martin Luther King had written the Bill of Rights.

Myself, I was still on the job trail. Sort of. There were openings everywhere, but only small ones; jobs for housewives, jobs for kids, jobs to supplement Social Security. None of them paid even half what I needed to get myself back on track. And unless I could borrow some money somewhere, fast, I wasn't going to make the rent. I had tried to contact my father, twice, but his secretary said he was in Tampa, giving a series of speeches on zoning. I couldn't go to my mother because she had been unemployed herself ever since my father ditched her. And Jessica wouldn't speak to me. When I banged on her door one night, she called the cops. They asked for a college ID, and when I couldn't produce one, they told me the next time they saw me near the dorms I would go to jail.

I had no choice: I went to Peng.

"Money? My money? From me?" he said. We were eating dinner, sharing a pot of twigs and tar that I was too poor and hungry to refuse. "What do you want money for? You *pig man*."

"Peng," I said, "be reasonable. We're friends."

"No, not friends," said Peng. "Not ever friends. You steal from me for the telephone. I caught you. The money you stole for the phone is what I want." His face had changed color, a terrible sight. I thought he was going to stab me with a chopstick.

"What if I sell you my bed?" I said. "The mattress and box spring are worth a couple hundred."

"Why do I need a bed for? I like floors. Only lazy pig men like the bed."

I looked around the apartment, adding up the worth of my possessions. Nothing but trendy, depreciated junk. A three-speed German coffee grinder I would be lucky to get five bucks for. A halogen desk lamp I'd never dared use because you had to send away to England for replacement bulbs. A box of Kleenex, brand-name Kleenex, when toilet paper would have done the job. Maybe my father was right: Maybe I was spoiled. Maybe I was actually a caveman, squatting in the forest, naked, dreaming up this world of brand-name tissues to make myself feel safe.

"I guess that's it," I said. "I'll have to move. I don't know where I'll go, but . . ."

I rose from the table and crossed toward the door. Peng stuffed more twigs into his mouth and watched me. I was putting on an act, of course, but a dangerous act, an act that might turn real. I imagined bluffing my way out the door, down the stairs and out to my junker Pinto wagon, where I would have to sleep that night, curled up next to the spare.

Peng cleared his throat and put the chopsticks down. "If I borrow to you," he said, "what interest?"

"Forget it." I lifted my coat from the doorknob. I couldn't believe my courage, my stupidity. I couldn't believe Peng's balls.

"Twelve percent interest," said Peng.

"I'm going."

"Ten," said Peng. "And the bed for what you stole."

"Go to hell, you gook," I almost said. "We should have nuked you bastards in the Fifties. Eisenhower had the right idea."

But I caught myself. Just in time. I said, "Okay."

Then rent day came and I was broke again.

I had been at the ski shop for less than a week, working in the stockroom, when I got bronchitis and coughed for four days straight. I had lost my infirmary privileges and didn't have any health insurance, so I couldn't get antibiotics from a doctor. I telephoned Jessica to see if she had a prescription left over from one of her infections. Jessica was a delicate girl and always had an infection of some kind.

"Where are you?" she said. "At work?"

"Lying down in a closet," I said.

"I thought you found a job."

"I did. *I'm sick*!"

I heard someone talking to Jessica, a guy. I recognized his voice, a hockey player, big in the college Republican club. I heard him say to Jessica "Get back under the covers, I'm freezing," and then I heard Jessica say, to me, "I'm sorry. Even if I had any erythromycin, prescriptions aren't transferable. In fact, I think it's a felony to do that."

"In that case, I'd like my heart pendant back."

"Don't worry," Jessica said, "I threw it out."

Two days later, all coughed out, I reported for work at the ski shop. My check was taped to the time clock and my name was not on the schedule. I cashed the check—only $98—and drove to a navy recruiting station. I think I was trying to scare myself, to see how it would feel to be so desperate that joining the navy was my only option. I sat in my car and watched two officers laughing it up behind a plate-glass window. I found myself wanting a haircut like theirs, uniforms like theirs. I found myself getting out of my car. I found myself standing in front of a desk, facing a portrait of President Bush.

The officers, it turned out, were women. They looked like they'd been on vacation. Perfect tans. They acted like I was interrupting something, a top-secret recipe conference maybe, and treated me like a reject from the git-go.

"You abandoned your degree," the tall one said. "Was it the work? The structure? How do you feel about structure? In general."

"I ran out of money. My father cut me off. We had a fight about how poor he was."

"Your father and you—do you quarrel a lot?"

I think I said no. Or maybe yes.

The short one picked up a pen and a clipboard. "Be honest: Do you have a problem with authority?"

"No," I said. "Not in general. The thing of it is, I'm broke. It's that simple. I know my clothes look nice, my haircut, but all I've had to eat today is—"

"You're wrong," said the short one. "Your clothes do not look nice. Your hair is a mess. You look like you've been drinking."

I laughed in a way I hoped was "with," not "at." "I thought you people *wanted* guys like me. I'm offering to die in combat."

"The navy these day has standards," said the tall one, apparently immune to humor. "Wanting in is not enough. Needing money is not enough. We can afford to pick and choose now. If that idea offends you . . ."

"It doesn't," I said. "It just amazes me."

The officers looked at each other. Dykes. I wanted to think they were dykes. They were being tough on me, and I had to think something tough about them. *You lousy fucking dykes.* It was a private, silent thought—a notion. The kind of thing I think but never say.

Except I really did say it. The words. It was like one of those bed-wetting dreams where suddenly you wake up soaked in urine. Only this was with words.

The house I grew up in had so many bedrooms that one of them was used for storing junk. There were parts of our yard that never got mowed because they were so far away from the house. There was a drawer by the sink in the kitchen where my parents dumped the dimes and quarters they couldn't be bothered to carry in their pockets. I stole from the drawer all the time, but it was always full.

My family was middle-class. That's what we were. I knew this because I asked my mother once how much money my father made. "The same as everyone else," she said. "A comfortable middle-class income." I knew it, too, from when I'd asked my father why we couldn't drink Pepsi for breakfast, the way a few of my friends at school did. "Because we're a middle-class family," he said, "and we happen to give a damn about nutrition." From listening to my parents talk, I got the idea that being middle-class was something that had simply happened to them and would happen to me when I was their age.

That is what I told my father, sitting in his office, all worn-out, offering to work for him.

And this is what he told me: "We live in a new America, Kirk, with no guarantees. There are no guarantees. Even professionals have it hard—this suit I'm wearing is four years old. My stocks are in the toilet. I used to eat all my lunches out, but now I brown-bag it. You understand?"

I had eaten nothing but Fritos for days, ever since Peng had changed the locks on me and I had moved into my Pinto; I had to understand. "I do," I said. "I understand."

My father said, "I doubt that. What's more, I don't think you have any idea how much you've cost me over the years. I added it up the other day—room and board and medical. Transportation, miscellaneous. It comes to over $100,000."

"You win," I said. "A hundred thousand dollars. A hundred million trillion dollars."

"And you can't pay it back."

"I can't pay it back. A hundred trillion zillion jillion . . ."

"You'll have to excuse me," my father said, standing. "I'm late for a dinner appointment. Good luck."

"Good luck," my father said, and I stiff-armed him backward, through a plate-glass window.

He fell thirty stories. They found him in the parking lot, spread-eagle on the roof of his Buick. The change had flown out of his pockets as he fell and had rained down on top of him, spangling his body. At the autopsy, the coroner cut him open and found a condom stuffed with precious gems lodged in his large intestine. The government stole it, my money. My inheritance. I threatened to sue, but no one would take my case. No one would go up against the government. To block an investigation of the theft, the government ruled the death a suicide and kept the enormous fortune meant for me.

You think all kinds of crazy things, say all kinds of crazy things living on the street.

You just let go.

It makes you feel better somehow, and besides, people expect a good story for their money.

Bruce Craven

Fast Sofa

After reading Catcher in the Rye, *most GenXers turned to* On the Road *for the real scoop on how to conduct one's rite of passage in the coolest manner possible. Bruce Craven's first novel,* Fast Sofa, *is nothing if not cool. Its cover beckoning the reader to "play this novel loud!" the book is a GenX answer to Kerouac's now-traditional visionary road trip. Rather than looking for anything in particular, though, Craven's hero almost aimlessly wanders the mall and motel-dotted desert highwayscape in search of the remnants of American culture lying in the bottom of a tequila bottle or in the crusty bed of a porn video. As far as their cultural heritage goes, Craven's characters build their Jungian identities out of the archetypal imagery available to them: TV's* Kung Fu *and the comic* The Mighty X-Men.

"This has to be the lamest machine I've ever seen. You call this a car?"

"Yeah, I call it a car. It's an *American* car," Rick said. "Remember them? Big, fast? Buick Skylark GS. Automatic transmission, oil leak . . . but we'll deal. Now you getting in or what?"

Jack pulled the door but it failed to latch. He shook his head with disdain and looked at Rick. Jack's face was sunburned from riding his motorcycle. His eyes strangely lunar. What Tamara had once called *sensitive*. Jaw obstrusive. His body muscular from the weight room, but soft at the edges from too much beer. Girls had called him pretty when he was in high school.

Jack thought of high school too much.

Oakdale High in Burbank, California. Burbank. A wing tip of the San Fernando Valley caught smooth between the pressure of the Hollywood hills and the Verdugo hills. Concrete. Mediterranean flora. Strip malls marked with Western wear outlets, appliance stores, coffee shops. Promiscuous oak trees and their shrub relatives fenced back against the concrete channel of the Los Angeles River or pushed up into the foothills, where the really rich people lived. The hot stomach grid with its square lawns, white sidewalks, freeway greenbelts. Then sometimes it would rain. Leave the brown sky blue. Chains of tight, well-kept houses. Algebraic apartment complexes, stairwells stacked up around fat jungle plants. The movie studios. The TV studios. The shiny corporate aeries.

Jack and Rick had been friends since that fourth grade recess when Jack had put his red Jansport daypack down on the concrete and punched two fifth graders who had shoved Rick against a fence. That was a different time. A different Los Angeles. Shooting caroms. *Johnny Appleseed* flickering in an air-conditioned grade school auditorium. Weird music blasting out of some big kid's house down the street. Throwing rocks at cars. The best of times, the worst of times. But when it was time to ride your Schwinn Sting-Ray bicycle home, you still couldn't make it all the way without lying down in the ivy to gasp. Your lungs like pink sea anemones. The air like water you'd never want to drink.

Yeah, things hadn't changed that much.

And it had not been the last time Jack had helped Rick around violence.

"Tamara's car's in the shop. Like permanently," Rick explained, peering over his green Ray-Bans. He handed Jack the free end of a bungee cord. "Hook it in there." He pointed to the lattice of shredded vinyl and soldered steel that was the passenger door.

Jack stared. "You've got to be kidding?"

Rick reached into the pocket of his flannel shirt. "Got you a present last night." He pulled out a pair of inexpensive aviator-style sunglasses with metallic purple lenses. DISCO war printed upon each glittering ellipse. "Tamara and I went to Magic Mountain last night to ride the roller coasters." Rick pointed out the window at the white sky. "Figured you can always use extra protection. The sun-god is cool, but he *kills*."

Jack nodded, slipped the sunglasses on, and opened the glove compartment. "No smokables?" He was wearing a blue, wrinkled button-collar shirt and a tie with frayed edges and thin blue and yellow stripes. Underneath, his dark blue T-shirt was visible. Jack yanked the tie loose and struggled out of both the tie and the wrinkled shirt.

"Too bad," said Rick. "You looked real nice."

"No *ganja*?" Jack scrunched the shirt and tie into the seat crevice.

"Nope. Not with. Tamara's been giving me a hard time about it. You know, *adulthood*. But back at the ranch . . ." Rick grinned.

Jack removed a transparent plastic folder from the glove compartment. Flipped through it. The folder was filled with math tests. Xeroxed math tests with scribbles, doodles, and different names. Scores inked in with red felt-tip. "I'm really burnt. I *need* to get baked." His blue T-shirt fluttered as the '71 Buick Skylark rolled down Sunset Boulevard. The under-inflated tires sucked at the cement. The door rattled. "Can you dig it? First lunch with my dad and then the Suzuki gacks." Jack shook his head. "I'm too old for this grief."

Rick nodded. "How's work going?"

The twin DISCOs were tinged with a patina of gold. "More misery, more grief. Nothing but assholes. Drunk business types. The scene is a *serious* stress."

"We need gas."

Jack shrugged. *"We?"*

"You. Unless you're into walking." Rick loved this Buick. "Like what's the evil dad doing in Hollywood anyway?"

"Nothing." Jack looked out the window.

"What do you mean, *nothing*?"

"He wanted me and Jennifer to meet the mystery siblings this time. The *stepfamily*. Like what am I going to say to them, right? A bunch of fucking ugly people I've never met in the past fourteen years. Like what am I going to say to my *stepbrother*? Hey, dude, nice face, looks like mine. But no, Dad said it was *time*. Time to talk. Time to clear the air. Time to make amends. Major error. *Dad* drives a DeLorean now. Got a *deal* on it. Can you believe it? A *DeLorean*?"

Rick was silent.

"Mom hated sports cars."

"Good eats?"

Jack shook his head, looked down, and flexed his forearm. "All right . . . I guess, but it was like art food. Three scallops, a spear of asparagus, and a little thing that looked like a root."

"Yum. What'd you talk about? The last fourteen years?"

Jack grinned flatly. "We talked about *him*. And the price of his favorite champagne. We talked about anything he wanted to talk about. Just like when he invited Jennifer and me at Christmas, only this time Jennifer figured it out. Jen won't even deal with him. So I got to *entertain* the *family*." He reached over and turned on the radio. The speakers implanted in the dash emitted a solitary whine. "It's a short," Rick said over the noise. "A wire gig."

Jack thinking about his father and his weird disappearance fourteen years ago. The stepbrother only a few years younger. This bad scene his mother never had to face. For fourteen years, Jack and his sister, Jennifer, used to play a guessing game. Take turns. Their father was a CIA double agent. No, their father was a successful gun runner. Their father was on the lam. Maybe he was wanted for political reasons. Maybe he was a criminal. But their father would be saved. Rescued someday, maybe even by them.

They never guessed that he was on the run from Burbank. On the run *from* them. From Jack Weiss. From Jennifer Weiss. From their mother.

They never guessed that he would just pop up a year ago on Easter and invite Jack out for a round of golf. He had joined some new church. The church of assholes, thought Jack. Let's have lunch. He said it was the first he had heard about their mother's death. Yeah, they never guessed their father was just living in Thousand Oaks. Living at the other tip of the San Fernando Valley, making his loot in software.

Rick watched the Hollywood Bowl drift past on the left. The whine increased as he accelerated. "Yeah, definitely some wires crossed," he explained professionally. "It's a three-fifty," he added, "Power central."

Jack swept his hand through the air. "They made four fifty-fives . . . where'd you get this piece of shit anyway?"

Rick turned the radio off. "It was a gift. Sort of. Kind of a *deal*."

"Yeah?"

"Yeah. Remember Estelle Maddox? *Mrs. Maddox?*"

Jack shook his head as the Buick window filled with slopes of manicured lawn and the flapping pennants of a condominium complex.

"Sure you do. Taught geometry at Oakdale. I saw this Xeroxed ad tacked up at K mart and gave her a call, you know . . . just to remind her of all the good times we'd had and clue her to how good I was doing these days thanks to her teaching. Before I knew it we were talking about her car and I had myself a deal." Rick smiled. "She said she'd rather give me the brother-digit 'cause I was cool, you know, *meant something to her*. Like I wasn't just some Cal Worthington used-car dealer dude."

"Did you write her a check?"

Rick looked from the tangle of approaching intersection and turned up the corner of his lip.

"And she signed the pink slip?"

"It's not my fault. If she really knew how to *teach* I'd probably be some big finance wizard or fat-cat computer lord like your dad . . . besides, her doctor was tense about her driving 'cause of her eyesight."

"How much?" Jack turned the radio back on.

"A hundred bucks, plus change. I figure I can make it in the next week and then I can square things. The problem was wheels. That was *crucial*."

Jack shrugged. This was Rick. Things were always *crucial*.

"Besides," added Rick. "It's like survival of the fittest. The old and weak are weeded out by the young and strong. It's all part of the evolutionary process. Darwin full-on. I'm just the wolf doing the weeding . . . getting blind ancient cunts off the road." He cackled and looked up in the rearview, showing his straight teeth. His eyes glistened behind the sunglasses, the bridge of his nose like a finger pointed straight at your face.

He guided the Buick toward the red stripes of a minimart service station. Then a Highway Patrol car edged up. Fat, black, white. Predatory.

Rick checked the speedometer. He hated this scene. Cops with monster engines going twenty-seven miles per hour in the fast lane.

"Fuckers," he whispered. Nursed the Skylark to the right and crept past the mirrored gaze of the officers. *Robo-squids*. He knew they did this just for kicks. Just daring you . . .

Rick stepped on the gas and passed the black-and-white with a rush, tires bouncing over the curb of the service station entrance. The back fender scraped.

The Highway Patrol car glittered away into the sunlight.

Jack stared at the gas pumps. Oblivious.

"Fuck the police," Rick said.

"What?"

"I said, fuck the police. They're fascists. Nazis with a license."

Jack nodded. Stared out the window.

"Forget your dad, man. Just get over it. He's a loser. A squid. He's not your fault . . ."

Jack's eyes were heavy in his face. That Jesus Christ look. But what was really starting to get on Rick's nerves was the sad grin Jack cultivated. A grin that crawled out and said everything was over. A grin that said *I give up.*

And it was just 'cause Jack couldn't get laid. Like the night the two of them blew out to Santa Monica on Jack's Suzuki to catch the Red Hot Chili Peppers. Dancing with these girls with chopped hair, pointy hipbones, and red lips. Smoking some bomber joint in the parking lot. Rick finally turning up his eyes into the stained morning, checking out the stuffed animals and posters of the Cure in some strange bedroom. Jack back in Burbank, passed out. Drunk, sweat-soaked, alone.

"I said I'm broke," Rick added.

Jack had put in extra hours in the gym. It showed in his arms as he shifted. "Yeah?"

"*Yeah,*" Rick explained.

Jack dug into the pockets of his Levi's and handed Rick eight dollars. "I think you're just scared."

"What?"

A man in tennis shorts fumbled with the gas nozzle.

"Cops. They're tough and they don't take shit and that ticks you off. You don't like that someone can tell you what to do. You don't like that people can stand for something."

Rick made an *oh wow, perceptive* face. "Is this bartender philosophy or *what*? Shit, I'm not scared of shit. I just don't like people who get *off* on messing with my life. Nazi clerks. They're losers. They're a waste of tax-payer cash. The only reason to have cops is 'cause of those real-life TV cop shows. Like great, so they're cheaper than *actors*. Big deal. But like are you safe 'cause they're *around*? No. The whole city's rolling with all these *sets.* Tool down to catch a Laker game and next thing you're buzzing up to a stop-light and looking at a lot of pissed-off gangbangers in a cherried-out Pontiac filled with semiautomatic ugliness. Just out taking a break from all that bliss of subsidized housing and unemployment. Yeah, cool. AK-47s, Uzis, Mausers, Brownings, Glocks. Ordnance Central. Just the Krenshaw Mafia Bloods or the Ghost Town Crips our *frontin'.* Good thing the police have been stick-whipping people for speeding. Look at someone wrong . . . and *later. Smoke.* And forget all these fucking *cholo* dudes. Or the Koreans. The Chinese. The Vietnamese. Am I forgetting anyone?" Rick looked up at the torn ceiling up-holstery. "Oh yeah, *the white people.* We're the best. We just drive around in Japanese sedans with stupid-ass computer-babble names like *Sentra* and

Integra. The white people? Forget it. Just hiding up in the hills or at the beach." Rick reached into the ashtray and pulled out a stubbed Tiparillo. He hit the cigarette lighter with the heel of his hand. What the fuck was he talking about? Oh yeah. "And the police? *Fuck the police.* Jesus, this city is a hardware store. One big raging Western hardware store. The only difference is you've got *these* Nazis tooling around and messing with your fun. And I don't care what color a cop is, they're all Nazis. They all speak the same language. They all speak the language of Handcuff, Nightstick, Stungun, Bullet. And I hate that language. I like driving. I like the wind at one hundred miles an hour. I like it fast. I like it loud. Fuck those squids telling *me* what to do!"

Jack shrugged. "Yeah, a real *outlaw.*"

Rick got out of the car, strolled in to prepay, then filled the tank, digging behind the license plate for the nozzle aperture. Got the air hose and pumped the tires up. The tire gauge on the pump was busted. He filled them good. Better gas mileage, better handling. Ran his fingers down the smears of steel belt that showed through the tread. Wiped the excess gasoline on his Levi's. Thinking, strangely enough, of that old TV show *Kung Fu.* Something about this Buick Skylark made him think of *Kung Fu.* Maybe it was the flayed '71 gold paint, maybe the used-car scent of metal and defeated leathery vinylish upholstery. Something about this car reminded him of the desert and being a kid in Los Angeles. Kawi Chang Caine walking under the hot yellow sky. Leaving no mark on the rice paper. One lone dude hiking across the desert. Or how about the episode where he gets shot by the assassin? Arrow buried in his back. Yeah, that'd been one of TV's *crucial* episodes. Sonic wildness. *Adventure.* Mano a mano. Or like the time Caine was a prisoner with this young dude with greasy hair, real predisco, post-Woodstock hair, and they were in this corrugated miner's shack, left to die of dehydration. Except Caine had taught the young dude how to dream of rivers. To dream of fields of snow. Their bodies cooling, surviving in a fiction of cold waters. The bad guys outside spitting plug juice. Waiting.

Rick pulled the Buick into the Jack in the Box parking section across the street from the liver-colored Disney Studio building. He found a space next to a white AMC Matador with a bumper sticker that went MY KID BEAT UP YOUR HONOR STUDENT. Jack and Rick walked in and each ordered a couple of Super Tacos. Rick took Dr. Pepper and onion rings. Jack took skim milk. No onion rings. No fries. He paid. "Ugh," said Rick. "Can't get over that white stuff, huh? That'll kill you, Logan." Logan was one of the aliases of

Jack's favorite Marvel Comics character. Wolverine. A member of the good mutants. The Uncanny X-Men. *Logan* and *Patch*. Patch was the recent alias Wolverine was working under in doing whatever it was comic heroes did all day long. *Logan* and *Patch*. Rick liked to interchange them.

Jack nodded, "Can't work out on sugar." He squinched his stomach. "Got to lose a few."

"So where are we these days, Logan? Where are the bad guys, the foes of freedom and righteousness? In the Canadian Rockies? Japan? Fresno? Or that other place . . . where the dinosaurs hang . . . what is it called . . . the Savage Land? Where goeth the fierce Wolverine? Supertough hombre of the mighty mutant team of X?"

Jack took a mouthful of taco. "Stith en Mattlesore."

"What?"

"Madripoor. Still there. Low Town. We've bought an interest in the Princess Bar. It's a crime-infested island where Tyger Tiger, alias Jessan Hoan, lives, remember?"

Rick nodded professorially. "Yeah. I forgot my notes. What about that other nectar, what's her name, the Japanese wayhone?"

Wayhone was Rick's supreme term for an attractive woman, although he would rely on *nectar* and *scruff* for punchiness. For rhythm. Wayhone was Rick's creation, a combination of the Hawaiian *wahine*, with *very honed*, i.e., in shape and aesthetically pleasing. *Hone* was also an intransitive verb meaning to whine, moan, and yearn for. Rick had looked it up once in *The American Heritage Dictionary. Way*, of course, was also just *way*, critical modifier to Rick's vocabulary.

"Mariko." Jack explained. "She's our love. We are her champion. She is a woman of culture and breeding. We are a superhero and outlaw. A mutant with the power to heal our body. We are both loner and psychotic. A guardian of society, yet an outsider. Beast and man. Problem is after being forced to kill her father, Shingen, who brought shame to Clan Yashida and who was being a real pain in the ass, we were given the honor sword but Mariko left us at the altar while under the spell of Mastermind. Called us *gaijin*. Which means sort of like *hessian. Mondo-valley*. Foreigner. This was cold and we took it hard. It was right after we'd joined the X-Men and used these characters Silver Samarai and Viper . . . saving Mariko's life. Thus, the betrayal was particularly harsh."

"And?" Rick licked his fingers.

"Anyway, we're in Madripoor. It's our kind of place. Lots of action. We use our adamantium claws, our keen wolverine sense of smell, and our mutant healing factor whenever necessary. We like the tradition and ritual of the East."

"You like the submissive wayhones," said Rick. "Like Mariko."

Jack finished his milk. Mariko. Proud, strong, beautiful Mariko. And Rick dared call her *submissive*? "Duty holds her back. The time is just not right. We respect that ..."

"I don't get it."

Jack looked at Rick. "We're sort of into this idea of mastering the vicious part of us ... the animal thing that makes us such an awesome X-Man. We are a natural killer. We go into *berserker* rages. We can defend the common good. But this is not enough. We are tormented by inner suffering. Mariko offers us something different."

Rick looked out the window at the neon sign for the Pago-Pago Bar. He looked back at Jack and shrugged toward the doorway. "In Burbank, we go to the Pago-Pago. It's like the Princess Bar 'cept you don't have to fly to distant Madripoor. Burbank's cool that way."

As they were walking out the door, Jack thought, *The garden has been wrecked, its pattern broken. Order turned to chaos. The story of my life.*

The tradition and ritual of the East ...

Like Wolverine, Jack was burnt on the West. Burnt on wilderness.

Darius James

Negrophobia

Writing for radio and television as well as his own performance pieces, Darius James brings a uniquely multimedia sensibility to his work. His first novel, Negrophobia, combines poetry, screenplay, narrative, and found objects but still manages to tell a frightening story in an altogether amusing way. However couched in format and media savvy, the book makes a ripping indictment of the racist hallucination that our culture has constructed into a reality. The book follows the dream visions of Bubbles Brazil, a blonde, white teenage sex bomb who, under the curse of a voodoo spell, imagines herself tortured in an alternate reality where the white race will eventually be exterminated by spontaneous combustion. The following scene occurs in the early, fairly linear phase of the story.

INT. Donald Goines Senior High—Classroom—Day

Fade up on the punkadelic blond dreads of a black-skinned GIRL. Slowly pan left to right, overlap dissolve, and pan right to left across the faces of the other STUDENTS seated in the classroom, each face a frightening caricature of the grotesque.

BUBBLES
(v.o.)

My high school was overridden with niggas. Not the slow-witted, slow-shufflin', eyeball-rollin', flapjack-flippin' niggas in the brownstones off Central Park West. Or the upwardly mobile, paper-bag-colored Klingon niggas of the bougie boogahood. But nigger niggas—the *nightmarish kind*.

Mindless angel-dusted darkies slobbering insane single sylla-
bles, flicking switchblades and flashing straightrazors. Hip-
hoppity jungle bunnies in brightly colored clothes, carrying
large, loud radios we white wits call "Spadios," who drank
bubbling purple carbonates and ate fried pork rinds and bag
after bag of dehydrated potato slices caked with orange dust.
Crotch-clawin' niggas who talked *Deputy Dawg* and shot
dope. Saucer-lipped ragoons who called me the "Ozark Mountain She-Devil" and asked to feel my lunch money. Percussive
porch monkeys who fart with their faces to a heavy-metal
beat.

These were the kind of niggas my daddy warned me about.
The kind of niggas my daddy said would whisk me off to the
Isle of Unrestrained Negroes far, far away, and turn me into
a coal-black pickaninny with a nappy ribbon top and white
button eyes if I wasn't a good girl and didn't do as daddy said.

At the close of the Ku Klux Cartoon Coon Show in the classroom, stop on
Bubbles seated at her desk.

SFX: Hammer of electric school bell.

Bubbles stands up from her desk. Instantly, she's swept into the rush of students jostling their way through the door. As she wrestles against the press
of bodies, a finger swiftly slides between the cheeks of her behind. Bubbles
recoils, and her eyebrows rise in surprise.

                              BUBBLES
        Leaping lizards!

INT. Donald Goines Senior High—Corridor—Day

The Corridor's physical structure combines the utilitarian interiors of a public school building with the depressed exteriors of a ghetto slum. The mood
is chaotic circus funk.

Tin whistles toot. Bass lines wa-wa. And students bark woof-woof-woof.

At the rear of the seemingly ceilingless corridor is a gun tower, enclosed by barbed wire, a cyclone fence, and a pack of slavering Doberman pinschers. Inside the gun tower, a GUNNER sits behind a brace of machine guns. The sign of the gun tower reads in punctured block letters:

DONALD GOINES SENIOR HIGH

The corridor's column of lockers is a dazzle of wildstyle designs: multicolored sprays of Vaughn Bodé nymphs entangled inside gnarled, Escheresque girders who fellate duck-billed home boys with floating thought balloons of musical notations and fried chicken parts above their heads. Huge posters of Marcus Garvey, Malcolm X, and Bob Marley are wheat-pasted all along the hall. Black, red, and green sewer steam billows from a manhole cover sunk into the floor. The front end of a car with a drinking fountain built into its toothy chrome grill projects from a wall. Iron grates are pulled across the doors. Sections of the wall are crumbling, and bricks are strewn about the floor. Neon BAR, PAWN SHOP, JESUS SAVES, and HOT PORK CHOPS AND COLD BEER signs flash in distracting sequence.

Throngs of students congest the corridor smoking resinous Rasta spliffs; inhaling in brown paper bags sticky with airplane glue; snorting smack from tiny, waxed-paper sacks; drinking pints of Wild Irish Rose; sucking tubes of crack; fighting with razors; firing pistols; dry humping each other against lockers; hawking stolen goods; miscarrying half-formed fetuses: singing gospel; and wailing the blues.

A 200-pound BLACK MUSLIM, in a well-tailored suit and maroon bow tie, stands, like a ringmaster, in the center of the corridor's confusion, with a bundle of newspapers under his arm. He holds up a copy of *Muhammad Speaks*, with a "Whitie the Devil" cartoon on its front cover: A horned Uncle Sam stabs a pious black minister in the ass with the prongs of a flaming trident. The cartoon is captioned, "Amerikkka is *hell*, nigger!"

200-POUND BLACK MUSLIM
Paper, brutha? Don'cho' wan' a paper?

Whatsamatta? Whyte man stole y'mind 'n' put a hole in yo'
soul? C'mon, brutha—*do fo' sef! Ah buys
a bundle ever' week! Ah jus' luz doze cartoons! D'way
dey be makin' d'whyte man look lak d'debil 'n' shit—
y'know, wid dem horns, dat tail, 'n' dem freakie feets—
ah be laffin' 'till my ass shake!*

The Muslim bursts into laughter, his rotund ass shaking like a bowl of Jell-O.

Bottles, bricks, and Afro picks whiz past Bubbles' head as she wanders
through an assemblage of robotic POPLOCKERS. A HUMAN DRUM MACHINE
belches to the beat.

> 200-POUND BLACK MUSLIM
> Or how 'bout some Shabazz Bean Pie, brutha? It be good fo'
> stabilizin' yo' blacktitude. Did you know, affa eatin' a slice o'
> bean pie, some bruthas have been known to fart all four sides
> of Brutha Miles' *Bitches Brew* out dey butts? The stench be
> so foul and unholy, the Honorable Elijah Muhammad hisself
> awakes wide-eyed in his coffin!

The Gunner fires a spray of bullets into the crew of POPPERS, LOCKERS, and
HEAD SPINNERS. Blood spurts. Eyeballs fly. Heads explode. Jaws shatter. Intes-
tines dangle. All in disgusting *Dawn of the Dead* detail.

SFX: Machine-gun fire from the soundtrack of the 1974 SLA shoot-out news
footage.

The 200-pound Black Muslim is riddled with bullets from head to toe. Blood
oozes from his wounds and down his suit. Half his face is ripped away. With
ribbons of flesh flapping against exposed bone, the Muslim quakes with
laughter. He then falls face forward to the floor. And farts. Loudly. The seat
of his pants flutters in flatulent winds. A brown nuclear cloud hangs over
him. He utters—

200-POUND BLACK MUSLIM
... *bean* pie, brutha.

—and dies.

Unharmed, unbloodied, and, apparently, invulnerable, the oblivious Bubbles doesn't even notice. Three grunting, pig-snouted POLICE OFFICERS blackjack a black-bereted student with a "RESURRECT HUEY!" button pinned to the lapel of his black leather jacket. A gush of his brain pulp flies by. Bubbles doesn't notice this either.

A CHICKEN leaps from behind and lands on her shoulder. She cringes. The chicken squawks and drops to the floor. A lanky TEEN with a protruding Adam's apple steps around Bubbles, following the chicken. He leans low to the floor with his hands shoved in his pockets, his elbows crooked and flapping. He has one eye open and the other eye closed.

SFX: Hard, metallic whir.

Bubbles' ears perk to attention. The whir builds to a grating metal-grinding pitch. The sound sets Bubbles' teeth on edge.

A ROLLER DERBY QUEEN skates behind Bubbles, circling around and around. On the front of the Roller Queen's black, red, and green jersey, embroidered around a soft-sculpture relief of Aunt Jemima's face in a waxing crescent moon, are the words:

AUNT JEMIMA'S FLAPJACK NINJA-KILLERS FROM HELL

A pair of crossed gold spatulas tattoo a breast thrusting through the jersey's elastic opening. The Ninja Queen grins. Her nipple stiffens. The Ninja Queen rolls around and around. She appears and disappears. Her wheels slow to a stop. She and Bubbles stand nose to nose.

The Ninja Queen spits.

The worm of spit doesn't squirm down Bubbles' cheek. It *sticks*.

The Ninja Queen turns and rolls away. Bubbles stands in the corridor with the clot of mucus stuck to her cheek, fumbling for a tissue in her pockets. Finding none, she tries to finger it from her face. As she stares in disgust at the viscid slime on her fingertip, a firecracker snaps above her head.

Bubbles walks through a hail of bottles, bricks, and more Afro picks to a door marked "GIRLS" The letters on the door have been slashed with a pen knife and the word "HOZE" has been carved in its place. She opens the door and walks in.

INT. Donald Goines Senior High—Girls' lavatory—Day.

EIGHT FLAPJACK NINJA QUEENS—outfitted in shoulder and knee pads, roller skates, and one-breast jerseys—slouch against the back wall. Joints are passed and smoked.

> FLAPJACKS 0
>
> *. . . an apple in a baby's fist, my ass!* It looks more like a gross green grub wif a marble in its mouf! I mean you shoulda *heard* dis nigga! He say "Ah knows d'ham hocks mus' be hot, 'cause d'grits be bubblin' in d'pot!" Da nigga's eyes roll back in his head, his lashes start to flappin', an' da nigga screamed, "Good Gawd, girl! D'greens is greasy now!" An' I thought "Would you listen to dis no-dick country fool!"

> FLAPJACK 00
> Den why you give him some den?

> FLAPJACK 0
> Well, girl, you know how it—

As Bubbles walks into the lavatory, the Ninja Queens turn and greet her with icy stares. Bubbles pauses with her back pressed against the door.

Ignoring them, Bubbles walks to the row of porcelain sinks lining the right wall. Above the sinks, a horizontal mirror extends from one end of the wall to the other. In the mirror, she examines the stiff blob stuck to her silver disks.

FLAPJACK 25

I see Miss Ann's come to use the can!

Bubbles watches the Ninja Queens' reflection in the mirror.

FLAPJACK 6

She act like she don't shit 'cause she can't find paper soft enough to wipe her ass with.

FLAPJACK 0

I wonder if she know how?

FLAPJACK 6

Miss Ann—you know how to *shit*?

Bubbles' mouth is a jittering black line. Watching the Ninja Queens' reflection in the mirror, she cautiously reaches inside her jacket for the straight razor. Suddenly realizing this could prove quite fatal, especially to herself, she lets the razor slide back.

FLAPJACK 25

Looks like this girl could use a little toilet trainin'.

FLAPJACK 42

Yeah? Funky entertainment—*steamin' hot*!

FLAPJACK 25

Drag her hunkie ass over here and let's get on with it!

The Ninja Queens separate into two groups. Four skate to the middle of the lavatory. The remainder roll to the row of sinks.

Flapjack 13 rolls to Bubbles and grabs her by the braids, yanking her around. Bubbles shoves her across the floor. Rolling backward, Flapjack 13 falls on her ass.

> BUBBLES
> *Get your filthy monkey paws off of me!*

Flapjack 13 heaves herself off the floor with a gleeful bloodlust in her eyes.

> FLAPJACK 13
> Miss Ann wants to jump baad! G'on widja pale, assless self,
> Miss Ann. *Jump!*

With a deft Ali shuffle on her roller skates, Flapjack 13 spins her fists, giving Bubbles a push. Bubbles pushes back.

> BUBBLES
> I said *keep your fucking monkey paws off of me!*

Flapjack 13 stops. Frowns. *Pouts.*

> FLAPJACK 13
> Who you callin' "monkey," hunkie?

> BUBBLES
> Who you callin' "hunkie," monkey?

> FLAPJACK 13
> *You!* BITCH!

Grinning, Bubbles squints in defiance. She boldly walks up to Flapjack 13. The two girls stand tit to tit.

> BUBBLES
> *Felch me.*

The Ninja Queens goad them on in the background.

FLAPJACK NINJA QUEENS
(o.s.)
Whoooo-ooooo! That's nasty! Tonja, you gon' take that offa whyte girl?!

Flapjack 13's eyebrow cocks in confusion.

FLAPJACK 13

What " 'felchin' "?

BUBBLES

A verb! Y'dumb, corn-bread-crunchin' *coon*!

The remark churns fears, frustrations, and animosities that Flapjack 13 cannot name nor Bubbles understand. She slaps Bubbles across the face, streaking her hand with the clot of snot. The rope of snot finally drops.

FLAPJACK 13

Corn bread *good*! Tonja like corn bread! And pig tails, *too*!
Like dat funky singa say, It make Tonja happy!

FLAPJACK 25
(o.s.)
You talk about Tonja's corn bread and pigtails, it's just like you talkin' about Tonja *mama*!

FLAPJACK 13
Don't you talk about my mama!

Bubbles' eyes are round with disbelief. She backs away.

BUBBLES

Oh, shit! This steroid-swollen *he-bitch* is about to go berserk!
(Help!)

Flapjack 13 swings her arms in blind fury, charges like an angry bull, and stumbles over her roller skates. She hits the floor.

FLAPJACK 13

Umph!

As she get up, Bubbles jumps on her back and rides her like a rodeo bronco-buster.

The gang of Ninja Queens tosses lit matches at Bubbles as she lurches on the enraged Flapjack 13's padded shoulders.

FLAPJACK NINJA QUEENS

Kill that bitch! Kick the whyte out her ass! Where's the lighter fluid? Let's set that bitch on fire!

Flapjack 13's back bucks up and down. Bubbles pulls her hair, gouges her eyes, and bites her nose. Choking her in a headlock, Bubbles leans over and bites her exposed black breast.

BUBBLES

Chomp!

FLAPJACK 13
(screaming)

D'biddie bit m'tittie!

Flapjack 13 swings her shoulders back and forth like a set of tavern doors. As she attempts to flip Bubbles to the floor, jerking her back in a downward swoop, Flapjack 13 falls to the floor herself. Bubbles lands in a tangle on top of her, scissoring the Ninja Queen's head between her thighs. The Ninja Queen bites Bubbles in the V of her Spandex crotch. Blond hairs sprout from the tear.

In disgust, Flapjack 25 shoves Bubbles off of Flapjack 13. She points to the middle of the floor.

FLAPJACK 25
(o.s.)

Enough of this bullshit. Drag her hunkie ass over there.

Six Ninja Queens drag Bubbles across the tiles by the braids of her hair. Flapjack 25 watches with her fists propped on her hips. Flapjack 13 whimpers in a corner, massaging her bruised breast. The Ninja Queens form a half circle around Bubbles. Switchblades are flicked in a clockwise direction.

Click! Click! Click!

FLAPJACK 25
(o.s.)

Stand up!

Bubbles stands.

FLAPJACK 25
(o.s.)

Now *piss*, bitch!!

The Ninja Queens prod Bubbles with the points of their blades. Dewlike gold drops glisten on the blond shoots of her pubic hair. And trickle down her leg.

Bubbles sinks into the widening yellow puddle on the floor. Tears bead on her ovals of silver greasepaint. Medium shot of Bubbles folded in a fetal ball on the floor with a row of muscular brown legs behind her.

FLAPJACK 19
(o.s.)

What is that devilish mess caked on her face?

FLAPJACK 54 *(o.s.)* Magically converging uteri equalizing her aura's balance of negative and positive energies.

FLAPJACK 19
(o.s.)

Why she do that?

FLAPJACK 54
(o.s.)
What else is a whyte girl to do in a school full of jigaboos?

FADE

Hate

Peter Bagge

This Seattle comic book artist steers well clear of the superhero tradition and instead focuses his monochrome inking talents on the gray world and ongoing saga of Buddy Bradley, artist, slacker, outcast, and failed lover. What distinguishes Hate *from other "real-life" comic books is Bagge's disarming honesty. He shares his most intimate and most self-condemnatory thoughts and attitudes: when he'd like to cheat on his girlfriend, what he really thinks about his friends, even doubts about his own talent.*

Bagge says that Hate *is not meant as a GenX comic book, but busters do constitute the core of his following. Given that his protagonist seems stuck in limbo between the educational nest and full adulthood, it's no wonder he has caught on with a generation that has graduated from college but can't find a job. In this short sequence we catch up with Buddy Bradley's sister (from Bagge's earlier series,* The Bradleys*), who leads a singularly depressing existence. Lacking the slacker skills to surf the dangerous waters of consumer culture, she drowns in it.*

"WHATEVER HAPPENED TO BABS BRADLEY?"

...YOU REMEMBER HOW **GEEKY** AND **NERDY** SHE WAS BACK IN THE ELEVENTH GRADE? WELL, SHE WAS SO DESPERATE FOR **MALE ATTENTION** BY THEN THAT SHE STARTED DRESSING LIKE A **SEX—CRAZED SLUT** —A **NERDY, RETARDED LOOKING SLUT**, BUT A SLUT NONETHELESS.

THIS "LOOK" AT LEAST WORKED ITS MAGIC WITH THE **GREASER-TYPES**, WHO STARTED OFFERING TO GIVE HER RIDES HOME FROM SCHOOL. AND SHE WOULD AL- WAYS ACCEPT, EVEN IF SHE DIDN'T EVEN **KNOW** THE GUY!

THESE "RIDES" RARELY MADE IT OUT OF THE SCHOOL PARKING LOT BEFORE THE GUY WOULD STOP AND TRY TO COP A FEEL. BABS WOULD THEN **PANIC** AND JUMP OUT OF THE CAR, ONLY TO ACCEPT THE **VERY NEXT OFFER** FROM SOME OTHER GUY.

SHE EVENTUALLY GAVE IN AND WENT ALL THE WAY WITH A GUY NAMED **ALFRED**, WHO WAS, LIKE, THE **KING OF THE GREASERS**. SHE LATER TOLD ME THAT SHE LET HIM DO IT PARTLY OUT OF **FEAR** AND PARTLY BECAUSE SHE FELT "**HONORED**".

WITH TYPICAL BABS LUCK SHE GOT **PREGNANT**. AND WHEN SHE TRIED TO TELL ALFRED ABOUT IT HE ACTED LIKE HE'D NEVER **SEEN HER BEFORE**, WHICH WAS ESPECIALLY DEVASTATING FOR HER, SINCE SHE HAD CONVINCED HERSELF THAT THEIRS WAS A "**TRUE LOVE**".

HER PARENTS MADE HER GET AN **ABORTION**, WHICH WHEN YOU THINK ABOUT IT WAS THE ONLY **SANE** THING TO DO, BUT BABS MADE A **HUGE STINK** ABOUT IT AND CALLED HER MOTHER A **HYPOCRITE** 'CUZ SHE'S SUPPOSED TO BE A DE-VOUT **CATHOLIC**, WHICH I GUESS IS TRUE, BUT, LIKE, SO **WHAT**?

AFTER HER ABORTION SHE BECAME **SEVERELY DEPRESSED** AND STAYED IN BED FOR WEEKS. SHE WAS TOO **MORTI-FIED** TO GO BACK TO SCHOOL (AS IF EVERYONE WOULD "KNOW") AND WOUND UP DROPPING OUT ALTOGETHER.

I DON'T KNOW WHERE ALL THIS **CATHOLIC GUILT** SUDDEN-LY CAME FROM, SINCE WE USED TO ALWAYS MAKE FUN OF PEOPLE WHO TOOK RELIGION SERIOUSLY, BUT NOW SHE WAS ACTING LIKE SHE WAS DOING **PENANCE**, BUT FOR WHAT? HAVING **TOO MUCH FUN**?!? IF SHE'S GUILTY OF ANYTHING IT'S BEING A **GULLIBLE SAP**, AND THIS BED-RIDDEN ROUTINE COMPOUNDED THAT FACT.

143

ANYHOW, ONCE SHE GOT OVER HER DEPRESSION SHE GOT A JOB AT A *BURGER KING* (OR WAS IT A *WENDY'S*? I FORGET WHICH). HER GOAL WAS TO SAVE ENOUGH MONEY TO MOVE OUT OF HER PARENTS HOUSE, WITH WHOM SHE WAS NOT GETTING ALONG *AT ALL*.

THIS TIME SHE ABSOLUTELY *REFUSED* TO GET AN ABORTION, SO BOTH THEIR PARENTS FORCED THEM TO GET *MARRIED*.

THEY LIVED WITH HIS FOLKS FOR A WHILE BUT THEY HAD TO GET OUT BEFORE THE BABY ARRIVED, SO THEY RENTED A *MOBILE HOME* WAY OUT IN THE BOONIES, FROM WHERE HE HAD TO COMMUTE AN *HOUR EACH WAY* TO HIS STUPID JOB AT TACO BELL. (OR WAS IT JACK IN THE BOX? OH WELL, ONE OF THOSE.)

WHAT SHE DIDN'T PLAN ON WAS GETTING *KNOCKED UP* BY THE ASSISTANT MANAGER ONLY A FEW WEEKS AFTER SHE STARTED WORKING THERE. SHE WASN'T USING ANY BIRTH CONTROL SINCE SHE *SWORE* SHE'D NEVER HAVE SEX AGAIN, BUT, WELL, YOU KNOW HOW *HOT AND STEAMY* THINGS CAN GET IN THE BACK ROOMS OF THOSE PLACES.

THE WEDDING WAS *SHORT* AND *EMBARRASSING*, EVERY-ONE COULD TELL SHE WAS PREGNANT, AND MR. BRAD-LEY ENDED THE RECEPTION BEFORE ANYONE COULD POUR A SECOND DRINK! THE *CHEAPSKATE*!

THEIR'S WAS NOT A HAPPY MARRIAGE. HE SPENT ALL OF HIS TIME AND MONEY ON HIS *CAR* WHILE BABS NAGGED HIM ABOUT BEING *BORED* AND HAVING TO TAKE CARE OF THE KID ALL THE TIME. STILL IN THEIR TEENS AND AL-READY THEY WERE ACTING JUST LIKE *THE KRAMDENS*!

I SAW HER ONCE AT A SUPERMARKET DURING THIS TIME. SHE LOOKED LIKE **HELL**, AND SHE WAS PREGNANT WITH HER **SECOND KID**. SHE WAS PUSHING HER SHOPPING CART FULL OF JUNK FOOD AND SODA POP LIKE SHE WAS IN A **TRANCE**, WHILE HER KID THREW A **FULL-SCALE TEMPER TANTRUM**.

IT WAS SHORTLY AFTER THAT THAT THEIR **TRAILER HOME** BURNED DOWN. THEY SUPPOSEDLY HAD A **BIG ARGUMENT** EARLIER THAT DAY, AND A LOT OF PEOPLE THINK HER HUSBAND WENT **NUTS** AND SET THE FIRE ON PURPOSE.

THEY HAD TO MOVE INTO HER PARENTS' HOUSE, AND THAT'S WHEN THE SHIT **REALLY** HIT THE FAN. THE FAMILY NEXT DOOR SAID IT WAS THE WORST FIGHTING THEY'VE HEARD SINCE **BUDDY** MOVED OUT. LIKE LAST THANKSGIVING BUTCH WENT AFTER BABS' HUSBAND WITH A **FORK**, AND A WEEK LATER I WAS TOLD THAT MR. BRADLEY TRIED TO **RUN HIM DOWN** ON THE STREET WITH HIS CAR!

NO ONE'S SEEN BABS' HUSBAND SINCE THEN, THOUGH HE CALLS UP EVERY NOW AND THEN AND THREATENS TO **KIDNAP THE KIDS**. I DOUBT HE'D EVER DO IT THOUGH, SINCE NOBODY IN THEIR **RIGHT MIND** WOULD WANT TO BE SADDLED WITH THOSE **LITTLE MONSTERS**!

BABS MUST'VE TAKEN HIM SERIOUSLY THOUGH, BECAUSE SHE MOVED INTO ONE OF THOSE HOMES FOR ABUSED WOMEN. ONLY THIS PLACE WAS RUN BY SOME **FUNDA-MENTALIST CHRISTIAN CHURCH**, AND THE LATEST I'VE HEARD IS THAT SHE'S BEEN TRANSFORMED INTO ONE OF THOSE **BRAINWASHED, SCRIPTURE-SPOUTING ZOMBIES**...

Eightball

Dan Clowes

Twentysomething Dan Clowes's protopunk-entitled monthly comic book (what does "Eightball" mean? we're supposed to ask) is an anthologized artist's journal. Less realistic and story-driven than his Fantagraphics Books colleague's Hate, *Clowes's work examines and stretches the limits of the medium itself. He plays with character and context, defying our attempts to categorize his work by changing drawing style and narrative technique from piece to piece.*

In this piece, rather simple by Clowes's standards, the reader experiences a party literally through the eyes of the author. By the end, this style and Clowes's meaning merge as the artist realizes that "I used to at least feel comfortable with my place as an 'outsider,' but now EVERYBODY seems to be an outsider . . . The divisions are all blurred."

The PARTY
by Clowes

IN COLOR

Here it is... Maybe I should just wait outside in case they aren't here yet... Fuck, I'm an hour late... I better go up there...

What the fuck was the name of the guy who lives here?..fuck fuck fuck... I'll go in with these creeps and it'll look like I came with them... I think the guy's name was 'Teddy'...

I can't say 'I'm a friend of Teddy's'...That might be him... I'll never be a friend of a guy named 'Teddy'...

Is this the host or was he just the closest one to the door?...

HI!

HELLO THERE, SON, I'M ROSS PEROT...

...HEH HEH

...What a jerk.

Come on... where are you fuckheads?...

Those MOTHERFUCKING ASSHOLES! I KNEW they wouldn't be here!

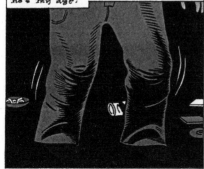

Is he one of those "Rave" guys? What is with that shit, anyway?... Those PANTS-- It's one thing for some dumb high schooler to be suckered in by a lame fashion trend, but this guy looks like he's my age!

...And why do they all wear those stupid ski-hats with the logos?...What are those logos all about, anyway?

I don't even want to know... Just the thought of talking to one of those creeps gives me a headache...

MR. CLOTHES!

Uh-oh, who is she?

HEY, HOW YA DOIN'?

HI! WHAT ARE YOU DOING HERE? ARE YOU A FRIEND OF PETER'S?

ACTUALLY, NO...

DO YOU KNOW IF MICHAEL'S COMING?

WHO? WHAT ARE YOU TALKING ABOUT?

NO, I DUNNO... ACTUALLY, I'M JUST MEETING SOME PEOPLE HERE...

I HAVE A FRIEND WHO'S DYING TO MEET YOU...ARE YOU GONNA BE HERE FOR A MINUTE?

Some big, fat guy with B.O. and acne, no doubt...

YEAH, I GUESS...

DAVID!... DAY-VID!

Jesus, what a motherfucking asshole I am! I should be eternally grateful that anybody gives a shit about anything I have to say... Where do I get off being such a smug, egotistical, critical bastard!...They're the ones who are happy and well-adjusted, not me... I need help...

HEY, ARE YOU THE ARTIST?

5.

149

HEY, HOW YA DOIN'?

SO ARE YOU THE GUY WHO DID THE SLEEVE ART FOR THE MEANINGLESS MOLECULES LP?

YUP.

NO, NOT REALLY... I MEAN, I TALKED TO 'EM ON THE PHONE A FEW TIMES, BUT...

SO DO YOU KNOW THOSE GUYS?

'CAUSE LAST WEEK I TAPED AN INTERVIEW WITH MITCH OF THE BLACK DOGS AND HE SAYS THERE'S AN UNRELEASED '7-INCH FROM '89 WITH HIM, DALE FROM THE BLADDERS, AND HARLEY, PRE-MOLECULES, ON VOCALS!

I GUESS THEY DO A GUITAR VERSION OF "MOODWRENCH"... ALSO HE HAD AN ADVANCE OF THE NEW SPINE PUPPIES DISC WHICH IS PRODUCED BY DOUG... I SAW 'EM IN '88 WHEN THEY SUCKED, BUT THIS IS KINDA LIKE EARLY SUNROOF...

Jesus Christ, ask me if I care!

I ALSO HEARD THAT DILDO OF THE INSIGNIFICANT SPECKS IS PRODUCING TWO TRACKS ON THE NEW GLOVEBOX 12-INCH WITH TWO OF THE HOSEBAGS SINGING BACKGROUND VOCALS AND DON ROTH PLAYING...

'SCUSE ME FOR A MINUTE - I REALLY HAVE TO TAKE A PISS!

Whew! I better stay in here for awhile so he can find another victim... Man, what a menace!

... This reminds me of that gag Rick and I thought of a few years ago where you crash a party and lock yourself in the bathroom and when people start to knock on the door you start crying and saying you're going to commit suicide...

HEY MAN, WHAT THE FUCK!

BAM BAM BAM

GO AWAY! SOB! I'M GOING TO KILL MYSELF!

... so they have to break down the door and then you act all emotional and grateful like they saved your life.

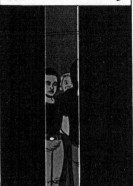

Hmm... Looks like the coast is clear... Those girls seem to find him fascinating...

6.

Holy mother of Pearl! Don't stare... Don't stare...

God, it's so frustrating! I hate trendy, club-hopping scenemakers like her, but it just TEARS ME APART that she won't validate my huge opinion of myself...

This whole "scene" is frustrating! These are just average upper-middle class kids and yet they all envision themselves as alternative 'fringe-dweller' types...

I used to at least feel comfortable with my place as an 'outsider', but now EVERYBODY seems to be an outsider... The divisions are all blurred... How can I like something when creeps like this also like it?

The only way to really separate yourself from the mainstream is to contrive an extreme persona...and all that gets you is a pathetic fashion show of freaks and assholes with made-up opinions...

Somebody my parents' age would probably lump me in with this crowd, but I'm not one of-- I don't know... I mean, I've got my own friends...

...Where are those fuckers?

Jesus Christ. What am I doing? I've got to get the fuck out of h--

HEY, MAN!

WHERE THE HELL WERE YOU GUYS?

WE'VE BEEN UP ON THE ROOF DOING 'ECSTASY'!

Fade to Black, roll Credits.

7.

151

bOING!
bOING!

Mark Frauenfelder

Reports from

Toys "Я" Us

Downscale, inexpensively produced, and almost adless, this California 'zine is free to explain illicit technologies and express irreverent notions usually whispered in the back row of the classroom or the back table at the coffeehouse. Amusing, alarming, and always insightful, editor Mark Frauenfelder's essays and stories share the experiential moment-to-moment quality of the worlds he is describing. Whether it be the effect of smart drugs, the feeling of virtual reality, or, as in this piece, a visit to a modern toy supermarket, his readers are always in for a ride.

Toys "R" Us was America's first chain of superstores and retains a respected position on the cultural totem pole in Dreg City. For this reason, as well as the fact that GenXers have maintained a deep interest in the ways the toys of our youth shaped our adult personalities, Frauenfelder chose to do a "you are there" piece from the front.

What are the toy stores selling these days? I hadn't cruised through one in a while, so I decided to check out a Toys "Я" Us late one evening, when most of the families had cleared out. I started at the front of the store and weaved my way up and down every aisle, taking notes when I saw something either really cool, really stupid, or really weird.

Unfortunately, almost everything I came across fell into the "yawn" category. I'm not interested in infant and toddler toys. Baby furniture is in-

visible to me. I hate hate hate sports. And the girls' doll section is pink over-
load. Every box is pink colored, with a smiling or crying plastic girl inside.
I'm pretty sure that most of the human body functions are simulated in one
doll or another, but the pinkness of it all forced me from staying long
enough to find out.

The good news about my visit is that the few things that caught my interest were just dripping with absurdity. Take, for example, goo. It's in a
child's nature. It brings them joy to fondle germ-laden ooze, mud, caterpillar
guts, and other types of natural glop. Fifty years ago it was impossible to
keep junior from smearing hirself with insect egg-clusters or slapping co-
coons between hir hands in hir quest for fun, but today's toy makers have
developed an entire market of simulated filth that's way more fun. Toys "Я"
Us stocks gallons of designer goo, including Gworms (gelatinous worms that
grow when you drop them in water), ooz balls ("The pod of intergalactic
ooz"), and Gak Splat (a handful of gooey putty). The packages scream "Look
kids! Gross goop to play with!" To their parents, they whisper "These toys
are sanitary substitutes, safe illusions that enable your offspring to act on
their urge to wallow in slime."

Animal cruelty was another opportunity for the toy companies to offer
clean versions of odious childhood pastimes. As a kid, I enjoyed burning
ants with a magnifying glass and taping grasshopper "astronauts" to pop-
bottle rockets. However, I drew the line at bugs.

The toy makers crossed it, with an animal torture simulation kit called
"Frog Baseball." It comes with a plastic boat oar and a green plastic ball
with frog legs sticking out from it. The object of the game is to pitch the
frog in the air and squash it with the oar. It seems frogs are low enough on
the cute 'n' cuddly animal list to prevent parents from complaining. If "Frog
Baseball" is successful, maybe they'll introduce a plastic "Kitty, Gasoline 'n'
Matches" kit next.

The step from frogicide to homicide is just an aisle away, in the large
weaponry section, where kiddies are given a million ways to pretend to kill
their friends. While the selection of firearms is greater than ever, they just
aren't realistic looking anymore. Today's toy weapons are made from
brightly colored plastic with fat red plugs on the barrel ends. During my
cork-gun commando days, toy firearms looked like smaller versions of the
real thing. Once, a friend and I were breaking in our new cap pistols by firing them at people on the street through the rear window of the station

wagon his mother was driving. A woman at an intersection saw us take aim at her and she dropped down flat on the pavement. My friend's mother didn't see what happened, and we saw no reason to tell her about it. She did ask us for an explanation (in a downright ungenial tone of voice) after several squad cars forced her off the road and screamed at her through a megaphone to come out with both hands up. (So, you see, Steve Jackson isn't the only one who's had to put up with illegal confiscation of property. The cops took our toy guns twenty years ago, and they STILL haven't given them back!)

I wished that Toys "Я" Us sold real guns when I got to the "plush" animal department, especially after seeing Barney the Dinosaur, who has taken over not only Toys "Я" Us but every kiddie brain in the country. If any dinosaur ever looked like a child molester, it has to be this fat purple freak. "We're a happy family." I'll bet we are. Did you know that Barney's producers actually ripped off Barney's mind-bogglingly vapid theme song from a school book written ten years ago? That's like stealing from a manure truck! Now why can't they come up with a Barney Baseball kit or a Barney you can squeeze until ooze leaks from his orifices? I'd buy that.

Other hideous toy animals include the "Disney Babies" series of dolls, games, books, tapes, cassettes, cartoons, etc. The Disney Babies look like the adult Mickey, Donald, etc., but have even fatter heads, tinier bodies, more idiotic grins, and (I'll bet) squeakier voices. This is cuteness overkill. Toys "Я" Us had better consider installing barf-bag dispensers in the "Disney Babies" section.

Moving quickly (to avoid the janitor coming over with his trusty can of odor-absorbing pellets), I found myself in "Farm Country." This company sells kits of little plastic animals, sheds, tractors, and feed silos, so you can "Build the Farm of Your Dreams." Finally! I can stop feeling sorry for those children who have been losing sleep over not being able to build a realistic miniature farm. The stuff did look realistic, I have to say!

So far, everything I'd seen was a simulated something-or-other. I like toys that don't pretend to be something else, especially ones that burn gas or solid fuel and make a lot of noise and move fast. Estes rockets, for instance. While they might be modeled after big rocketships, they are in fact real rockets and operate on the same aerodynamic principles. The same goes for the Cox gas engine planes. They're real airplanes, tiny as they may be. I used to play with a .049-cubic-inch Cox engine toys when I was a kid, and I enjoyed looking at the new products: hovercrafts, helicopters and dune buggies. The boxes said that Cox has sold 50 million .049 engines in its forty-year history. That's one for every child in America. (Where's mine? Some little fucker out there must have two!)

Almost—but not quite—as cool as the rockets and planes was the Spy Tech line of toys. They're designed for kids who want to play sleuth and are watered-down versions of what you might expect to find in the briefcase of a real covert intelligence agent. The "Tracker" consist of a small transmitter that you can surreptitiously plant in a purse, backpack or pocket to "help trail suspects and locate them when they are hiding" and a receiver unit with a speaker that emits a tone. The speaker's volume is proportional to the distance between the two units. The Spy Tech "Tracker" operates within a tiny range—under 50 feet—so it uses as a tracking device are limited. Another interesting Spy Tech toy is a small hollow plastic rock and a "special frequency" whistle. Here's what you do: put something in the compartment of the fake rock and hide it in a park or forest or some other place that has gray rocks that look like the phony one. Then your partner walks around in the general vicinity and blows on the whistle. A microphone built into the rock picks up the whistle signal, and if the frequency matches, the rock will beep, so your pal can locate the rock and the goodies inside.

The trouble with both of these spy tech toys is that they make a lot of noise and a real spy doesn't want to run around in the woods blowing a whistle or walking down the street holding a weird looking baton that emits a whooping siren noise.

Where there're spys, there're soldiers. The fall of communism was welcomed by everybody except arms and toy makers. The geniuses behind the GI Joe line of action figures had to come up with a new enemy, fast, before children forgot how to use violence to solve conflicts. They still sell the normal-size Joes with "lifelike hair"—I couldn't find any with the "kung-fu grip"—for fighting foreign enemies, but a new gang of teeny-weeny Joes has two new sets of villains to contend with: drug dealers and litterbugs.

These 4-inch warriors come in cardboard-backed blister packs, complete with a weapon, and sometimes a dog or even a dolphin. The art on the blister packs is great: on every one, whether the Joe is a good guy or a bad guy, the illustration depicts him screaming with rage, wildly firing his weapon from the hip. This, plus the fact that these subminiature GI Joe dolls show "battle-damage" when splashed with water, is enough to make me want to run down and buy the whole set right now.

The drug-menace fighters are called the DEF (Drug Elimination Force). The drug dealers are called the Evil Head Hunters. The back of each package explains the situation: "After taking the Headman's drugs, victims are unable to perform the easiest task, such as tying their shoelaces." I also learned that "GI Joe is proud to be a member of the Partnership for a Drug Free America." Somehow it seems right that a person with a hollow plastic head and an IQ of zero would want to join the Partnership.

The GI Joe Eco-Warriors also scream with rage on the packaging, but instead of firing exploding bullets from their weapons, the good guys shoot big clean water guns and the bad guys squirt toxic sludge. It took some creativity on the part of the toy makers to come up with reasons why a person would want to intentionally pollute the environment. Take the sad case of the head eco-villain, "Cesspool." He was the head of a corporation until he fell into a tank of chemical waste while giving an environmental group a tour around his plant. The poisonous concoction mutated and deformed him, 60s Marvel comic book style, and now Mr. Cesspool blames environmentalists for ruining his life. He carries a big tank of filthy liquid on his back and squirts it at anyone who comes within range. The biographies for the other Eco-Villains don't go into detail about how they became so untidy; they're simply called "Sludge Viper" and "Toxo-Viper."

It was interesting to note that in both scenarios, the bad guys have some kind of scarring or physical damage. This was probably done to teach children that people who have been maimed or have a disfigured appearance will never amount to anything.

My final stop was to check out the Nintendo and Sega section. One day, Toys "Я" Us will be nothing but game cartridges and plush smiling Barneys. This is the nineties, and the "play" experience provided by toys has become "simulated play." Now you can actually hear the people scream with rage and watch them fire their weapons. That's progress. Right before I left, I scanned the rows and rows of cartridges for sale. Shoot-the-enemy games were most prevalent, then sports simulations, then cute 'n' cuddly animal quests. There was even a bright pink card for, you guessed it: Barbie "Gamegirl."

Lemme outta here!

CHAPTER 5

Metamedia

Metamedia

A GenXer I know has the word "VIRUS" scrawled across his TV screen in indelible ink. He believes that if he simply stays aware of this medium's ability to infect him, he will be able to resist the cultural programming emanating from the tube.

While most GenXers don't resort to these measures, we are particularly attracted to media that use bracketing devices to comment on media methodology. Built into our favorite shows are characters and narrative techniques that constantly remind us of our relationship to the program we are watching. Our television heros are characters like Bart Simpson and Beavis and Butt-head, who demonstrate proper aloofness toward media iconography as well as the skills to dissect and reconstitute television imagery against its original purposes.

More than a case of form reflecting content, GenX self-reflexive art and media use forms within forms as the basis of content. Employing VCRs, computers, photocopying machines, and other "cut-and-paste" technology, the GenX artist creates an impact through his or her ability to keep the audience aware of its relationship to media. For us, a "junk culture" of screens within screens is a self-reflective societal looking glass.

Finally, then, the people whom we entrust with the future of our culture are those who understand the basic principles of the datasphere and who can help us continue to disengage from the hypnotic spell of the sociomarketing machine. Our key activists are media educators who teach us how to view the datasphere as a living organism that can be attacked with advanced programming techniques, as demonstrated by the shows highlighted in this chapter. If we can really use these media "viruses" to reprogram the propaganda beast right down to its DNA coding, then we will have become capable of genetic engineering on a societal scale.

Ren & Stimpy

Dan Persons Analyzes
"Stimpy's Invention"

Left with nothing but the postmodern entrails of a meaningless junk culture, today's animation artists have developed an aesthetic of borrowed and recycled imagery. Unlike Warhol, who simply framed objects to create art, GenX artists frame media: We reframe things that have already been framed.

Originally marketed as a children's cartoon, Ren & Stimpy provided safe passage for extraordinarily virulent social satire. Characters often made references to homosexuality, satirized boomer ethics, and poked fun at the government. The show quickly became a buster cult classic, and many analyses like this one appeared, granting each episode the attention and thoughtful deconstruction it deserved.

With rare exceptions (Barry Manilow albums, the *Friday The 13th* series), you can't get much lower on the aesthetic scale than kidvid animation. Even when the occasional savior comes along—a Paul Reubens, a Ralph Bakshi—the network suits are always there, conspiring to make sure that the wee ones aren't confronted with anything that would take their minds off the next wave of Fruity Pebbles ads.

That's the way it's been. And if you think that's the way it will forever be, then, buddy, you've never seen "Stimpy's Invention."

Appearing as one segment of Nickelodeon's popular "Ren & Stimpy Show," "Stimpy's Invention" initially does little to telegraph the dangers that lurk within. The setup is pure "Ren & Stimpy": Stimpy, the dim-witted cat, goads his Chihuahua friend Ren Hoek into helping him test some of his latest inventions. Predictably, the upshot is an enraged Ren, who struggles mightily to reach Stimpy's throat. The ever-slow feline comes to a remarkable conclusion: "Say," he confides to the audience, "you don't suppose Ren is *unhappy*?" With tears brimming in his eyes, Stimpy declares that he has found his one, true calling: to use his "gift of invention" to alleviate Ren's pain.

Here's where things start to get nasty. What Stimpy invents is the Happy Helmet, a chrome gadget that looks like a cross between a toaster and a bit of Flash Gordon headgear. Stimpy wastes no time in permanently affixing the thing to Ren's skull, informing him, while proffering a remote control box, that never again will the Chihuahua be unhappy. His pal has time for one obligatory insult ("You sick, little monkey . . . !") before Stimpy punches a button, and Ren is plunged into a mortal struggle with the device.

It's a losing battle, of course, even with Ren's best efforts at a Bill Shatner imitation ("Must . . . fight . . . it . . . Can't . . . lose . . . control . . ."). When the Chihuahua finally surrenders, what he winds up as would give the Pod People nightmares: "SO . . . HAPPY!" he shrieks, his face broken into a strained, toothy grin, his dialogue punctuated with a fearsomely hysterical laugh, "Must go do . . . good things for Stimpy!"

This, for Stimpy, is an unqualified victory. For Ren, it's pure hell, made worse when he's forced to dance to Stimpy's favorite song—an idiotic ditty called "Happy Happy, Joy Joy." Pushed to the limit, the Chihuahua finally cracks, zealously taking a hammer to his helmeted head, freeing himself just in time to grab his friend by the throat. The only thing that saves the cat from certain death is a flash of realization on Ren's part: "Hey," the Chihuahua shouts, "I feel *great*! I *love* being angry!"

It's pretty wicked stuff, and way out of the norm for standard kidvid. In fact, *everything* about "Stimpy's Invention" suggests that all involved knew they were working on something special. The visuals—from Ren's temper tantrums, to a transformation sequence that has the Chihuahua's face fracturing into a riot of angles, to the following sequences in which every portion of Ren's body seems determined to go in a different direction—contain some of the best animation the program has yet offered. Even the cost-cutting static shots, employed mostly in the central inventor's montage, exhibit a sophistication not previously seen.

But there's more to "Stimpy's Invention" than just technical proficiency. There have been frequent hints that director John Kricfalusi and company have been pushing for more than mere giggles with their dark, little cartoons. Here, they come out of the closet with a comic horror story that speaks volumes about free will and the dangers of forcing one's own bliss upon others. There's an unusual reversal of roles in this episode, with the usually benign Stimpy taking an almost sadistic delight in controlling Ren's moods, while Ren—normally too short-tempered and violent to win much sympathy—becomes a figure of pure tragedy, condemned to a brainless euphoria not his own, and not under his control. The dog's plight is capitalized on magnificently, with the impressive "Happy Happy, Joy Joy" sequence offered as the curdled icing on the poisoned cake.

The song itself is a piece of work: it's nothing less than the aural equivalent of the Happy Helmet, complete with semi-subliminal audio over-lays and singer Stinky Wizzleteats' (Kricfalusi, again) I've-skipped-my-medication-today interjections ("I don't think you're happy enough!").

Even after Ren has saved himself, there's no easy out. As if it isn't a clear enough contradiction that a short-tempered Ren could achieve happiness only by indulging the worst of his anger, Kricfalusi underlines the moment with one of the most bizarre fade-outs the series has yet provided: an abrupt cut from a two-shot of Ren and Stimpy to a static close-up of the Chihuahua grinning maniacally while Happy Helmet laughter echoes in the background. Ren's freed himself from one brand of enslavement, perhaps only to deliver himself into another. The character comes full circle—Beckett would have been proud.

Maybe that's too heavy for what's supposed to be a simple kid's cartoon. Maybe it's also too extreme to suggest that not only is "Stimpy's Invention" the best segment of the series so far, it may be the best bit of made-for-television animation in decades (and, just in case I forgot to mention it, it's also screamingly funny). It's a revelatory few minutes—as challenging to one's preconceptions of the medium as Walt Disney's *Snow White and the Seven Dwarfs,* or Chuck Jones' *Duck Amuck.* With only 18 "Ren & Stimpy" episodes under their belts before they were canned by Nickelodeon, the artists of Spumco never got to demonstrate all they were capable of.

Beavis and Butt-head

A Rolling Stone *Interview*

by Charles M. Young

Beavis and Butt-head themselves are too young to qualify as GenXers, but their television show is pointedly metamedia. Much more interesting than their famously violent exploits (exploding frogs, et al.) is their nonstop media commentary: They teach people how to watch MTV. They demonstrate proper aloofness toward their television intake, criticizing videos they think "suck" and praising the ones they consider "cool." Also, however idiotic this pair looks to adults, they exhibit tremendous wit, irreverence, and, most of all, their creator's ability to frame media within media within media.

The stupid and ugly have one advantage in life: Teachers expect nothing from them, so they can fly under the usual indoctrination that accompanies education. Thus the stupid and ugly—if they aren't entirely stupid—have a greater chance of being original. They are allowed to speak the truth because no one cares what they say. *Because they are stupid, they are free.* The major disadvantage, among many, is that uneducated behavior is often just rotten.

Beavis and Butt-head, two thunderously stupid and excruciatingly ugly pubescent males who live somewhere in the Southwest, do rotten stuff all the time. They are cruel to animals. They vandalize their neighbors. They torture their teachers. Their libidos rage unchecked, except by the uniform unwillingness of the female sex to associate with them. And they are the biggest phenomenon on MTV since the heyday of Michael Jackson. Where a normal video draws a .6 rating, Beavis and Butt-head draw up to a 2.4. Kids are memorizing their dialogue and throwing Beavis and Butt-head parties. Their laugh—low and breathy variations on "huh-huh"—has superseded Wayne and Garth's "Not!" as the comic catch phrase of the moment. An album and a movie are in the works, and their merchandising campaign is sweeping the malls. Yes, Beavis and Butt-head are America's Inner Teenager. *Because they are free, we will make them rich.*

Every weeknight at 7:00* and 11:00, they set out on their mundane, sordid adventures, usually inspired by a commercial or soap opera plot that no non-stupid person could take seriously. Simultaneously they have become the most acute commentators on TV. For half of their 30-minute show, they sit on the couch and tell the truth about music video. They are the complete viewer service, right down to channel surfing for you. Butt-head's philosophy of aesthetics goes thusly: "I like stuff that's cool" and "I don't like stuff that sucks." For Beavis, it's even simpler: He agrees with Butt-head. What's cool is explosions, loud guitars, screaming and death. Who are cool include the Butthole Surfers, Corrosion of Conformity, Metallica and babes. What sucks is everything else. And they say so, suggesting that aging purveyors of pop metal like the Scorpions join the Hair Club for Men and that Edie Brickell, when bent over and straining at her deadly serious lyrics, looks like she's "pinching a loaf."

That Zen perfection—stuff that's cool being good and stuff that sucks being bad—has caused an earthquake in critical circles. Kurt Andersen, in *Time*, says *Beavis and Butt-head* "may be the bravest show ever run on national television." And Chris Morris, in the L.A. *Reader*, sees them as the wonder drug to dissolve the great clot of semiotic theory clogging contemporary rock criticism, as capturing the true essence of rock: "volume, abandon, radicalism." Seeking even deeper wisdom, we caught Beavis and Butt-head on their couch for their first in-depth interview. *Because they're going to be rich, we must study them.* Series creator Mike Judge and writer David Felton joined in for interpretive purposes.

* * *

You're selling more posters than "Jurassic Park." You're getting all-time high ratings on MTV. What does your success say about the current culture of American teenagers?

*Editor's note: Because of its provocative nature, this show now airs only late at night.

BUTT-HEAD: Huh-huh, huh-huh.

BEAVIS: He said "suck." Huh-huh, huh-huh.

BUTT-HEAD: Huh-huh. Uh . . . could you repeat the question?

What I'm getting at is, there's a whole new group of kids in junior high now, and your success—

BUTT-HEAD: Huh-huh. He said it again.

BEAVIS: Yeah. Huh-huh, huh-huh.

Let me put it another way. Just this morning I watched a psychologist on TV talk about the horrible effect that heavy metal has on kids. Do you ever consider the influence you're having on today's youth?

BUTT-HEAD: Uh . . .uh . . . well, I like to burn stuff, but that doesn't mean—

BEAVIS: I like it when stuff blows up and knocks people over. Huh-huh.

BUTT-HEAD: [*Smacks Beavis on the head*] Shut up, Beavis. I was saying something. Huh-huh. Uh . . . what was I saying?

Your influence on today's youth.

BUTT-HEAD: What's today?

Tuesday.

BUTT-HEAD: Oh, yeah. What was I saying?

Your effect on young people. You said you like to burn stuff.

BUTT-HEAD: *Whoa!* You must have one of those pornographic memories! Huh-huh. Uh . . . I like to burn stuff, but that doesn't mean *you* have to. Huh-huh, huh-huh. It would be cool if you did, though.

BEAVIS: Yeah. Huh-huh. Fire! Fire! Fire!

So what's the coolest thing you've ever burned?

BUTT-HEAD: Uh . . . Beavis's eyebrows. Huh-huh.

BEAVIS: Yeah, that was pretty cool. Huh-huh. It smelled cool, too.

Why was that so cool?

BUTT-HEAD: It was, like, unexpectant? We were torching a June bug with a can of Lysol and a lighter, an it ended up burning Beavis's face. Huh-huh, huh-huh. It was like a bonus.

BEAVIS: Huh-huh. I burned my bonus.

Well, let me ask you this: Do you guys find anything funny that isn't scatological?

BUTT-HEAD: Uh . . . sure. Lots of stuff. Like, uh, butts are funny.

Anything besides butts?

BEAVIS: Farts are funny. Because they come out of your butt. Huh-huh.

BUTT-HEAD: Did you know any time anyone is born, they come out right next to a butt? Huh-huh.

BEAVIS: Yeah. Even the president of the United States.

So what's your point?

BUTT-HEAD: Well, uh . . . that's pretty cool. Huh-huh, huh-huh.

What do you think of the disclaimer MTV sometimes runs before your show?

BUTT-HEAD: It's cool.

Do you know what I'm talking about?

BUTT-HEAD: Uh . . . no. Huh-huh.

Those words MTV runs before the show warning people about you.

BEAVIS: Words suck.

BUTT-HEAD: Yeah. If I wanted to read, I'd go to school.

BEAVIS: So, like, what do they say?

They say you're crude, self-destructive and anti-social, but for some reason you make them laugh.

BUTT-HEAD: Cool! Huh-huh.

BEAVIS: Yeah. MTV's cool.

Even though the censors in their standards department won't let you say certain words?

BUTT-HEAD: Yeah. MTV's cool—for a bunch of wussies. Huh-huh, huh-huh.

BEAVIS: We can say "ass wipe."

BUTT-HEAD: Not very often.

BEAVIS: We can say "asshole."

BUTT-HEAD: No, we can't, Beavis.

BEAVIS: Are you calling me a liar?

BUTT-HEAD: No, I'm calling you a waste of bum wipe.

BEAVIS: We can say "butthole." Butthole! Butthole! Butthole!

BUTT-HEAD: Shut up! MTV will fire you!

BEAVIS: Fire! Fire! Fire!

BUTT-HEAD: Settle down, Beavis!

You seem to watch a lot of TV. Do you think television depicts an accurate view of the world?

BUTT-HEAD: Uh . . . like, are you really with the Rolling Stones?

I'm with "Rolling Stone," the magazine.

BUTT-HEAD: So, uh, do you get lots of chicks?

BEAVIS: Hey, Butt-head, when chicks find out we know someone with the Stones, we'll get some helmet. Huh-huh, huh-huh.

I'm with the magazine "Rolling Stone." I'm a writer, not a musician.

BEAVIS: Wuss.

BUTT-HEAD: So you don't get any chicks?

Not like Mike Jagger.

BEAVIS: Mick Jagger's not a chick.

BUTT-HEAD: He didn't say he was a chick, Beavis. He said he doesn't *get* chicks.

BEAVIS: He said he doesn't get chicks like Mick Jagger.

BUTT-HEAD: That's right. Not like Mick Jagger.

BEAVIS: But Mick Jagger's not a chick.

BUTT-HEAD: Don't make me kick your ass again, Beavis.

BEAVIS: You know who looks like a chick? Huh-huh. Vince Neil.

BUTT-HEAD: Yeah. Huh-huh. And Dave Mustaine.

BEAVIS: Yeah. That's why he wears glasses. So he doesn't look too much like a girl. Huh-huh, huh-huh.

What do glasses have to do with masculinity?

BUTT-HEAD: You know what you should do to, like, get chicks? Since you're a wuss? Huh-huh, huh-huh.

What?

BUTT-HEAD: You should get some binoculars and stand outside this apartment building we know and look in the windows. Huh-huh.

How would that help me get chicks?

BUTT-HEAD: Sometimes you can see 'em naked. Huh-huh, huh-huh.

BEAVIS: Yeah. Huh-huh. Or you could go to Bible camp and hug chicks when they find Jesus.

BUTT-HEAD: That would be cool. Huh-huh. "Give us this day our morning wood." Huh-huh, huh-huh.

What kind of music do you like?

BUTT-HEAD: Uh ... uh ... all different kinds.

BEAVIS: Yeah. Like *loud* music.

BUTT-HEAD: Yeah. And music that *rocks*! Huh-huh.

BEAVIS: Music that *kicks ass*! Huh-huh. And fire music! Fire! Fire!

What's fire music?

BEAVIS: Oh, sorry, I was thinking about videos.

BUTT-HEAD: I also like music that's about stuff. Huh-huh.

BEAVIS: Yeah. Like that rap song about that guy who likes big butts.

BUTT-HEAD: Yeah. That one speaks to me. Huh-huh, huh-huh.

The rumor is, you guys have the same father.

BUTT-HEAD: Uh . . . we're not sure. It's possible. Huh-huh.

BEAVIS: Yeah. Huh-huh. He used to come around a lot.

Are the two of you friends with anyone besides each other?

BEAVIS: We're not friends.

BUTT-HEAD: Beavis has a special friend. Huh-huh.

BEAVIS: Yeah. Huh-huh.

BUTT-HEAD: Sometimes he shakes hands with Little Beavis.

BEAVIS: Yeah. [*Pathetic attempt at Pakistani accent*] "Hello, Meester Monkey." Huh-huh, huh-huh.

BUTT-HEAD: Huh-huh. That was cool.

Well, you two sound pretty friendly.

BUTT-HEAD: We just do lots of stuff together. Huh-huh.

BEAVIS: Just cool stuff.

BUTT-HEAD: Yeah. I like stuff that's cool.

Well, there must be a lot of cool stuff to do, because as far as I can tell, you two spend every moment of your life together.

BUTT-HEAD: That's 'cause Beavis follows me around.

BEAVIS: *You* follow *me* around.

BUTT-HEAD: Only when I'm gonna kick your ass.

BEAVIS: When you're gonna *lick* my ass?

BUTT-HEAD: Shut up, booger wipe!

BEAVIS: Peckerwood!

Hey, break it up! Butt-head, I have a question for you. I noticed that you often say, "I like stuff that's cool!" But isn't that circular logic? I mean, what is the definition of "cool," other than an adjective denoting something the speaker likes?

BUTT-HEAD: Huh-huh. Uh, did you, like, go to college?

You don't have to go to college to know the definition of "redundant." What I'm saying is that essentially what you're saying is "I like stuff that I like."

BEAVIS: Yeah. Huh-huh. Me, too.

BUTT-HEAD: Also, I don't like stuff that sucks, either.

But nobody likes stuff that sucks!

BUTT-HEAD: Then why does so much stuff suck?

BEAVIS: Yeah. College boy! Huh-huh, huh-huh.

BUTT-HEAD: Huh-huh, huh-huh. Uh, I have a question for *you.*

Go ahead.

BUTT-HEAD: Pull my finger.

That's not a question.

BUTT-HEAD: Huh-huh. Uh . . . would you please pull my finger?

Oh, all right.

[*Butt-head farts loudly.*]

BUTT-HEAD: Huh-huh, huh-huh. That's cool.

BEAVIS: I taught him that joke. Huh-huh.

BUTT-HEAD: I taught *you* that joke, bunghole!

BEAVIS: But I taught you the part about where you fart.

BUTT-HEAD: Oh, right, you did. Huh-huh, huh-huh. That's my favorite part.

I just have a couple more things I'd like to cover.

BUTT-HEAD: Huh-huh. He said "things."

BEAVIS: He said "couple." Huh-huh, huh-huh.

When I was your age, the big event that formed the values of my entire generation was the Vietnam War.

BUTT-HEAD: Yeah. Huh-huh. Rambo was cool!

So I was wondering if there was some similar experience, some unifying event, that has affected your life.

BUTT-HEAD: Uh . . . well, once we bought this bullwhip at Stuckey's? And we went around looking for stuff to whip. But like we couldn't find anything. No frogs or lizards or nothing.

BEAVIS: We tried a bag of charcoal, but it wasn't alive.

BUTT-HEAD: Then we found this big old grasshopper in the middle of the road. It was really big. It was like a freak grasshopper. Huh-huh. We whipped it and whipped it.

BEAVIS: Yeah, yeah. And then I kicked it. Huh-huh.

BUTT-HEAD: We slapped it around like a red-headed stepchild. Huh-huh, huh-huh. And then it looked like it was dead 'cause it hadn't moved in like an hour? And then all of a sudden these little white worms started crawling out of its butt, one by one. Huh-huh, huh-huh.

BEAVIS: Yeah. They looked like long-grain rice. It's like they were trapped inside this grasshopper, and we came along, and set 'em free.

BUTT-HEAD: Huh-huh. Uh . . . they crawled out of its *butt!*

You're comparing the Vietnam War to worms crawling out of a grasshopper's butt? How could that affect your life?

BUTT-HEAD: Well, uh . . . if that hadn't happened, we would have had to, like, do something else.

Well, I suppose it's pointless to ask this, but—

BUTT-HEAD: Huh-huh. You said "butt."

What advice do you have for America's youth?

BEAVIS: Uh . . . sometimes at the arcade? If you rub your feet on the ground and touch the coin slot, it makes a spark and you get a free game. Huh-huh.

BUTT-HEAD: Huh-huh. Uh . . . I got one. Like if you go to school and, like, study and stuff? And grow up and get a job at a company and, like, get promoted? You have to go there and do stuff that sucks for the rest of your life.

BEAVIS: Yeah. You'll be trapped, just like those worms in that grasshopper's butt. Huh-huh, huh-huh. And then people will whip you, and you'll come crawling out and—

BUTT-HEAD: Shut up, Beavis! Huh-huh. But what I was saying is, if you act like us and just do stuff that's cool? Like sit around and watch TV and burn stuff?

BEAVIS: And choke your chicken. Huh-huh-huh.

BUTT-HEAD: Yeah. Huh-huh. And choke your chicken. Then, ROLLING STONE magazine will come and kiss your butt!

Huh-huh. You said "come."

BEAVIS: Yeah. Huh-huh, huh-huh.

BEAVIS AND BUTT-HEAD: Huh-huh, huh-huh. Huh-huh, huh-huh. Huh-huh, huh-huh. Huh-huh, huh-huh.

BUTT-HEAD: That was cool!

Seize The Media

The Immediast

Underground

Twentysomething Greg Ruggiero and Stuart Sahulka began the Immediast Underground as students at New Jersey's Rutgers University. Extending the principles laid down by the European situationist movement of the 1950s and 1960s, the Immediasts are a network of media activists intent on overthrowing consensus reality. Greg and Stuart print an Open Pamphlet Series, which includes lectures by media and social theorists ranging from Noam Chomsky to Helen Caldicott. "Seize the Media" is their original pamphlet/manifesto and carries the following anticopyright notice: "Immediast projects are against all forms of coercive communication, cultural monologue and media control. We acknowledge non-violent public insurgence as a legitimate response to sustained violations by media and state. We recognize the air as public property, and the signals that travel through it to be the domain of the public."

Asian philosophy instructs enlightenment. But given our daily exposure to a barrage of persuasive messages, monologues, sales pitches, come-ons, and uninformative hyper-sensational news, common sense and sanity are tough enough a struggle to maintain.

We each see how extended exposure to television and mass media dulls people with a sense of numbness and nausea. At every turn a monologue of coercion penetrates our senses and rapes our attention. Wherever we look, wherever we listen, wherever we go: the pornography of billboards, bus-side placards, subway cards, glaring storefront signs and displays, the glut of junk mail, stupid fly-by beach planes and blimps, coupons, obnoxious bumper stickers and breast pins, embarrassing service uniforms, plastic banners and ribbons, absurd parades, streetcorner handouts, windshield wiper flyers, matchbook ads, business cards, screaming radios, the daily papers, every nanosecond of television, the package wrapped around everything we buy—from the label in our underwear to the robot computer that calls us in our homes—only the upper atmosphere and the ocean floor offer any sanctuary from America's ecology of coercion. And at every turn the monologues drone on, imbedding the psychological mutagens that coax us to become pathetic customers and unquestioning flag wavers. At every turn, we are under subtle attack.

The media serve the interests of the State and other corporations, but never the interests of the public. The media's screen of aggression and seduction is designed to mesmerize and captivate the largest possible sector of a population whose attention is then sold like scrap metal to advertisers and gang raped by their slogans, jingles, and manic images. Protected by an uncrossable media moat, agents of the State profit from war and relax behind a web of information laws, censorship powers, and vapid explanations that swat the public of detailed intelligence and mass resistance.

So long as we do not control our own government, our own state, and our own broadcast media—the mirror with which we reflect on the reality of life—we will continue to be forced to see fun-house mirror distortions of ourselves projected onto a Dumpster of products that promise to make us each desirable, sophisticated, and correct. At every turn we are under attack.

INCEST OF CORPORATIONS AND THE STATE

The State controls information, debt, and violence and targets collective identity. Corporations control commodification, work, and media and target individual identity. Both deploy the same psychological strategies for imbedding the public with their messages and directives. Never were their common strategies more transparent than when US disinformation and propaganda service, the infamous USIA, decided to step up its psy-warfare campaign against the people of Cuba in the Spring of 1989. Until then, attempts to psychologically destabilize the Cuban people were concentrated in the broadcasts of Radio Martí, the Florida-based, Government-owned pirate radio station that to this day illegally transmits propaganda and disinformation into domestic Cuban radios. In the Spring of 1989, the USIA added images to their psy-war arsenal and began transmitting tele-broadcasts from a hot air balloon controlled from the Key West signals station. Sibling of Radio Martí, the project was dubbed TV Martí.

A few things are to be held in mind here. First, after the Creel Commission saturated Americans with pro-war propaganda during World War I, the level of public disgust was so intense that laws were enacted forbidding the State from ever subjecting the public to its propaganda again. Thus, the USIA's Voice of America propaganda broadcasts that we can hear today in Amsterdam, Berlin, and Prague, we are protected against hearing here on our own turf. Propaganda is so disorienting and confusing that Americans have actually passed laws forbidding it here in its crude verifiable forms.

The fact that we must now face and destroy is that advertising, entertainment, and news have become the government's Trojan horse into the psyche of the public. What was TV Martí's first propaganda broadcast aimed at destabilizing the minds of Cuban people? MTV! Think about it: The USIA's first broadcast of tele-propaganda delivered MTV's corporate rock videos! At every turn we are under attack.

METHODS OF MIND CONTROL

Immediast research has turned up two invaluable sources revealing State tactics of behavior modification, subliminal manipulation, and mind control. The first is the psychological warfare manual authored and distributed by the CIA to the Nicaraguan terrorists, the Contras. The instruction manual directives state:

> In effect, the human being should be considered the priority objective in a political war. And conceived as the military target of guerrilla war, the human being has his most critical point in his mind. Once his mind has been reached, the "political animal" has been defeated, without necessarily receiving bullets . . .
>
> This conception of guerrilla warfare as political war turns Psychological Operations into the decisive factor of the results. The target, then, is the minds of the population, all the

population: our troops, the enemy troops and the civilian population . . .

Communication is a way to ask and give the answer to the same question.

The manual goes on to instruct its readers how to effectively deceive, blackmail, and assassinate individuals antagonistic to the imperatives of the State.

THE SEMANTIC DIFFERENTIAL

Our second source of documentation exposing State-led programs of media subversion is found in the video documentaries and published articles of Fred Landis. Landis first discovered the presence of mind control tactics in commercial broadcast media by monitoring daily newspapers produced by the CIA in Chile in 1973. His resulting Ph.D. dissertation outlined CIA tactics of subliminal manipulation and mind control and was used against the CIA in Volume 7 of the 1975 Hearings of the Senate Church Committee; "The CIA and the Media," and in the 1977–1978 Hearings of the House Intelligence Committee. Landis' observations and research exposed a now easily identifiable method deployed by the State to psychologically destabilize and subliminally coerce a given population. Based on the crosscultural linguistic theory and research generated by Charles Osgood (funded by the CIA), the government deploys the following method, called the *Semantic Differential*:

• First, media Agents identify cultural symbols which have deep emotional associations within a target population's everyday domestic, cultural, and spiritual lives. Agents then use these symbols as inroads to the people's unconscious and manipulate these symbols as subliminal imbeds which can be antagonized or resonated in accordance with situations being manufactured by the CIA:

Indirect attacks on government ministers employ the juxtaposition of photos of the targeted official with unrelated headlines, subliminal propaganda, and pre-selected word associations. By simply placing the key word near a photo of government leaders, a crude behaviorist attempt is made to

condition new associations and new values to familiar personalities.

The combined effect of word associations (derived from
the semantic differential) with subliminal imbeds is so strong
that it displaces any other message . . .

—even ones which disprove the connotations and meaning of the effect.

State tactics of media control deliver subliminal and disinforming directives in the guise of news. Targeting deep psychological imbeds present in
every culture, the State instills shock, terror, confusion, sexual arousal, awe
or uncertainty by antagonizing or coupling these imbeds with sensational
headlines associating such things as Satanism with enemies, and religious
miracles and good luck with leaders implanted or puppetted by the State.
The symbols change from culture to culture. During the US Supreme Court
Nomination Hearings of Clarence Thomas, *The New York Times* ran a cover
photo (Sunday, October 13, 1991) of Senator Hatch holding up a copy of *The
Exorcist* and associating it with Anita Hill! This was not an accusation, it
was a psychological tactic. According to the semantic differential, the deep
and negative feelings experienced in people by such associations outlast evidence which demonstrates their falsehood and perversion.

IMMEDIAST TACTICS

Asian philosophy instructs self-realization and awakening, but when
under attack, Asian philosophy also instructs methods for overpowering an
assailant with the force of his own assault. We herald this approach.
Immediast tactics aim to neutralize the key images and text being imbedded
into the public by the media and the State. Our work is the liberation of public space from the broadcasts of corporations, businesses, and departments
of the State; and the abolition of public captivity as spectators to the ceaseless barrage of billboards, manipulative images, State constructed news and
propaganda. The question is, how we can lockjaw the spectacle with its own
force?

Returning all airborne commercial broadcast media to public direction,
access, and control will naturally release cultural forces difficult at present

to imagine—the mind turned inside out won't be a viral image slogan on a Gannet billboard. It will be living people on the airwaves and in the streets.

We interpret Freedom of Speech to mean the facilitated ability to both access and produce information and cultural material through the development of public production libraries where we can each and all produce cultural print, radio, television, and radio broadcast materials in library studios equipped with desktop publishing facilities, graphics technology, multi-track audio recorders, film and video cameras, and editing equipment. Freedom to broadcast can be in the power of the public. Corporations can be evicted from the airwaves. We can charge them staggering rent for the low-end frequencies if we want to. The State, under relentless public scrutiny, can be kept nude of its power to hide from, indebt, and subvert the public. Democracy can be as open and dynamic as our public libraries.

Of course we anticipate struggle on the part of the State and corporations. Let them struggle. Doing so opens up new fissures and points of access. In the meantime, we call on you to engage in your own actions. We call on artists, writers, posterists, activists, and networkers from all countries to assist with our project. Vocalize your disgust. Speak up. Fight back. Liberate the public spaces in the zones that most need it—the ones in your everyday life. Organize indigenous Immediast groups. Organize Networker Congresses. Strike. Send to our journal, *Noospapers*, your statements, manifestoes, critiques, tracts, tactics, poetry, posters, collages, documentation, graphics and art. Together we can begin the liberation of public spaces and end our forced captivity in a spectator democracy.

REVOLUTION AND INSURGENCE

Revolution is the overthrow of government; our aim is to overthrow the media. Armed insurrection is unnecessary in so far as it is words and images which are shot at us, not bullets. But the words and images which keep us in bondage, which inundate us with the political muzak of disinformation, half-baked scandals shock, empty desires, and subliminal imbeds are what enable State and corporate men to shoot bullets at people outside our borders, slaughtering people like you and me by the thousands in Iraq, in Panama, in Grenada, in El Salvador, in Libya, in Nicaragua, in Africa. With the media in the hands of the public, State agents who order secret wars, election riggings, destabilization programs and other covert actions will be forced into open view and the democratic control of the public.

THE NEW SERVANT CLASS

Establishing democratic legitimacy in America begins not with overthrowing our governments, but with diminishing them to the role of public servants. After all, in America, State agents are still employees of the public. The Immediast goal is to make government officials the only servants in our society, the audience of public expressions, the assistants of public cultures, economy, and the archivists of public histories. The legitimization of democratic government will come from multicultural public movements, not State initiatives. The airwaves are public domain to be used by and for the public— and public movements will converge through the establishment of national public media—liberation of the airwaves. This is our work for the nineties.

THE CASE OF USA VS. JOHN POINDEXTER

The outcome of the federal court case *USA vs. John Poindexter* has pushed us from long-standing civilian silence to insurgent Immediast action. Look carefully: North and Poindexter reversed their felonies by proving that extended media exposure destroyed case witnesses' ability to think independently of the words and images the media had saturated them with. This is now American history, a legal precedent. Admitting the mind-control action of mass media protected State felons from public law. The precedent of *USA vs. John Poindexter* thus establishes that:

1. Spectacle representations derived from actual public events manipulate perception and control the natural outcome of our events.
2. Spectacle media disables the public to think and perceive freely of the biases imbedded by exposure to mass media noise and images.

Spectacle media serves as a moat protecting the National Security State from public participation and democratic scrutiny. Meanwhile, North and Poindexter, both felons, are back on the streets again.

These crimes and their accomplices in the White House, CIA, NSA, CNN, DOD, ABC, USIA, MTV, CBS, etc., are too much to tolerate given the increasing violence, debt, recession, and systemic deception forced upon us every day by the government and consumer media.

Our drive to connect, to create, to love and make love, to play, to communicate, to share, to live freely, to participate or be left in peace, to represent our own desires and author our own cultures and live with meaning that we together create are under relentless invasion and constant assault. The time to change has come.

We no longer tolerate being besieged with manipulative messages that we don't want to hear and cannot respond to. We no longer tolerate an inaccessible State that censors, blocks, and denies information to the public. We no longer tolerate the spectacle that ultimately serves to absolve criminals like Poindexter, Bush, North and their lickspittles from crimes of international violence and domestic debt. The time has come to turn the ecology of coercion in on itself. The time has come to veto, overwhelm, and subvert the messages of all airborne commercial broadcast media until they are returned to complete public direction, access, and control. How long should we wait to liberate public spaces from the blister of billboards and advertisements? The air is public domain, and the airwaves are ours to hear our own voices, see our own colors, enjoy our own conversations, and celebrate in the vast community of our cultures. Remember: dialogue offsets the hegemony, and intimacy empowers.

The time has come to restore the democratic power and public space that have been coopted and colonized by commercial media.

Celebrate public culture. Reconnect. Seize the media. The air is yours.

In 1992 we begin the work that needs to be done. Asian philosophy instructs enlightenment [*v. 1.1, March 1992*].

Mark Kriegel

Fear and Loathing in Atlanta

Nominated for a Pulitzer Prize in his twenties, sports columnist Mark Kriegel, now thirty-one, brings a unique media awareness to his coverage of the coverage of sports. He was originally hired by the New York Post *because, his editor told him, "I want them to hate you." Now with the* Daily News, *Kriegel has become famous for his wry wit and dead-accurate humor. Kriegel's first novel, about the son of a gangster from Carmine Street, will be published by Doubleday.*

ATLANTA—A mindless many-headed beast are we who chew the cud and spit it out, again and again and again, delighting in bad taste, requiring only that endless buffet line from which we feed, from which we get our coffee, our danish, our Dewar's, our hors d'oeuvres (always, those chicken things) and, of course, our quotes. This is not to say we shirk our duty. We suffer, too, gathering in the humming bowels of the Hyatt Regency, the media lounge like the Port Authority of Journalism. Did we not come off that buffet line for **Leon Lett** of Fair Hope, Ala.?

I pick up *USA Today*, official paper of the Super Bowl, and learn again that I am right. More right than ever. We are the story, the dimwitted engine of this whole machine. There's a picture of **Jim Kelly** wearing a spiked crown of microphones. And **Tonya Harding**: she films us filming her. And **Leon Lett.**

"Can't hear you in the back, Leon."

Did we not make him sweat?

Damn sure did. We hyperventilated that sumbitch.

Shoot, we made Leon famous. A *bona fide* celebrity from Emporia State. And how we love celebrities. They are our gruel.

Before long, we'll make **Marv Levy** and **Jimmy Johnson** into **Adlai Stevenson** vs. **John Gotti**.

We say goodbye to **Pat Summerall** as if he were **Edward R. Murrow**. He'll be back, but what the hell. Weep for him anyway. **Rupert Murdoch** pays **John Madden** $8 million a year, but not a penny for those he fired from the Post, many who once worked faithfully for him, one of whom recently died of self-inflicted asphyxiation. Won't read about that in **Rudy Martzke**'s *USA Today* column.

Sorry, didn't mean to bum you out. This is a happy time, America's televised Sunday service. They're all here, those children of **Donny** and **Marie**, the happy people, their movements choreographed by cliche: Whoomp, There it is, and We Will Rock You, the Coke Jingle, and anything at all by MC Hammer. Don't Worry, Be Happy. I mean, **the Bud Girls** are here. I love them very much, in their most severe shades of blonde.

What we have is a movable Vegas, though the sense of sin is as yet uncultivated. **Frank** is in town. The thing is—and this is a true story—Frank is still looking for **Jilly**. Even the hookers have come in from Vegas. "That's where I live," she says. "But I own property here." I don't get it. Takes an ex-boxing writer, an old Vegas hand, to straighten me out. "Stupid," he says. "She's working."

Maybe she's here to audition for **Up With People**. Remember them? The halftime show with all the dancers high on dopamine. Can't bust on the halftime shows, though. They're what you call Classics.

Like the **Michael Jackson** halftime show. Remember that? Didn't he parade about 2,000 children on the field? How do you like that one now?

Every year the ghoul in me watches halftime from the Super Bowl. And every year I feel like the guy in *A Clockwork Orange*, the part when they force **Malcolm McDowell** to watch all that bad stuff. It was good for him.

* * *

One day when I'm at Fox, I'll produce my own halftime show. There will be no country music. There will be **the Delphonics** and **the Manhattans,**

Barry White and **Al Green.** There will be a moment of silence for **Lenny Bruce**. And for **Jilly Rizzo**, too. **Allen Ginsburg**, a hell of a Super Bowl guy, will say the team prayer. He will recite from his own classic, the poem "Kaddish." Yeah, they'll hurry off the buffet lines for that sumbitch.

Seven Days and Seven Nights Alone with MTV

Hugh Gallagher's
Experiment in Terror

Gallagher wrote a college application essay so original that it was re-printed in Harpers *and read on National Public Radio. Now twenty, Gallagher brings his unique world view and expressive style to* Rolling Stone *and other media-conscious magazines, where he writes with a pro-totypically GenX mixture of cynicism and innocence. Gallagher's insights are matched only by his ability to convey them; he is surely hard evidence that GenX presents no threat to the survival of the written word, even when it's used in media about media about media.*

TUESDAY, DECEMBER 29TH, 1992

8:18 P.M.

And so it begins . . . for seven days and seven nights I will watch MTV. I will not change the channel, I will not turn off the television, I will not walk out of this room. There will be no visitors. There will be no phone calls. All contact with the outside world will come through the MTV. The only adjustment I left myself to stave off complete insanity for at least a couple more months is the volume control.

I asked for this assignment, and for my sins, they gave it to me. MTV and I grew up together. We kept in close contact through high school, but when I went away to college, we lost touch. I was busy finding my identity in the culturally cluttered streets of New York City, while MTV was becoming more cosmopolitan, diversifying its musical and programming tastes. I saw brief flashes of this new MTV at parties and bars, but I never had the chance to really take a good look at it.

What I saw of it, though, released a vague, uneasy feeling. What had started with a couple of bucks and a smoke machine was rapidly growing into a fully strapped, double-barreled cultural force that was storm trooping the planet. Then I began to be identified in the media as part of the MTV Generation, which I found disconcerting. If the only thing that was holding my generation together was this slashing confusion of fashion ads and hip-hop jammy walks through swirling cyberspace, what hope did we have?

I decided that this beast must be challenged. That decision led to this hotel room and this MTV. Moments ago I checked in and had my last contact with the outside world. "Hope you enjoy your stay!" the Dorset Hotel desk attendant said as I walked toward the elevator. I entered the room and turned on the MTV and set up my computer to begin writing. But something on the screen dragged my eyeballs up into it, and I was lost in the mesmerizing swirl of editing until something clicked in my head and I realized that *I was being entertained against my will.* I looked at the clock—a half-hour had passed.

This was a development I hadn't considered. Perhaps there is a defense mechanism lodged in the MTV to foil any in-depth investigation. If that is the case, I am determined to break through. I must be strong, like Jean-Claude Van Damme.

11:30 P.M. Room service just came up with a salmon dinner, and I'm taking a break. Spent the first hours of the experiment trying to track images, but my typing skills couldn't keep up with the MTV. This channel moves at the speed of thought, in electric snap jumps of the neurons. I am in a room with the pulsing, beating brain of pop culture.

WEDNESDAY

1:30 A.M. A bunch of big-sweater alternative rockers are lanking across a cliff in the Netherlands, wearing Gilligan hats in the purple sunset. Hours ago I watched *Yo! MTV Raps*, and it seems like these white boys are millions of miles from Ice-T and his urban shootout. In *Yo!*, ninety-nine percent of the vids are in an urban environment with a camera frame that cages and confines. But out here in Alternative Land, the camera is panning with these floppy rockers from a leisurely distance over the wide-open space.

How long is hip-hop going to stay confined in its hostile urban sets while the white rockers prance carefree through verdant, breathtaking scenery? The channel is time-slot segregated and dominated by white acts. Latinos and Asians are nearly nonexistent, almost all hosts are white. Black music gets a minimal slice of air space, except when it's being used in the background of fashion ads where white women prance across the screen, setting the standard of beauty. Riots are imminent on MTV unless programming is changed, and I don't think there's much of a doubt that *Yo!* could kick the whole channel's ass if a full-out broken-bottle brawl busted out.

In order to preserve harmony on the channel, I'm proposing the MTV Cultural Exchange Day. We'll toss Toad the Wet Sprocket into the riot-wrecked inner-city set of Ice Cube and have En Vogue walk the wind-swept plains of Guns n' Roses video, and we'll give Naughty by Nature a fat, red Cadillac to drive through Kansas.

3:38 A.M. I tap off the volume and wheel the MTV into the bathroom, where I take a long bath in its eerie glow. Soft shades of TV light silently chase each other over the porcelain walls and dance across the water to the echoing drip of the faucet. I take out my razor and shave, then slowly wash my body. I'm twenty years old, and I'm locked in a hotel room watching MTV. Duh?

4:10 A.M. An unsettling 'MTV News' interview with U2 has been in rotation today. The band does not appear in flesh but chats down to Kurt Loder from four enormous TV screens. Projecting the measurements of their head size, if Bono and friends were released from the TVs, they could King Kong through Times Square, singing "One" as they toppled buildings and crushed fistfuls of screaming citizens. They loom magnificent over Kurt the mortal—pathetic in his need to urinate, his desire for a ham sandwich.

That's what happens after heavy enough rotation on MTV: You shed your body and become a spirit in the videodrome. As we destroy the environment to make more MTVs, we will need to evolve into something non-meat in order to survive. Porcelain teeth, metal rods and pacemakers are the initial steps in the process. U2 is among the first to go, existing now as pulse beats and energy patterns in our massive network of cables and screens, cavorting blissfully with Michael Jackson.

And it seems like only yesterday they were running around the winter landscape with little snare drums. . . .

4:38 A.M. There is unbound energy and flailing anarchy on the screen, but I feel unanimated and stupid. I don't have the power or hope that I did eight hours ago, eight minutes ago. Who are my viewing companions at this hour? Dazed and confused, we are isolated in sunken couches, empty beds and cheap hotel rooms across this crumbling nation, one through MTV but fated never to meet. Rest, my little Smurfs, there is nothing for us here.

12:27 P.M. The words "safe sex" flash on, then disappear, and I am whisked away to a commercial of three statuesque white women in a white space, laughing and winking, hair in exploding fans twisting in the air behind them. The camera shakes and zags over their bodies in epileptic eye tracks, never giving me a chance to really *see* who they are.

Beauty ads clutter the MTV universe: beautiful people riding subways, beautiful people dancing in the twilight, beautiful people in tuxedos shooting arrows . . . an army of beautiful bodies kayaking on an ocean of come, hitting the beach to conquer the Land of Average-Looking People. Swinging broadswords and maces, laughing out loud as they chop through the ranks, sprays of blood hissing up onto their immortal faces . . .

I have lived in New York for three years, and I have yet to see one of these men or women on the streets. I'm beginning to wonder where they are kept. Perhaps there is a complex, subterranean network of tunnels that they use to move about the planet, from poolside to Paris runway show to video shoot to dinner party in the Hollywood Hills.

2:17 P.M. Ozzy is in a white suit, standing on some sort of Dick Clark rock & roll metal scaffolding with a trio of cavorting dwarfs. What happened? I remember the hard-core Sabbath days: Ozzy breaking puppies' necks and chugging gasoline, shooting third graders in the head onstage. Now here he is, a man who still thinks midgets are funny, belting out another forgettable metal anthem for Jersey. MTV is a terrible place to grow old.

3:32 P.M. Something about the Black Crowes' anti-heroin song makes me want to try heroin.

4:00 P.M. A Malcolm X video calling for revolution. But it just isn't possible on this channel. Even the revolution vids are too choreographed and formulated to strike up the fists inside of anyone. The images are like dope, temporarily satiating the desire for destruction and radical action, keeping us all watching and buying and watching and buying. The spirit of rebellion taped, canned and rerun over us again and again.

4:35 P.M. And here comes Madonna again, deeper and deeper. . . .

My God, the woman is completely insane. She's a national-security threat—you can see it in her eyes, howling orbs of vacant, heavy rotation. One of these days she's going to whip out a Cobray submachine gun and mow down a roomful of fashion freaks at a Jean-Paul Gaultier runway show. It looks like the years of physical-fitness abuse are starting to take their toll on Madonna. Her friends tried to help her kick, but she couldn't. Now her eyebrows have fallen off, and she's wandering dazed through some chthonian nightclub where screaming, diamond-eyed snakes in double-breasted suits kiss her face. She's wearing a Muppet frock and running with balloons through the crowd . . . driving in a Studebaker and looking either drop-dead gorgeous or hideously ugly. I can't tell which one it is.

Oh, Madonna, what's happened to you? I remember you back in the day, carelessly flip-flopping around on doinky keyboard beats, wearing neon socks and Day-Glo shoes, your hair a wild mop, a little girl's mane. And now . . . who are you? What are you? And who are these new friends of yours? Young gentlemen in underwear and combat boots, obese cross-dressers and mocking, laughing women with chain-saw-blade eyelashes.

Madonna, MTV, I don't know why I've turned to you. I don't know anything anymore. The end of school races closer, friends and relations drop in and out of my life, everything is transitory, the world is spinning out of control, and no one can give me answers about anything.

But I want to be like you, MTV! You don't hesitate, you don't regret, you don't stumble, you don't care if they like what you say or not. You just scream and spin and howl all day, all night long.

5:46 P.M. You don't know heavy rotation. I know heavy rotation . . . a bronze hammer slowly revolving on a creaking wooden wheel, pounding into my skull again and again.

I do deep-breathing exercises in front of the silent screen in hopes of pulling my mind back together. The shards of color and screeching angles sear directly through my eyeballs, videos pour out of the television, and I inhale them deep into my body. It is like a form of meditation, two hours speed-skating by in seconds.

6:11 P.M. It's 'Classic MTV,' and they're showing a video from three years ago. That's how fast this operation moves—three years and you're in the fucking archives.

Now they're spinning a Blondie vid from the Cold War years. The backup band is dorking through a video that looks like an afterthought to the song, filmed by some AV kid from the local high school for twenty bucks. If Debbie Harry turned that in to the MTV board these days, she'd be told to get breast implants and a buff backup band and then maybe they'd consider it.

6:30 P.M. And now we're at 'The Grind,' MTV's dance club. I've been to clubs before, and this is the best-looking crowd I've ever seen. They are young, happy, clean, sober. I don't have to dance—they dance for me, with more finesse than I ever could hope for. The camera swirls about, and I am omnipresent—fifteen different places in as many seconds. I don't sweat and get stinky. There is no cover charge. I don't have to deal with coat check. These are my friends. They're all smiling and reaching out to me, shoving their breasts in my face, grinding their young bodies in a rhythm sweat for me, all for *me*.

But now the host comes on, an Al Jolson update. Some white-boy graduate of Homeboy 101 who erased the suburbs out of his voice and moves his hands in the hip-hop style but is still lovably, huggably white.

Wait a minute! I just caught a glimpse of a really ugly kid bobbing in the background of the dance show. It was a split-second blur as they focused on another grinder, but I saw him! *You can't hide him from me!* The whole show they were angling cameras in a panic to keep him hidden, and they almost got away with it. Someone's head is going to roll for that one. MTV does not tolerate ineptitude.

7:33 P.M. This is the fiftieth time I've seen the Super Hoghead Mario Scooters commercial. Nintendo and MTV must have some sort of racket going—to keep the youth of the nation plugged into an MTV set by their eyes and thumbs.

8:47 P.M. This experience is making me feel dirty, like I've been eating fast food in a mall for the past twenty-four hours. I don't know how much this is going to help my development as a responsible citizen....

I caught myself pretending that I was being interviewed by *MTV News*. That square-hair dude with the Merry-Go-Round look is asking me: "So, Hugh, as an MTV Generation population sample, what was it like in that hotel room . . . ?"

Well, it was kinda like . . . BLAM!BLAM!BLAM!BLAM! Blood and hunks of VJ brain fly onto the MTV screen, as I pull shots from the sawed-off concealed in my overcoat. *It was just like that, Johnny. It was just like that,* OVER AND OVER AGAIN, *with a couple of Cindy Crawford commercials thrown in.*

9:58 P.M. This is the third time I've seen the mighty Nirvana play on *The Ed Sullivan Show* in the early Sixties. But I'm down with it....

That's what it's all about to be alive today. We'll take what we want from 1957 and slap it into a 1985 scenario, mix it up with a drill bit from 1977 and smash it all together for a late-'92 release.

THURSDAY, NEW YEAR'S EVE

12:17 A.M. I heard a young, laughing couple jingling their keys and switchblades in the hallway as they skipped to the elevator for a night on the town. Outside, the city moves, people streaking out to evening getdowns. I push my head through the wet window frame, and to the left, I see a wash line of white headlights in the street, stretching out from the East River westward in an arching line straight under my nose. Don't they understand? There is nowhere to go except MTV. I walk to my chair and strap in for the late-night programming.

Around midnight, the VJs desert me, and fashion ads drop off the screen, replaced by promo spots for Time-Life Books on serial killers. Sally Struthers is ubiquitous in this universe; she seems to endorse every product formed by the hands of men. I am in the tub again, and the chaotic, jabbering images that this channel won't stop pushing on me are rampaging around the room, tearing the tiles off of the wall.

From the hours of midnight to 6:00 A.M., an endless river of beer-commercial rock flows past on MTV, and what little variety exists here vanishes. It's the long, lonely journey into Guitar Rock Land, a numbing, pointless ride, like a drunken missionary fuck that just won't end. Young white men in cowboy boots and faded bluejeans strumming guitars in the dusty heartland roads, then driving off in an old, red Cadillac convertible with a couple of babes in the back seat.

But judging from the number of these vids, there can't possibly be any room left in the middle of nowhere. I imagine droves of young rockers cruising the heartland in their red '57 Caddies, looking for the scant scrags left to strum upon. The competition is vicious, and mad packs of young rockers streak down the highways, blood in their eyes, white knuckling the steering wheels and flooring the accelerators. They scream at each other over the roaring wind, swerving in and out of lanes, ramming rival video crews off the road. The blond babes in the back seats fashion Molotov cocktails from Jack Daniel's bottles and toss them into enemy convertibles, causing thundering explosions and massive pileups that snarl the landscape. The wind blows dust devils and tumbleweeds over the scenes of carnage, where bro-ken babes in tiny cutoff shorts are strewn across the roads, moaning in pain, and a young rocker, burned black and crushed behind a mangled steering wheel, reaches with a trembling hand toward a shattered Gibson for one last riff, then dies. The wind kicks up in a mournful howl, and the sun blazes red as it sinks down over the rock & roll wasteland. Life is a bloody highway, and only the strong survive.

3:45 A.M. I am a pioneer; this is the life of the future. MTV is the wheel, my computer an abacus and a piece of coal compared to what is coming. I feel at peace now, I have no anxieties, and my reality is consis-tently beautiful, well lit and wonderfully edited.

Editors ... the oppressed craftsmen who make this whole universe go round. In darkened rooms across the city, strange dwarfs with bleary eyes and crooked necks wade through the chaos of images and construct a man-gling bridge of sound bites and flashing teeth. They are the true power—not these pompadoured pretty-boy rockers and saucy women.

But there are not enough editors in this country to keep up with MTV. The beast is expanding, moving into the Third World, where industrial-safety standards can be ignored. In Mexico, thousands of peasant editors labor in crumbling, poorly lit factories. With outdated gasoline-run video equipment, they splice together images and sounds of a society they could not possibly understand. Naked pipes hiss steam from the ceiling, cords dangle over sweat-slicked floors, and the seething stench of slavery chokes the air. MTV editing supervisors walk through the rows of creaking machinery in jodh-purs and riding boots, pistols dangling from their hips. They bark commands and snap whips over the hunched backs of those who have dropped from exhaustion or finally gone blind from the tedious toil. Hundreds of editors die each year, smothered by noxious fumes or ripped to pieces when their ponches are pulled into the grinding wheels of the machinery. They sell their souls for a mere two pesos a week, weaving a shrieking quilt of commercialism so that we in the U.S. might take our hand out of a bag of Cheetos, punch the remote and click on the latest video from Bell Biv DeVoe.

4:08 A.M. "Only elephants should wear ivory," the MTV says. Elephants will be extinct in ten years if we don't stop killing them for their tusks. Then a Metallica video comes on.

Kill the elephants, what do I care. It'll give us more space to build more stadiums for more Metallica concerts. I think I heard that the band has demanded a 60,000-capacity stadium constructed entirely of ivory for the *Metallica Goes to Africa* tour movie.

4:28 A.M. Little Richard is scaring me.

5:19 A.M. Decided not to stay up tonight. Tomorrow is a big day— *Top 100 Countdown* and then the New Year's Eve blast. I need to rest up. It's going to be so exciting. I can hardly wait.

2:16 P.M. Good morning! MTV greets me with screaming blue faces and interconnected naked bodies. The incessant imagery burned through my eyelids and seeped into my eyeballs last night, distorting my dreams. I have a feeling I'm doing something terrible to my body in this experiment.

6:07 P.M. The vid for a favorite song of mine has convinced me that video is detrimental to the cause of music. MTV gives me mass-marketed images of Hare Krishna bell-bottoms, Princess Leia haircuts and apocalyptic cliffs for me to remember. But it's my own memories of that song I want to hold on to.

That CD came out the weekend I went to visit my older brother in D.C., and we had it spinning as background music the whole time. The image of us zooming through the city of white marble monuments on his motorcycle as the wind blew over our bodies will never leave my mind. As I was watching the sunset that day, sitting on the steps of the Lincoln Memorial, it suddenly hit me that I was getting older. Here I was, coming from New York to see my brother in another city, the same brother who used to kick me around in a backyard that isn't even ours anymore. The smells, the thoughts, the crystal, CD image of that weekend comes to mind whenever I hear that song. I don't want the video—put it away, put it away, put it away now.

9:37 P.M. I'm beside myself in anticipation of the New Year's Eve extravaganza. I think Kurt Loder is back from his winter break in time for the party—I'm glad, he's so much fun at these events. Sometime this morning I caught a blurred view of him at the news desk, his sober voice and sensible haircut such a relief in this circus of flash.

FRIDAY, NEW YEAR'S DAY

12:11 A.M. I can hear those little blooty horns all over town, "Happy New Year's" squawks of celebration up and down the block. Here I sit, bottle of champagne on the desk, sharing the moment with MTV. I set a stemmed glassful on the television and in moments will lead a toast to this glorious institution. Outside is mayhem; I can hear people screaming, engines revving and bones breaking all across the city. On the MTV, some dooby-bop band is singing the hit of the year. I can hear Times Square in the distance, a faint but resonating roar from down the city blocks.

I stood at the window at midnight, when the city erupted in vibrating thunder. Fireworks exploded in Times Square, and I could see the soft red-and-green flashing of pyrotechnic color on the sides of buildings. On the MTV screen a confused announcer was trying to figure out when the ball was dropping amid the confusion, and jogged camera frames just managed to get a picture of the flashing 1993 sign in the Square. Then the balloons fell, and the band went on with the latest hit to bring in the year.

I was almost enjoying the crazy, anything-could-happen vibe of the party until I remembered that it had been taped months ago. The chosen bands file onstage to play their hits, with absolutely no variations on the music. They have just enough cameramen and editors working on the fly to make it look just like a video. Why even bother?

The façades are falling off of MTV faster and faster. Brand names are fading into the buzz, names of bands are fading into the wash of a world that is eight floors below me and 80,000 dog years away.

I watched MTV for ten hours straight today—*straight*. I did not turn down the sound. I did not turn away. When I went to the bathroom, I rolled the MTV on its wheelie cart into the doorway and watched as I dumped. I'm doing this for you.

The MTV party just ended, and they're showing it again.

I'm starting to get angry.

4:05 P.M. I awoke an hour ago with these words falling out of my mouth: "Don't think. Just watch." That is the key to survival. My initial joy at waking up late and missing hundreds of minutes of commercial flash and malice was immediately sunken by a dark, sweeping feeling of dread as I realized that this means another lonely trek through the Guitar Rock wasteland.

I've just realized that I've yet to write a single word about the music on this channel. It's all image—keep my eyes busy, and the ears fall right off my head.

More beautiful creatures on the screen. Tight, taut strings of sexuality whipping and flexing along the beach. I think this channel only exists to remind me how much I'm not getting laid.

I don't know if I'll make it through the day.

5:37 P.M. The room-service guy has been my only human contact in this ordeal, and I've been monitoring his relation to the MTV since we began. Upon entering the room, his eyes invariably become sucked in to the whirling screen. He stands dumbly and watches while I search for a pen to sign the check. I have to break him away from his trance with my voice, and he always emerges as if startled, unsure of his bearings.

Tonight, however, a new waiter comes up with my dinner. I immediately become suspicious when he does not give a second glance to the jabbering box. I fumble for a pen, hoping to find it quickly and get him out fast, but as I turn to give him the check, he says something:

"You have someone coming?"

"What?"

"Someone come in before?" he repeats with a leering grin.

"The room service came."

"No, *some*one . . . heh heh . . . ," he says, pointing to the bottle of champagne in a bucket in the far corner of the room.

"Uh, yeah, sure," I answer.

"I bring up another bottle tonight. No charge."

I thank him, and he whisks out of the room.

Now, as I eat my salmon and watch MTV for the third straight day, the pieces are falling together. I am getting into something huge. MTV does not want this article written. The United States government does not want this article written. Through their agents at Rolling Stone, they have found out about my plan and made their move to crush it.

An MTV agent is placed on the Hotel Dorset wait staff. While inside my room, he ignores the trap of the blathering videoscape and peruses the room with his trained eye, trying to assess a report on my mental condition. The seasonal MTV agent can draw deductions from the slightest pieces of information—the track marks on the carpet, the angle the bathroom door stands ajar. He takes a critical look at my hand as I sign the bill—does it shake?

Seeing the empty champagne bottle bobbing in the bucket of melted ice, he chooses the method. Writers love to drink, right? I'll slug his complimentary bottle down later tonight and either (A) fall out of the window or (B) choke on my own vomit. And that will be the end of the MTV article. Threat nullified, the beast runs on.

But when that bottle of champagne comes up here, my friends, you can be sure that I will thank him kindly and pour it right down the drain. I can't play with *room service* anymore—tonight I'm stockpiling. I'll order thirty club sandwiches and leave them in the bathroom with a hot shower running to keep the bread from going stale. I'll make it out of here with this article one way or another.

6:15 P.M. Once again, I'm trapped in the MTV 'Top 100 Countdown.' I've lived a hundred lifetimes in the *Top 100 Countdown*. I remember how lucky I thought I was on that day, years ago, when They started the countdown. "Yes, variety!" I shouted, sobbing with joy. After the recycling and reshuffling that govern this channel, 100 *different* videos seemed like a boon from heaven. But I was a fool back then. Now I realize that seeing a new show only means having to endure it fourteen more times before I leave this room. I don't know what is worse, the madness of seeing the same videos again and again in different orders over the course of one day or the madness of seeing the same videos in the same order on different days.

7:32 P.M. I walk to the window and tilt my head to see outside. People on the street: tops of head, shoulders, feet. I can almost hear in my head their petty conversations. It's cold out there. . . . I put my face against the window, a pane of freeze. On the MTV, L.L. Cool J is going back to Cali.

7:55 P.M. Gum commercial. Music starts, and a platoon of sparkling white youth hits the beach for a day of rock & roll, water-skiing and gum chewing. A speedboat is towing a world-class-model Olympic skier. She hits the wake at full speed and flies into an aerial spin, the camera zooms in between her legs, and it's rotating, slo-mo pussy flying through the air.

Juicy Fruit.

8:23 P.M. Prince is trapped in a giant glass cylinder. I hope there is proper ventilation.

9:01 P.M. Just saw a game show where average-looking people lip-sync to MTV hits for big, big prizes. Can't even tell you how much that show made me want to spit and break things. Yahoos, applause signs, canned orchestra hits and laughing, whooping, stupid, fat, ugly everyday people. I asked for normal people, and I got them for a half-hour; now bring back the beauties. I'm beginning to understand the wonder of MTV. Every day I see dorky people with lame haircuts on the street, farting, sweating and spilling things on their cheap shirts. I endure and make it home to the MTV for an endless hip-hop, heavy-metal parade of the finest-looking human beings nature has to offer. What a fantastic creation. I love this channel. I want to move into MTV, meet a nice girl and raise a family. I look forward to every new video day, and just like Boyz II Men on the MTV New Year's Eve celebration, I got to thank God and my producer that I'm alive.

9:11 P.M. I am turning into some sort of alligator. The lack of air circulation and the constant input of central heating is drying up my face and turning my lips into scarred tracks of hardened flesh. I have no lip balm, and unfortunately I used all the aloe skin moisturizer to show myself a good time the other night. . . . Hey, it was New Year's Eve. I poured myself a glass of champagne, kicked back with the lotion and hit a stroke.

With the help of the MTV, I slipped into a video sex fantasy to satisfy my needs. I jazzed on over to *The Grind* and picked up a couple of dancers, took them back to my loft in the Real World and got busy in a quiet storm.

After my virtual sex, I opened my eyes, cleaned up the essence of jojoba and watched more MTV. I see no blame in this. Like the Buddhists say, attachment is suffering. With no friends, I have no one to challenge my beliefs, no one to force their beliefs on me. Within a few more months, there will be no memory of my former life, and all will be well.

SATURDAY

1:26 A.M. "Everything needed for real party fun: The Collective Unconsciousness."

That statement just flashed on the MTV, each word interspaced by chaotic camera shudders, leather hands, snakes—I think I saw Donnie Wahlberg in there somewhere. . . . WHAT THE FUCK IS GOING ON?!

I think I'm beginning to get it. They don't want us to know what's going on; this isn't entertainment, this is a front for global domination.

As the nation-states erode and the global village is connected via satellites orbiting the planet, the New MTV World Order becomes possible. MTV is hooked up in Europe, Japan, Brazil, Australia and soon the Third World. Gifts of MTVs are given to all the poor, starving nations that can't afford them.

Fiber-optic cables snake through the Amazon mud and traverse dense jungles, infiltrating primitive villages that have yet to control fire. The startled natives have no concept of telecommunications; they throw spears at the MTV when the image of Bono appears on the screen. They are given an explanation of its powers, however, by the magnanimous, godlike man with white skin who appeared with the magic box then flew away in a metal bird. A shrine is built around the set, forty calves are slaughtered in sacrifice, and the natives begin to watch MTV.

For the first time in their thousands of years of peaceful existence, a rape occurs. Then thievery blooms in the village, discord and envy. Soon, catalogs arrive in the mail for the wondrous products they see advertised on the MTV. Their gold and precious stones, the ancient onyx-and-ivory statues of the village ancestors are traded for cases of Crystal Pepsi. Bloody tribal wars ensue over a pair of Versace jeans. The elder sage of the village, protector of the Gameboy, is brutally murdered late in the night.

Meanwhile, thousands of acres of their jungle habitat are chopped down and dragged away to fuel more MTVs. Ancient customs are discarded, religions fall to pieces, wars and skirmishes erupt in pockets that have reigned in peace for thousands of years, as the whole planet is sucked into MTV screens. Don't watch the news, watch *MTV NEWS*. Don't watch movies, watch MTV MOVIES. Don't vote for the president, vote for the MTV PRES-IDENT.

Dear God, it's brilliance.

5:56 A.M. I'm scared.

10:35 P.M. You don't know pain like I know pain. And I mean suffering, in the classical, Hindu sense of the word. I just woke up in a ho-tel room, a double-bottle champagne hangover screaming through my veins and an MTV that is shrieking into my eyes. My head is lead, broken glass, charred cinders and dead cats. There are no pills or remedies in the room, and I can't leave. My body is sweating and shaking, my teeth are crum-bling, but something good will come of this, I keep telling myself. This is the physical ordeal I must endure to gain true vision. The Cause is greater than one man's trial.

Last night I saw the answer.

Near dawn, after the fourth viewing of the MTV New Year's Eve party, in my darkest hour of despair, I tapped off the volume of the MTV and turned to the I Ching. A series of strange circumstances had landed this ancient text of Chinese wisdom in my hands on my way to the hotel, and although I had originally planned on nothing but MTV, I turned to it in an act of des-peration. Upon opening the book, I became lost in a timeless dive into the deepest abyss of human thought, the pressure causing my nose to bleed and threatening to crush my skull after the shallow shuffle of MTV I had been snorkeling through. I read for hours, and a sense of peace began to envelop my being. Dawn was lighting up the Manhattan sky, and I walked to the win-dow to drink in the cold sunlight. The complimentary bottle of champagne was resting against the windowpane, where I had placed it to keep it chilled. Feeling an inexplicable sense of optimism, faith in mankind and destiny, I cracked the champagne, toasted the MTV and drank.

As I was finishing my final glass, I had an epiphany. The sunlight was beaming through the window and illuminating the glass of champagne I held in my hand. Bubbles were rising in the glowing, golden liquid, and at that moment, I finally understood what Don Ho was really talking about. *Tiny bubbles.* OF COURSE!!

My head swirling in a delirium of excitement and intoxication, I felt that this was only the beginning of something huge, calling for more juice. I swung around and looked at the clock—9:00 a.m.

Before the bellguy came up with the buzz, I dove into the bed and mussed up the covers, stripped off my clothes, wrapped myself in a towel, turned on the bathroom light and closed the door. I didn't want anyone to know that I was in a room at nine in the morning drinking champagne and watching MTV alone.

Within moments the bottle arrived with a cover of muffins, fruits and croissants. I ripped off the cork, tipped the bottle back, turned up the MTV and . . .

Now it's morning. Or night. I don't care. It doesn't even matter anymore. It's *Headbangers Ball* on MTV, and I'm dying. My body-clock system has been thrown out of jam, and my life has parted paths with everyone else. But I have found the answer.

The MTV is now on full volume two feet in front of me, but I am having no problem concentrating. It has been absorbed into my bloodstream. It is part of me. I am part of it. MTV is the force that runs through all living things. A butterfly lights a cigarette in Brazil, there's a tidal wave in the Philippines, Axl Rose's bride is struck by lightning. . . . It's all *connected*. WE ARE ALL ONE. WE ARE ALL MTV.

It is a divine force: the global-communications network and the primordial sway of music, the most thundering force in the world! MTV is God working through the hands of men and women. Don't you see it? No, of course you don't. . . . Everyone watches MTV, but no one really *sees* MTV. I am *seeing* MTV. I know MTV. I AM MTV. I aM TV . . . MeTV.

On the MTV, a correspondent is walking through Germany with the MTV microphone. It is nothing less than a talisman, a magic stick that enables instantaneous, global communication. We can learn! We can love! We can live through MTV!

But who controls this gift of the gods? Some old professional backslapper and back stabber, mauling millions across the globe with a stroke of his pen. Standing atop his desk, waving his club tie and beating down the masses.

Yes, it's clear now. The tyrant must be overthrown! We must band together, storm the controls and take MTV into our hands. There will be bloodshed, there will be terror and times of despair. Yes, some of us will die. But in the end, we the people will hold the controls of the MTV, and we the people will reign! The great races of this world will all be one, and as one we shall produce beautiful music videos until we don't need them anymore. For in the post-revolution future, there will be no need for cameras and televisions. You will step out of the door of your hut, and the streets will be filled with dancing and singing, a living, breathing, joyous music video that never ends.

Forget the White House—it's falling to pieces. The roof is caving in, and the pipes are all groaning and heaving, about to bust wide open. Insects and vermin are nibbling away at the crumbling foundation, and mountains of unpaid bills are piling up in the study. The man of the house is running his hands through his hair and popping pills, throwing bottles of Scotch against the wall and screaming at his wife, then grabbing a smile out of the desk drawer and SLAPPING it on his face to walk outside and say hello to the neighbors. They keep the Rose Garden trimmed and healthy so everyone thinks everything's fine.

How long are we going to fall for this? Another president . . . and this one likes Fleetwood Mac. . . . Suck my ass. Washington is *over*. DONE.

Those who want to cling to the rotting carcass of empty optimism are welcome to. But I am going back to India, I am going back to China. I am going back to Africa, the origin of all music, to join up with a band of music-video Jeet Kune Do warriors. There we will construct a temple in the fertile plains and form the bands that will infiltrate the machine and destroy MTV.

We will appear on heavy rotation as any other metal rap act or big-sweater bands do, but at the given signal, perhaps during the MTV Video Music Awards of the year 2000, we will throw off our haircuts, brandish our arms and let loose the war cry.

We will seize the controls, throw aside the curtain to the throne room and seat PRINCE at the top. Yes, he is the one to lead us all, I've seen it in his videos. Danzig will be sergeant-at-arms, leading the military of music-video Jeet Kune Do warriors. A huge task, but after his heroic feats of valor in the apocalyptic battlefield, there will be no question that he is worthy.

After the initial revolution and securing of the MTV network, several uprisings will occur, challenging our power. Madonna, enraged at not being appointed grand queen of the MTV, will form her own army of androgynous, voguing club freaks that will rise up from the island of Manhattan, sail across the great sea and attack our stronghold in Africa. This will prove to be our greatest, bloodiest battle. But Prince, in his divine wisdom, will deploy Danzig and the troops with calculated precision. The uprising quelled, peace will reign for a thousand years. The entire planet will rotate through space as one all-encompassing, well-lit, brilliantly directed music video.

SUNDAY

Midnight The MTV is on at roaring full blast, but it's not loud enough. . . . It can't possibly get loud enough tonight. My head is throbbing in resounding hammer strokes of dull, thickly wrapped pain, but it is good. Everything is good tonight. I WANT TO RUN BAREFOOT INTO THE STREETS OF THE CITY, WAVING MY HANDS IN THE AIR, SINGING AND LAUGHING AND CRYING AND DANCING, AWAKENING EVERYONE TO THE BEAUTY AND GLORY OF MTV! But I would miss the Danzig concert clips from the Circus Krone, in Munich, Germany, and there is no way I will pass up this gift from the programming gods. Danzig is one who has truly harnessed the power of metal. And he was wearing a V-neck sweater in his last video! A V-neck in a metal video?! Do you understand the innovative genius of this man?

1:23 A.M. This MTV commercial keeps flashing by: Light bulb swings into the TV screen and shatters. Voice-over: "Revolution now." Baby, you don't know revolution.

1:40 A.M. Just puked up the cup of coffee I tried to down as my only form of nourishment. *Headbanger Ball* is on the MTV, but there is no correlation. Despite my agonizing physical state, I am enjoying some of the finest hours of MTV programming since I've been in the hole. Sick of It All is playing a song called "Just Look Around." I think these men are on our side.

2:37 A.M. The phone rang, and someone asked me to turn down the television. Luckily, the Danzig special from the Circus Krone, in Germany, just ended. I will comply.

3:45 A.M. Shaking with excitement. Can't write anymore, can't sit still, can't stop . . .

1:19 P.M. Last night, the shock of knowledge threatened to blast open the fragile pinnings of my mind, but I was able to withstand. Four a.m., 5:00 a.m., last night—this morning . . . who knows anymore?

I lie soaking in the tub with the MTV turned away from me, hurling a silent massacre of entertainment against the wall. It doesn't care if you embrace it or ignore it; it keeps on going. We must do the same in order to defeat it.

This place is a mess. I've got to straighten up. The maids keep calling to ask what time I want the room cleaned. "NEVER!" I scream, slamming down the phone. I trust no one.

Today is the Sabbath, and I will rest. My work in this room is done—the wisdom of our ancestors has spoken. I can feel my mind slipping back into my skull, after helixing out into the depths of the universe. I spent today near the window reading the I Ching and drinking water, as the MTV spit the Spin Dorkters on me every other hour.

MONDAY

1:48 P.M. I woke up, wiped the snot out of my eyes and stumbled to the MTV. There was a news feature on the L.A. riots, quick flashes of footage dodging through hip-hop beats. Burned buildings, Korean store owners firing rifles from rooftops, shouting mobs shattering windows, black men lined up against a police car . . .

Then cut to a video: "It's Gonna Be a Lovely Day." A white, blond woman smiles and sings as nubile bodies perambulate in rhythm steps around the sparkling pool of her Hollywood bungalow.

Pass the ammo.

TUESDAY, THE FINAL DAY

12:11 P.M. Today I skip naked through the room, laughing and singing along joyously to all the MTV hits, which tried their best to destroy me but failed. In moments, I will turn off the MTV, give it a kiss and drop down into the stinking sweat of the city.

Be thankful that there are soldiers like me, willing to sacrifice ourselves for the benefit of all, in the hopes of finding an answer to our confusion. I did it for you, my children. I suffered for your—for our—sins.

I leave you now with our battle cry, a cry that must be heard the world around if we are to survive. May it ring through city streets and mountain passes, hamlets and jungles the world around, igniting the raging fire of revolution: I WANT MY MTV!

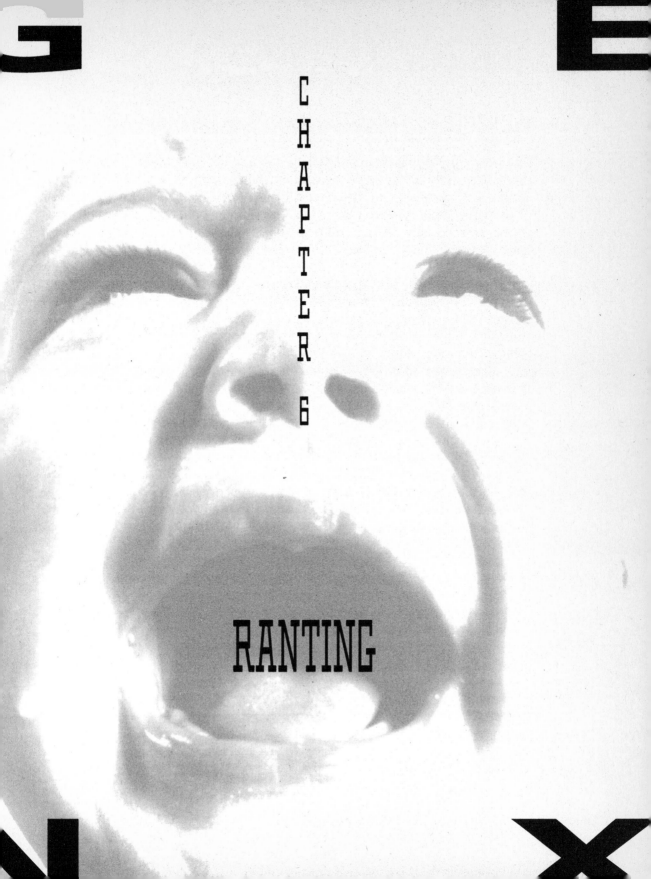

CHAPTER 6

RANTING

Ranting

Revolting against the "politically correct" boomer urge for peaceful co-existence and smiley-faced agreement, busters prefer dialectic to equilibrium and tooth-grinding debate to hand-holding sympathy. Emerging from the GenX dependence on telephones, computer bulletin boards, and other mediated communications technology is a new oral and literary form called the rant.

These long-winded GenX tirades have elevated the simple temper tantrum to free-form text-jazz. Whether they appear as editorials in 'zines, monologues in a stand-up routine, or three-screen-long diatribes on a computer conferencing system, rants invariably mix fiery passion with ironic distance, bold assertions with smirky nuance, and intellectual complexity with disarming simplicity.

The success of a rant is dependent on two things: the consistency of the internal argument and the creativity with which it is expressed. Like a slam dunk in basketball, the flourish and gusto of a rant are appreciated only if the argument scores a decisive blow against a worthy opponent.

Outsiders to GenX fail to appreciate the style and passion of the rant and interpret even our most creative vehemence as pointless whining. They fail to see that as a form, the rant is to GenX what the blues was to African America. And like the blues, no matter how angry, cynical, forlorn, or hopeless a rant gets, the underlying energy is a pure joy of expression, inventiveness, and a deeply felt urge to entertain those around us.

The GenX Computer Conference

People Try to

Put Us Down

The following conversation occurred over the WELL (Whole Earth 'Lectronic Link), a computer bulletin board based in the Bay Area. These conversations, called "topics," occur over a period of days, weeks, or even years as participants each read the responses so far and then add their own postings.

This topic began in the very popular Generation X conference, which is dedicated to discussions of interest to the on-line buster community. It begins with a heartfelt rant by Bob Rossney, whose on-line prose (this stuff is generally written on the fly) demonstrates his ability to maintain the thread of an argument, type it into a keyboard, and stay emotionally open, all at the same time.

(Each posting is preceded by a "header," which lists the topic name, the response number, the user's name or pseudonym, user ID, and the date of the response. In this topic "baboos" means baby boomers, and :-) is a sideways smilie, indicating that a response is meant as a joke.)

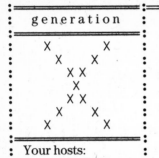

: generation :

: X   X :
:   X   X   :
:   X X   :
:   X   :
:   X X   :
:   X   X :
:   X   X :

: Your hosts: :
: (cynsa) & (jeffreyp) :

"YUPPIE WANNABE'S: An X generation subgroup that believes the myth of a yuppie lifestyle being both satisfying and viable. Tend to be highly in debt, involved in some sort of substance abuse and show a willingness to talk about Armageddon after three drinks."

Generation_X_, pg. 91

Topic 17 [genx]: People Try to Put Us Down
Started by: Bob Rossney (rbr) on Mon, Aug 17

Some late night thoughts about my generation. Listen up: that's you.

Topic 17 [genx]: People Try to Put Us Down
#1–#4 : Leisure of the Theory Class (rbr)   Mon Aug 17

My generation has come to realize that it will not be as wealthy, as comfortable, or as free as the generation that has preceded it. The people in it have come to believe, I feel, that they will be unable to live meaningful lives.

The generation's response, which I find more than a little alarming, is distrust—or even hatred—for anyone that they think might have wealth, comfort, freedom, or a meaningful life.

Let's look at one example. Let's look at an early topic in this conference, "The Revolting Yuppie Excess I Witnessed Today." There is not the slightest hint of self-consciousness here, not the faintest awareness that the topic is but one or two slim moral removes from "The Disgusting Nigger Laziness I Witnessed Today" or "The Mongrel Kike Degeneracy I Witnessed Today."

In this topic you will find a discussion of a man who slipped as he was stepping from his car to the curb and who became embarrassed when he saw someone looking at him. This could have happened to any of us. However, the person telling the story looked at the man and saw only his car and his shoes.

The view of boomers is similarly blinkered. To my generation, if what we hear here is to be believed, the boomers fall into two categories. One abandoned their principles and become yuppie scum, the other didn't and remain pathetic self-righteous Birkenstocked throwbacks.

I think I know what the problem is with my generation. We grew up at a time when the poisonous mythology of unlimited abundance was so deeply embedded in the culture that it seeped into how we think about the world the way that cigarette smoke gets into clothing. And just as a nonsmoker in a smoky club comes to smell of stale nicotine, our generation, even as it prides itself on its slacker rejection of materialism, stinks of greed.

We're jealous. We're deeply, deeply jealous. We're sure that our parents and the generation between us and them got a good education, made easy money, had fun, were a part of things, and that it wasn't a struggle for them the way it is for us. We hate it. Deep down, we hate it. We hate being on the outside and having to scratch for a living. We hate the plasticity of received culture. We hate all those shallow disgusting attorneys who are buying houses and raising children. We hate them because it's what we want more than anything else, and we're just not going to get it.

Topic 17 [genx]: People Try to Put Us Down
#6 : X-tant X-sistence (cynsa)   Mon Aug 17

Gosh, I couldn't disagree with you more. How cool to know we aren't homogeneous, as a generation, not that that comes as a surprise.

First of all, a yuppie is a yuppie because s/he chooses to be. Why may I not criticize them for choosing a lifestyle that celebrates greed and excess? I don't equate that with criticizing someone for being of any particular race or religion . . .

I have no desire to be a lawyer or any of that ilk; what's more, you couldn't pay me to be one. Which is, I guess, the point, getting paid that is. Sure, if you choose to have children you find you have to choose a career that will pay for that choice. But, once again, that is your choice. No one forces you to have children, at least not in this state, not quite yet, which brings to mind my greatest disappointment, the core of my dissatisfaction, and it's not that I don't "have things easy" or that I have to struggle harder than they did: THEY ARE TAKING AWAY MY CHOICES. That is what gnaws at me, kills me inside. I don't have a choice. I vote, I never win. My voice is not heard. No one is listening to me. Instead, they listen to the baboos, who are more numerous, and what do the baboos say? In the 60's they said "no more war." In the 60's the baboos had idealism and high hopes. But NOW, now when I really need them to speak out because no one will listen to me, now they say: "I have a HOUSE. For god's sake, don't raise property taxes. Prop 13 was a GREAT idea. Yeah!" Of course, since I registered for classes 2 weeks ago, narrowly squeezing in the credits I need, they have cancelled two of those classes due to budget cuts, because you know the state of California is in dire financial straits, but, hey, that's life, you know.

So my greatest dissatisfaction is not that I will never own all the stuff they have (and please don't blame me if I have to denigrate materialism in order to deal with that); my dissatisfaction lies elsewhere, in the mere fact that I will never have the *choices* they have had. And it really kills me that if they could have made those choices back when they had ideals, they might have made better choices.

btw: I wasn't laughing because that fellow tripped out of his own shoe. I was laughing because he felt he had to cover up by using his little car-alarm doohicky to reassert his sense of self-importance, and it wasn't until later that I equated him with yuppie excess.

Topic 17 [genx]: People Try to Put Us Down
#8 : will kreth (kreth)   Mon Aug 17

Si. Bob, I too have wondered when the f*** we will (might/might not) find our voice.

If I could shoot people with obnoxious car alarms (with impunity)—I would.

Topic 17 [genx]: People Try to Put Us Down
#14 : Madame X (thanne)   Wed Aug 19

Great posts, Bob, although I also agree with Cynsa's response. I do wonder if it's a mistake to assume a generation *can* have a "voice", though. A generation can have a *stereotype*, yes, but do we really want one?

The thing about feeling one's life is meaningless is interesting to me. I've struggled with that feeling for years, especially recently. A lot of what I end up doing (like trying to teach someone to read) is a direct response to that feeling. It never occurred to me it could be a symptom of my generation, rather than a phenomenon local to just me.

Topic 17 [genx]: People Try to Put Us Down
#15 : A firm grasp of the obvious (virginia)   Thu Aug 20

The feeling that one's life is meaningless is familiar to individuals in all generations. FWIW, I think people feel that way more *often* in their 20s and then again when they retire.

Topic 17 [genx]: People Try to Put Us Down
#16 : Jeffrey P. McManus (jeffreyp)   Thu Aug 20

A bell curve of meaninglessness. Interesting.

Topic 17 [genx]: People Try to Put Us Down
#17 : X-tant X-sistence (cynsa)   Fri Aug 21

Actually, I've felt that way ever since I read *Deathbird Stories* by Harlan Ellison at age 11. Around then I started having Nuclear Holocaust dreams, and thinking the only point was to have as much fun as possible. Now I feel the same way, although I think it's important to hedge your bet by doing good things for people, as much as you possibly can, because it's a way and a kindness, and to have fun while doing it, because after all, there really is no point.

Topic 17 [genx]: People Try to Put Us Down
#18 : ferretlike (magdalen)   Sat Sep 12

But that seems to say that there's some inherent point to "having fun" . . .

Topic 17 [genx]: People Try to Put Us Down
#19 : will kreth (kreth)   Sat Sep 12

Magdalen—ever heard the Gang of Four song that has a chorus that goes: "Having fun, gives me a reason for living"?

Topic 17 [genx]: People Try to Put Us Down
#20 : doing the things a particle can (cynsa)   Sat Sep 12

pleasure . . .

Topic 17 [genx]: People Try to Put Us Down
#21 : D. Joe Anderson, Jr. (justjoe)   Sat Sep 12

. . . little treasure

Topic 17 [genx]: People Try to Put Us Down
#22 : We're livin' in the age of cooties. (lorelei)   Sun Sep 13

I have to wonder if the reason that the boomers always seem to write articles about genx with negative slants isn't jealousy. They are no longer twentysomething and they resent it.

Topic 17 [genx]: People Try to Put Us Down
#23 : Jeffry P. McManus (jeffreyp)   Sun Sep 13

I have thought of that as well. But then on the other hand it could just be because we suck.

Topic 17 [genx]: People Try to Put Us Down
#24 : Triple X (leilani)   Sun Sep 13 '92

Naw, GenXers don't suck. I think there is a difference in values between the two groups, though. Maybe that's the source of some of the conflict.

Topic 17 [genx]: People Try to Put Us Down
#25 : Leisure of the Theory Class (rbr)   Sun Sep 13

Can anyone point to a period in history in which an older generation wrote approvingly of a younger one?

Topic 17 [genx]: People Try to Put Us Down
#26 : how the world works isn't a secret (jdevoto)   Sun Sep 13

It does seem to me that the baby boomers got quite a bit of praise, as a generation, from their elders. I'm thinking of articles during the late fifties, and more or less throughout the sixties, praising "the new generation" as "the best, healthiest, best-educated generation in our history; we expect great things from them." That sort of thing. And most of the stuff I've seen about the counterculture included praise for the moral stance of the participants—if there was demurral, it was along the lines of "Well, they have wonderful ideals, but they're just not realistic." Meaning the world wasn't good enough for these golden children to carry out their wonderful, worthy ideals.

Not that there wasn't condemnation too. But I think the above view was mainstream, and it was certainly common.

Topic 17 [genx]: People Try to Put Us Down
#27 : Consensus con carne (virginia)   Sun Sep 13

I don't think it was all that common—when and why do you think the term "generation gap" was coined? So much of the turmoil in the 60s had to do with deep, serious rifts between the boomer generation and their parents. It was the first generation that didn't march merrily off to war without thinking to Question Authority. That concept was a foreign one to our (meaning boomers') parents. And needless to say we had radically different ideas about sexual freedom, especially women's sexual freedom, than did our parents' generation. Polar opposite attitudes about the War and sex led to a heck of a lot of condemnation, on both sides.

Topic 17 [genx]: People Try to Put Us Down
#28 : doing the things a particle can (cynsa))   Sun Sep 13

But after the 60's were over, when people began to have a little perspective, they became more and more approving. They might not have been able to deal with the 60's while they were happening, but the baboos have received praise since, that is undeniable.

Topic 17 [genx]: People Try to Put Us Down
#29 : Andrew Mayer (iam)   Sun Sep 13

I think that's more a case of *self* approval. One thing about the Baboo gen is the amount of attention they lavish on themselves trying to achieve some kind of perfection. I have a little hint for them: when the last Baby Boomer dies, then they'll have *all* died screwed up.

Topic 17 [genx]: People Try to Put Us Down
#30 : is he a dot, or is he a speck: (riff)   Mon Sep 14

But—c'mon everybody, be honest—isn't it somewhat *reassuring* to be part of a generation that bothers people, that we're not just Partnership for a Drug-Free America programmed zombies?

Topic 17 [genx]: People Try to Put Us Down
#31 : how the world works isn't a secret (jdevoto)   Mon Sep 14

Is anyone *bothered* by the post-boomers or whatever the appropriate term is? Or are older people just contemptuous of us?

Topic 17 [genx]: People Try to Put Us Down
#32 : is he a dot, or is he a spec? (riff)   Mon Sep 14

Contemptuous, I hope.

Topic 17 [genx]: People Try to Put Us Down
#33 : Sid (sid)   Mon Sep 14

Contemptuous, confused, and attempting to constantly categorize, package and recycle.

Topic 17 [genx] People Try to Put Us Down
#34 : Consensus con carne (virginia)   Mon Sep 14

Most "older people" don't think about it all that much, to tell you the truth. I never hear this subject come up in conversation, and most people I hang out with are in the boomer generation or older.

Topic 17 [genx]: People Try to Put Us Down
#35 : Jeffrey. P. McManus (jeffreyp)   Mon Sep 14

—Exactly—my point.

Topic 17 [genx]: People Try to Put Us Down
#36 : We're livin' in the age of cooties. (lorelei)   Mon Sep 14

Most of the articles etc. praising the boomers are written not by their elders but by the boomers themselves. And when you try to talk to the boomers about the genx they seem to have a BT,DT attitude which I find extremely annoying . . .

Topic 17 [genx]: People Try to Put Us Down
#37: Triple X (leilani)   Mon Sep 14

BT,DT?

Topic 17 [genx]: People Try to Put Us Down
#38 : Andrew Nelson Hultkrans (drude)   Mon Sep 14

Been there, Done that.

Topic 17 [genx]: People Try to Put Us Down
#39 : Leisure of the Theory Class (rbr)   Mon Sep 14

lorelei, what if the reason that the boomers have a bt/dt attitude is that they have, in fact, been there and done that? Is this a problem, and if so with whom?

Topic 17 [genx]: People Try to Put Us Down
#40 : We're livin' in the age of cooties. (lorelei)   Mon Sep 14

It is a way of discounting anything that a non-boomer has to say. Not that they all do this, or that many of them haven't in fact BT,DT, but it is just another way of doing the "kids today know nothing" routine.

Topic 17 [genx]: People Try to Put Us Down
#41 : Underground Sexual Revolutionary (lamorte)   Mon Sep 14

If they had indeed BT,DT then they would have a different response from BT,DT.

Topic 17 [genx]: People Try to Put Us Down
#42 : doing the things a particle can (cynsa)   Mon Sep 14

ah, yes, if they had BT,DT maybe they would remember how it feels to have all your opinions and attitudes belittled for not being original or worthy of note? or maybe they wouldn't. After all, many victims of abuse turn around and abuse others when in positions of power. <append smiley if necessary>

Topic 17 [genx]: People Try to Put Us Down
#43 : Rik Elswit (rik)   Mon Sep 14

No smiley needed, but the dynamic must be heeded if we're going to communicate.

Topic 17 [genx]: People Try to Put Us Down
#44 : Andrew Mayer (iam)   Mon Sep 14

I definitely feel the BT/DT attitude is a cop out. One way of dealing with the massive Peter Pan syndrome that so many Baboos seem to be just coming out of as they hit their forties, finally realizing it doesn't pay to be a teenager all your life.

Topic 17 [genx]: People Try to Put Us Down
#45 : Soothing Pink Liquid (kreth)   Tue Sep 15

Why does it hurt to see people in luxury 4 × 4's—with gold-rim spoke wheels—driving badly and trying to run down bicyclists (yours truly) with a latte in one hand and the car phone shoulder-cradled against the ear?

Because—THEY'RE F***!

A "Thousand Points of Darkness"

"BT,DT. . . . . . . .BT. . . .but they're gonna get slapped"

(Thanks to Prof. I.B. Gittendown - inventor of Slapthology(tm))

—end of bitch—(eob)

Topic 17 [genx]: People Try to Put Us Down
#46 : P. Dilluchio (pdil)   Tue Sep 15

We're just jealous because you have faster metabolisms.

Topic 17 [genx]: People Try to Put Us Down
#47 : drifting in a space free of time (xoc)   Wed Sep 16

Sure, but what explains those ugly "gold" wheels?

Topic 17 [genx]: People Try to Put Us Down
#48 : We're livin' in the age of cooties. (lorelei)   Wed Sep 16

Too much money.

Topic 17 [genx]: People Try to Put Us Down
#49 : Andrew Nelson Hultkrans (drude)   Wed Sep 16

Those dirty rings . . .

Topic 17 [genx]: People Try to Put Us Down
#50 : Leisure of the Theory Class (rbr)   Wed Sep 16

Too much money *and* too little class. The people with gold rims on
their wheels are the same people that would put flamingos in front of
their mobile home, except now they've made it big and don't live in a
mobile home anymore.

Topic 17 [genx]: People Try to Put Us Down
#51 : doing the things a particle can (cynsa)   Wed Sep 16

If I had a LOT of money I would buy a plastic flamingo and put it in
front of my apartment.

Topic 17 [genx]: People Try to Put Us Down
#52 : We're livin' in the age of cooties. (lorelei)   Wed Sep 16

Once they get rich they replace the flamingos with those strange iron
horse hitcher things.

Topic 17 [genx]: People Try to Put Us Down
#53 : Riparian pother! (nexsys)   Wed Sep 16

And when they get even richer they tie a couple horses to them! :-)

Topic 17 [genx]: People Try to Put Us Down
#54 : Triple X (leilani)   Wed Sep 16

Ugh! My parents have an iron horse hitcher thing in their front yard. I had nothing to did with it. It came with their house when they bought it.

Topic 17 [genx]: People Try to Put Us Down
#55 : the creation myths of Lefforts Ave (pdil)   Thu Sep 17

I have big pink flamingos in front of my home! I have no gold rims on my car, nor wish for same . . .

Topic 17 [genx]: People Try to Put Us Down
#56 : doing the things a particle can (cynsa)   Thu Sep 17

This is the woman I want to be someday.

Topic 17 [genx]: People Try to Put Us Down
#57 : drifting in a space free of time (xoc)   Thu Sep 17

Yeah, Lawn Jockeys! A friend of mine used [in college] to make guerilla attacks on the suburban lawn jockeys. He'd go around painting 'em white . . .

Topic 17 [genx]: People Try to Put Us Down
#58 : Bruce H. MacEvoy (macevoy)   Thu Sep 17

There's a fantastic rustic home on Hwy 84 in the hills above Pescadero that has about forty or fifty pink flamingos in the front yard. It's set off the road amongst redwoods by a creek bed, and the effect is truly bizarre.

Topic 17 [genx]: People Try to Put Us Down
#59 : Underground Sexual Revolutionary (lamorte)   Thu Sep 17

Sad.

Topic 17 [genx]: People Try to Put Us Down
#60 : Riparian pother! (nexsys)   Thu Sep 17

au contraire! . . . a brilliant display of individualism!

ONWARD PLASTIC PELICANS!

Topic 17 [genx]: People Try to Put Us Down
#61 : Madame X (thanne)   Thu Sep 17

All this is making me think of Laurie Anderson:

"I came home last night, and *both* our cars were gone. And there were all these pink flamingos arranged in star patterns, all over the lawn . . ."

(Now back to our regularly scheduled drift)

Topic 17 [genx]: People Try to Put Us Down
#62 : Fleagle = Dog (cynsa)   Thu Sep 17

good drift!

The
I Hate Brenda
Newsletter

Slamming

Shannen Doherty

The 'zine explosion has fostered a different sort of rant. Entirely dedicated to dissecting and dissing "Beverly Hills 90210" actress Shannen Doherty, the I Hate Brenda Newsletter conducts a humorous but frontal assault on the Hollywood establishment through an extended insulting tirade directed against one of its perhaps undeserving stars. Utilizing tools of both the postmodern deconstructional media analyst and the good old-fashioned Los Angeles gossip columnist, these GenX publishers (Kerin and Darby, as they're known on the inside) are out to prove that our only use for the icons set before us by mainstream media is symbolic lynching.

I HATE BRENDA THE NEWSLETTER

1ST PRINTING: 10,000 2ND PRINTING: 15,000

© 1993 BEN IS DEAD MAGAZINE

SUBSCRIPTIONS: $2 EACH POSTAGE PAID. EUROPE & CANADA ADD $2.

SEND INQUIRIES, CONTRIBUTIONS, OR DONATIONS TO I HATE BRENDA, c/o BEN IS DEAD P.O. BOX 3166 HOLLYWOOD, CA 90028. ADVERTISING AND BRENDA SNITCH LINE: (213) 960-1042.

ALL MATERIAL SENT WILL BECOME OUR PROPERTY AND WILL NOT BE RETURNED UNLESS OTHERWISE ARRANGED.

MAKE ALL CHECKS OR MONEY ORDERS OUT TO BEN IS DEAD.

DOHERTY

$1.⁴⁹
cheap!

It's hard being America's new hip, nubile, teen-televi- – very trying, according to the numerous sources we Queen B of TV's *Beverly Hills 90210* soon developed into an

We understand that Hollywood changes people. placed upon one in the public eye. However, once at the pressures of stardom do not constitute an excuse to sour the world with such a blood-curdling personality.

sion starlet... yet, Shannen Doherty certainly is trying spoke to. What started as a generic dislike for the 80,000 watt transmission of protest to dethrone her.

We realize that it is difficult to cope with the demands top one must remember not to spit in that eye. The

Unfortunately, Shannen Doherty seems to be that personality, whatever that personality may be. How much of Brenda is Shannen Doherty? Do we really hate Ms. Doherty? Is she just a victim of her character, Brenda? Or is her character becoming a victim of Shannen? While asking these questions we have come to realize that her behavior must be stopped. People are fed up. One popular U.S. magazine even has an informal ban on publishing any photos of Shannen! The Doherty denominator seems to cross every social boundary, as thousands coalesce to end her reign of terror.

Welcome to the first edition of the *I Hate Brenda Newsletter*. This newsletter is the culmination of what began with our weekly *90210* gatherings, which over a period of time turned into informal "I Hate Brenda" discussions, and then evolved to highly orchestrated "I Hate Brenda" meetings.

As you read these pages, you will probably define your own perspective of this multi-faceted, yet strangely one-dimensional woman. Our newsletter is a forum for thoughtful analysis, as well as fun and expression. We're not out to change the world... just a star.

★ ★

Who *Likes* Brenda Anyway?

During a casual conversation one evening, I was taken aback when Curtis York revealed to me that he liked Brenda. Always striving to show the two sides of this complex phenomenon (trust me, it's been hard), I, Kitty-Lu Kemia, Los Angeles-based actress and columnist, pounced upon Mr. York for the following interview.

I guess the first question is why do you like Brenda?

It's a weird combination of liking Brenda Walsh and liking Shannen Doherty. It's hard for me to distinguish between Brenda Walsh and Shannen Doherty. I think in a lot of ways the role of Brenda Walsh was created for the actress Shannen Doherty. But sometimes I think the whole myth of Shannen Doherty was created for the character of Brenda Walsh.

I don't think the other kids at West Beverly High really understand how hard it is to go through your whole life being so tragically disfigured. She manages to be popular and have an okay attitude, even though she is a bitch some

continued on page 6

"The world we live in isn't safe for any woman." –Shannen Doherty

THE MISFORTUNES OF STARDOM

Pearl Jam's Eddie Vedder on Shannen Doherty, the Wanna-be Princess of Pop

"Someday, Doherty may have her own rock-and-roll groupies to distract her. A big fan of U2, Guns N' Roses and Pearl Jam (she would love to meet lead singer Eddie Vedder), she enjoys toying with the idea of having her own band." –People Magazine, November 9, 1992.

Darby: Could you tell us about your brush with Shannen?
Eddie: I'm the kind of person that I... I don't usually get into anybody's shit or anything. I don't worry about little silly things but she like... I didn't even know who this person was. See, I went to stay at this hotel in San Diego one night where I used to work the midnight shift as security. It was really cool because I lived in a shitty neighborhood, and pretty much had a shitty life but I could go and stay at this fancy hotel at midnight and check in and get a bottle of wine and go up on the rooftop and write songs and stuff.

How long ago did you work there?
Like three and a half, four years ago. I worked there for a long time. I'd done midnight shifts for like five years before I moved up here (to Seattle). It was a great thing – kinda like preying upon the rich. So, when we (Pearl Jam) were going to play at Iguana's (a club in Tijuana, Mexico), I thought it was going to be really cool, because I was going to stay in

continued on page 2

THE GOOD SAMARITANS OF THE I HATE BRENDA NEWSLETTER

Darby: We're just doing a public service – this is what the people want. It's all in good fun... good clean teen fun.

Kerin Morataya: Brenda leaves an awful taste in my mouth. This newsletter is like a huge swig of Scope.

Michael Carr: It's socio-political for me. For the first time in my life, I feel motivated to fight the Hollywood establishment. It's not her fault that they hired a no-talent with a bad attitude. But we have to start somewhere. We need to send a strong message.

Dave Ehrlich: By any means necessary.

Cliff Thurber: Our country purged most of the people who participated in the last Republican Convention... and Ms. Doherty should not be overlooked.

31

(sealed with a knife)

Dear Fellow Shannen-haters,

I know all too well how sweet that two faced bitch Shannen Doherty can be. She cost me a job.

It was years ago and I was working on *Heathers* as Wino Ryder's stand-in. OK, so it's not the greatest job in the world, but as the punch line goes, it's show biz. Anyway, Ms. Ryder was rarely on set (her temper tantrums could be a whole 'nother story) and consequently I was required to be on set during most of the rehearsals.

Everything was just peachy keen until the third day, which was the first day I came in contact with Princess Doherty. Which also turned out to be my last day on the film. Already at this early age, Shanny-poo was the prima donna we've all come to know and loathe. It seems she had just been dumped by her then-current boyfriend for some bleach blonde bimbo and Shannen decided all women were evil incarnate. She proceeded to throw a fit that earned her the nickname the crew gave her – the "BMW" (the bitch and moan witch).

Shannen took a particular dislike to my golden locks (never mind that I was probably ten years her senior) and proceeded to butt heads with me whenever she could. First she complained I wasn't doing my job. Excuse me, but standing in one place is not that difficult.

Next she demanded to know why I didn't have Wino Ryder's lines memorized. I explained to her that not only did no one inform me that the lines needed to be memorized, but in all my years of stand-in work, no one ever asked me to memorize lines before. Well, Shannen knew best, and she could not do the scene unless I was reciting Ms. Ryder's lines. Realizing we were at the brink of a major incident, the Assistant Director quickly handed me a copy of the script.

So we started. The next thing I knew Shannen ripped the script out of my hands and started another tirade. Seems Shanny couldn't rehearse with me if she couldn't see my eyes. Now I've had compliments on my eyes before, but never from a screaming, out-of-control young lass such as Ms. Dohead. Since I don't possess Marty Feldmen's eyes, I tried to explain to her that it was impossible to read the script and keep eye contact with her. This just would not do. Shannen proceeded to get in my face, yelling and pushing. And I wasn't about to let this young twit push me around.

cont. on page 4

EDDIE VEDDER continued...

this hotel and get drunk, just like the old days. So, I go and check in and I'm with my friend, who's the valet, and I'm embarrassed 'cause I'm checking in at the front desk and I'm having to use a fake name. And I'm checked in under Ruben Kinkade. Every once in awhile, there's problems or a pain in the ass. I put myself out in the public all the time and I just want to sneak away and play my guitar. So, here I am under this name and he goes "Let me tell you. This person [Shannen Doherty] has been trying to figure out when you were going to stay here and she has been fucking around with everyone at the hotel." And Shannen ended up fucking with him hard-core because she found out that we had been friends. It was like, she never said, "this person's cool, I like his music. Do you think we can hang out" or "I'm this person and maybe he knows my work or whatever." Maybe she knows that if I knew her work I would never hang out with her.

So when exactly did this occur?
It was this summer. She was staying in the same hotel, doing some TV movie.

You're talking about that movie "Obsessed"?
Something about a teenage whore.

It was like a fatal attraction type movie.
So she was probably using her obsession with me to get inspiration. Well, I heard that she was really rude to a lot of people. They have a concierge at the hotel and they said that she came up to him and said "I heard this band is playing in Mexico and I want tickets and I want passes. Make it happen."

So she wanted to go see Pearl Jam.
She demanded back stage passes. "Make it happen." That was the quote. I heard this from the valet and then they called the concierge. And then she was calling our office, and... I've had a girlfriend for eight years and we're like a total team and she just happened to be at our management office and was there the day that Shannen's office called and wanted to know if I had a girlfriend and wanted pictures and all this shit.

She was having her *office* call to find out your statistics for her?
Yeah. And my girlfriend who was with me at the MTV awards was looking out for Shannen just waiting to kick the shit out of her. And my thing was like "I would probably beat the shit out of a guy who was doing that to you, so go for it." Shannen Doherty would have been dead meat.

Did they get her tickets?
Yeah.

So did she ever end up meeting you?
No. But I know I would probably just spend the whole time puking if I met her anyway. I mean anyone who seriously wanted to meet me or gain my confidence would never show up at some Republican thing. I don't even know what she did.

She led the Pledge of Allegiance.
I've never read an interview with her. I've seen her on Arsenio a couple of times. I don't have any feelings for the person, but I just don't think you can get around in life or in this business by being a fuck. You can't treat people like shit. And everyone I know who treats people like shit haven't come from places where they've been shit upon.

SAN DIEGO, CA – During the recent filming of the TV movie, *Obsessed*, with William Devane, Shannen Doherty seemed to live the title of the television drama, obsessed with Eddie Vedder of Pearl Jam. And her obsession with being a bitch, unlike the cologne, smelled less than pretty. Even less pretty than alcohol-induced bile.

When she found out that Eddie was staying at the same hotel, she used an alias to call the front desk and said, "Oh, can you tell me what room he's staying in? He's a friend of mine and we're supposed to party together tomorrow night." Of course when Eddie was asked about this he said this wasn't the case. That he wasn't friends with and had no intention of "partying" with her. Later, when she attempted to telephone his room she was told by the operator that he wasn't taking any calls. "Oh, he'll take mine," she cooed. He didn't.

Shannen's make-up people who were there for the film related that she was a horrible bitch. It was witnessed that Shannen actually slapped a couple of them. A security guard said that if it had been up to him to calm her down, he would probably hold her head under water. He said that she was the worst person he ever worked with.

After the daily wrap was called on filming, Shannen would usually go out and get smashed on margaritas. She would return to the hotel in the wee hours of the morning in a condition that was "not tipsy, or tight, or even tanked. She was overflowing with booze, a wet-your-pants drunk."

The morning after the Pearl Jam concert, two friends smuggled alcohol into the room in vases. Observing the scene, a room service attendant commented that Shannen had probably gotten herself in over her head, "Oh that little Brenda Walsh is in trouble."

When the *Obsessed* stint ended (the movie), her temper escalated when it was time to check out of the hotel. Shannen Doherty apparently was not ready to leave. "The police were called. The hotel had to evict her," a valet at the time reported. "A friend of mine is a photo-journalist, and I called him to have him come down because we were going to sell this stuff to the Enquirer."

Shannen was told that the room was promised to another guest. She became verbally abusive to the general manager who stated that she had to pay for a pillow that her dog chewed to pieces.

"You probably chewed it yourself," the cleverly succinct starlet screamed in response. Shannen then telephoned her father, to no avail. The hotel refused to allow the vagabond vixen to dodge the bill. They summoned the San Diego police to have her forcibly removed from the premises. Shannen's boyfriend at the time, Chris Foufas, acted as the dean of diplomacy by mediating the dispute, and restoring Shannen to her normal, barely tolerable self.

All we can hope is that he was always such a gentleman throughout their on-again, off-again courtship. Opening doors, pulling out chairs, and raising toilet seats... It's never too late to learn about manners.

That makes it even more offensive to me that she's interested in our band and she did something for Slaughter. – Eddie Vedder

223

We almost came to blows, but the Assistant Director stepped in. Now I should point out that I'm all of 5' tall and weigh 98 lbs so I'm anything but a big girl.

To tell you the truth, if I didn't need the job so much, I would have slugged her. As it turns out, I should have punched her. At the end of the day, I was told that my services would no longer be required.

Thanks Shannen,

Nora Columbo

P.S. The only reservations I have in writing this letter is that it may discourage some would be obsessed fan to begin stalking her and make her life a living hell. To those lonely, schizophrenic men out there who are desperately searching for an object of desire, all I can say is Shannen Doherty is probably the greatest gal in the entire world, and is desperately in need of someone just like you to rescue her from the hells of her phony showbiz relationships. And remember, when Shannen says "no" she really means yes. Go get her boys.

Dear Ben is Dead,

I normally don't read your magazine but someone brought it in to one of our meetings to protest the incredibly offensive Ben is Sex issue. You'll probably be hearing more from us on that later... That same media watchdog also got your fax regarding Ms. Shannen Doherty and that's why I'm writing you today. We'll surely never see eye to eye with your ilk but one thing we do have in common is an intense dislike for the aforementioned. We were truly appalled with Shannen's shenanigans at the Republican national convention in Houston, let me tell you.

Young Republican Women's Caucus invited her to appear in the hopes that she would be able to capture the youth vote since she does, after all, appear in a very popular television show and we thought that someone so beautiful and talented would dispel the notion that Republican women are all pinched-up dowagers.

The first indication that Shannen wasn't all sweetness and light came when we had to negotiate with her manager at some length (we could clearly hear Shannen in the background screaming at him that she didn't have time to deal with "a bunch of drips like us") but she agreed to come somewhat reluctantly. When we balked at having to fly her and her dog first class and have a three page rider of food and cosmetic items available to her backstage she told us to "go sell some extra f**kin' cookies" She would only stay at the Four Seasons and we thought it was kind of odd her masseuse (male) was staying in her room but it did save a little money on another room.

Shannen was scheduled to do a speech to rev up the nation's youth the first day but she

cont. on page 6

Page 4 I Hate Brenda

★★

Cosmic Danielle Does Shannen

Hello, dolls! It's the Cosmic Danielle, Astrologer to the Stars, zooming in on Planet Hollywood for a close-up on Shannen Doherty. Here's the lowdown on that low-down little hussy.

Shannen is an Aries with a Leo moon. The sun squares Mars in Capricorn, which accounts for her being type-cast as a manipulative bitch, a role that she plays all too well. Pluto and Virgo shows that she can be real difficult to work with. Though charm and popularity are likely, extravagance, vanity, and exaggerated emotions come too easily. Projecting a forceful and energetic personality, she probably has an asteroid temper and some underlying emotional discord.

Her chart reveals that she is really a spoiled brat with Mercury in Taurus (always thinking about money). Venus is in Pisces, an indicator that she is a closet slut. The negative aspects of Jupiter in Saturn prevent her from making up her mind when it comes to love. Her Uranus in Libra may provide parking space under the bed for the shoes of some strange bedfellows. An attraction to foreigners with strange customs is sparked by Neptune in Sagittarius.

The good news is that the galactic stars have nothing really good to say about the Doherty star. Perhaps the full moon on January 8th, 1993 may bring the lights on the set crashing down upon her head during an earthquake (well, maybe not that lucky). Instead of Valentines in February, the mail may bring news of a financial catastrophe which just might spell the end to her career, when Saturn in Aquarius squares her Saturn in Taurus. 'Til then dolls.

The Cosmic Daniel Hernandez, professional Astrologer to the Stars, can be reached at 310.657.4903.

★★

RUMP!

INTERVIEW BY JONATHAN PONEMAN

With the upcoming release of their new 12", "Hating Brenda", Rump has become a household word. Their aggressive attack on Hollywood darling Shannen Doherty has created the trend of celeb bashing (known as celeb-core in the music world) and given birth to a knew genre of music soon to be known as "Grave" (a lethal combination of grunge and rave). I've known Darby and Kerin for years. I knew them through their respective bands, Mac Babe and Aye Mamacita, before they knew each other. Never have I seen them look cuter or sound as incredible. Kerin and Darby's entry into the fame sweepstakes had all the drama of a Lotto purchase at AM/PM. As record company moguls search for the next Rump, they have now become the standard-bearers of rock celebrity. What follows is a brief conversation with two of the most talented women the rock world has yet to meet.

JP: Tell me about this "Hating Brenda" project. What fueled the idea?

D: Well, the fuel was a eye-catching girl named Shannen Doherty. After watching her and her character on 90210 become more and more hateful, we decided we had to do something about it. First, we created this newsletter.

K: And then, we decided to dedicate a 12" to her.

JP: And what has the response been?

K: Incredible! Sub Pop loved it when we pitched it to them.

D: And all the other labels have been calling us. There seems to be an indefinite number of people who hate Brenda.

K: And love Rump.

JP: One thing about your music is that it's unlike anything that's been done before. How do you feel being the originators of GRAVE and the fact that Shannen had an unconscious part in it's creation?

K: I don't think Shannen had anything to do with the creation of our sound at all. If we weren't singing about

her, we'd be singing about something else. But, I do thank her for the inspiration.

JP: So what's next for Rump? Who's the next person on your hit list?

K: I've been hearing some great stories about Winona Ryder, so maybe she'll be next, although I loved her boob shot in Dracula.

D: We're working on a cover album of Disney tunes called "Yo Walt Yo" which will be released sometime in the middle of next year. We're really hoping Mayim Bialik [Blossom] will play bass with us – so we're working on that as well. I just hope this obsession with Brenda or, uh, Shannen doesn't absorb all of our attention. Maybe we're getting a little carried away.

MY BRUSH WITH BRENDA

BY CLIFF "JOE EVERYDAY NORMAL" THURBER

The circumstances surrounding my particular "Brenda" encounter are as follows:

On a Saturday night this past August, one stop on our party circuit itinerary was some soiree up on Mullholland Drive. Upon entering the party, I quickly learned that our host was none other than *Beverly Hills 90210's* Kelly (Jennie Garth). The occasion was Miss Garth's house warming.

My ever lucid perception caught a striking contrast to Miss Garth's generous food spread and hospitable disposition- the frigid presence of Shannen Doherty. While standing at the keg, my peripheral vision caught the equivalent of an Arctic ice sculpture. In the midst of the ensuing party, on the back patio, she stood alone like some taboo totem pole. Her face affected a tight lipped, straight ahead gaze intermittently disrupted by "Virginia Slims" woman style drags from her cigarette. These puffs were stiffly executed by forbidding folded arms. Oh, all that is glamorous in Hollywood.

The fact that she conversed with no one or vice versa led me to some general conclusions. One is that in public, she experiences a deep rooted frustration that there's no hi-lighting or make-up artist to hide her nicotine stained and poorly aligned teeth. I also surmise that Ms. Doherty was more than a little miffed that she was upstaged by the potato salad and brie cheese. Or, of course, I could be all wrong, and she was simple pondering the peculiarity that a medical world that could give her fake boobs still does not have the technology to remove her head from her ass.

"My parents always taught me to be honest." –Shannen Doherty

THE DON'TS OF Fashion

"Anyone who watches 90210 with an eye towards fashion can always pick up a few tips hear and there. It's just one more aspect of the show that makes it so much fun!" Taking the fun to another level we've picked some of our favorite Doherty costumes. Do it yourself Halloween fashions for the whole family!

"The way Shannen dresses is one major way she expresses herself. 'I'm not trendy. I do and wear whatever I feel.' She loves to wear combat boots and halter dresses with a motorcycle jacket." Personally, we just love that belt! Definitely not trendy!

The biggest fashion problem with Shannen is that she has somehow decided that black is her color and now wears it constantly. Wrong, wrong, wrong, Shannen! Especially with the white make-up. Please, honey, you can afford it – get your colors done!

"Shannen shares Brenda's liking for casual menswear, big shirts and blazers. Her look has streamlined over the two years, going from a lacy, more frilly look, to a more tailored style. As an illustration of how influential Beverly Hills is in setting trends, a recent article on the new fall fashion named Brenda's preference for wearing man-tailored clothing as a reason for the boom in the style."

"She takes advantage of the wealth of stores and boutiques surrounding her. Some of her favorite shops in L.A. are Armani and Fred Segal. When she visits Chris in Chicago, she favor Henri Bendel. Charivari is the draw in New York... Shannen can also be found scrounging the vintage clothing stores in nearby Melrose for unique pieces of clothing."

COMING NEXT ISSUE: HOW TO AVOID SHANNEN'S GLAM LOOK!

"Shannen certainly knows how to keep busy! Keep watching to see what she'll do next!"

R. U. SIRIUS

There's No Such Thing as An Original Debt: A Message of Hope to the So-Called Generation X

A boomer himself, the original editor-in-chief and humanoid mascot of Mondo 2000 *magazine jumped at the opportunity to participate in this GenX experiment. An avid on-line participant since computer conferencing existed, Sirius is a master ranter. Straddling both his 1960s sensibility and his 1990s one (Sirius was responsible for hatching many of the formerly fringe concepts now central to GenX philosophy), Sirius here both participates in a GenX-style manifesto and shares his own outsider's perspective on our economic plight.*

A baby with big sad eyes and a distended belly sits in the desert in Africa. She is hungry, sick and about to die. As a citizen of an emerging African nation state, she's several thousand dollars in debt to the World Bank. And *you* thought Generation X was getting the shaft.

Speaking of which. The legend goes like this. The boomer generation, a self-indulgent bunch of oversexed stoners lived it up through the '70s and '80s, leaving behind an ashtray full of roaches and a huge debt for future generations to pay off before they can go about the business of eliminating poverty, combating AIDS, getting educated and indulging themselves. Well, the legend is a crock of shit.

Aside from the fact that the future has *really* been ripped off by that welfare-for-the-upper-middle-class system for bureaucrats, engineers, discipline freaks and corporate contractors known as the military, the truth is that monetary debt is theft ... monetary debt is impossible.

While I have no wish to exume the tortured theories of Karl Marx, *real* wealth—whether it's food, medicine, housing, industrial products, consumer conveniences, information, ideas, entertainment, or interpersonal services—isn't created by lending institutions. The definition, control and issuance of tickets representing value is, at best, a macro-organizational tool and, by no stretch of the imagination need we credit the government-approved institutions that do this with generating more than a small fragment of what people need or value.

Wealth is generated by work, organization, invention, intelligent application, entrepreneurial fervor, creativity, service. The various central banks, in concert with the World Bank and the International Monetary Fund, *lend* nation states, business, and individuals tickets representing value. These tickets are promises that the value they claim to represent will be honored, a kind of worldwide semi-consensual agreement enforced by governments. The tickets help generate the confidence that, in turn, generates the activity that creates actual wealth. The problem, of course, is that as long as most of the wealth generated is tied to tickets that are created and monopolized by lending institutions, all the wealth in the world is—in a sense—on loan. But, arguably, it's the *symbol* that's owed. In other words, the national debt, et al., is *symbolic*, a virtual reality.

This is not to deny that this system has operated according to a fairly consistant internal logic or that there is a plausible necessity for a worldwide consensual symbol system that maintains some kind of equilibrium and therefore continues confidence that the symbol will be accepted as value. But the current system has already been thrown out of equilibrium by the removal of a physical governor, when Nixon dispensed with the gold standard in 1971, and has been further disarranged and overwhelmed by the worldwide near-speed-of-light trading and transference of virtual wealth—in the form of stocks, bonds, futures, currency exchanges, options etc.—in cyberspace. Indeed, according to Paul Glaser, chairman of Citicorp's Technology Committee, the nation's banks have approximately the same amount of money under their management as the nation's money management firms. In other words, half of the tickets representing value (They're not actually tickets anymore. They are more like bits and bytes in a data base. And there is no macro-accounting system. So they are actually *nothing* but numbers that are honored as tickets once were) are free-floating in international cyberspace. While the Central banks attempt to maintain equilibrium, they are overwhelmed by this currency trading market.

Joel Kurtzman, business editor for *The New York Times*, in his book, *The Death of Money*, writes, "Every three days a sum of money passes through the fiber-optic network underneath the pitted streets of New York equal to the total output for one year of all of America's companies and all of its workforce." Money, which always has been something of a virtual reality—a consensus hallucination, a symbol system—is spinning out of control in a world of nearly infinite and breathtakingly rapid symbol exchange. It's making an increasingly large, but nevertheless privileged elite, of players unfathomably rich by means of the rapid manipulation of symbols and perceptions. If we can let this privileged group accumulate riches and the social power that comes with it by pure symbol manipulation, then we can surely game our way out of debt and deficit. After all, did the lending institutions create so much actual wealth that we now must sacrifice our children's education or universal health care ad infinitum on the altar of our indebtedness? Must we continue to "tighten our belts" around the necks of the starving?

The Emperor Has No Dough

So fuck Ross Perot and balancing the budget. And fuck the big Clinton administration lie that the economy is on the upswing again and unemployment is going down. The standards that are used to measure economic growth, like postmodern money, mean absolutely *nothing*. Just take a look around. Been stepping over more ragged homeless bodies every week for the last two fucking decades? Noticed the sudden increase in corporate downsizing, big corporations laying off workers in the tens of thousands. And you really believe that unemployment is going down and the "economy" is going up? Unemployment figures only count people who are registered and looking for work. The real figures are at least three times as high. According to economist Hazel Henderson, over 50 percent of the American people are either unemployed, working part-time, or working at temporary jobs without the promise of job security or benefits. Robert Reich, the Secretary of Labor, recently said that 71 percent of Americans now live from paycheck to paycheck. Clinton goes around telling people that they will have to change careers eight times in their lifetimes. Forget it. Employment is obsolete. The GNP and GDP indicators are fat with the money spent on weapons of destruction, meaningless hype, and coping with the results of ecological and natural disasters, crime waves, drug abuse, etc. Federal and state budgets are so riddled with subsidies for profit-making megacorporations that if such subsidies were pulled, the entire edifice of so-called free enterprise would crumble, town-by-town and city-by-city. President Clinton talks about the "courage to change," but he barely scratches the surface of what needs to be done. And, fortunately, it needs to be done *right away.*

It's not "the economy, stupid." It's the *stupid economy.* We don't need family values, censorship of television, a movement of modern primitives based on tryptamine hallucinogens, the mass castration of males, or enforced vegetarianism. We don't *want* a perfectly nice world. All we need is to create a new economic virtual reality, a de-monopolized economic system based on complexity theory that democratizes government-supported mainstream financial institutions while allowing new forms of exchange to evolve with no, or limited, intervention, and to have that system reflect the creation of *actual* value. We only need to obviate worldwide debt by hacking the digital economy. We only need to set "free" enterprise free of taxpayer subsidies as well as bureaucratic controls, while at the same time moving certain parts of the economy into the commons without adapting the Orwellian ethics and aesthetics of collectivism. Well, it sounds easy to me, anyway.

So I propose the organization of a "post"-cyberculture think-tank dedicated to digitally remastering the world economy for maximum well-being with minimal coercion. Call it "Free World 2.0." And to escape the abstraction of futurism, the think-tank should resolve to create a reasonable political platform for the 1996 Presidential election, a document that would suggest how to effect this transition. It's not a question of utopia or oblivion. It's a question of a liveable-if-bizarre world or the grotesque living nightmare already extant.

Maggie Estep

Humping Hilda

Queen of the "Spoken-Word Movement" and High Times *cover girl Maggie Estep can be heard on the coffeehouse stages of New York's Lower East Side shouting, "Fuck me! Fuck me! Fuck me!" And a lot of busters have begun crowding into these tiny spaces to listen to her and other young poets do it. The herald of GenX's own brand of performance poetry, Estep works to fight the self-deprecating tendency of most female stage artists, instead concentrating on the power inherent in a good head-banging rant.*

So there I am, 21 years old, 5 foot 4', 115 pounds and a purple mohawk that stretches to the heavens and never quite gets there.

I've got a big bristly brush in one hand and a bottle of *A Thousand Flushes* blue shit for the toilet bowl in the other.

I'm sick,

I'm in Hell,

I'm in rehab.

One night I got so wasted, me and my friend Hope stole a shopping cart from in front of Key Food on Avenue A. We got on the thing and rode it down Avenue A, left on Houston, south on Allen, and smashed into a cop car.

Hope ran off as the cops got out, I was reacting in half-time and they got me and stuck me in rehab.

So now, as I flick the last speck of fudge off the toilet bowl, Michelle the Rehab Counselor comes in, stands there with her hands on her huge hips, gestures at a faint pee streak beneath the rim and goes:

"What's that?"

"Uh, I dunno, lemon juice."

"Watch your mouth, Margaret, I've had about enough of your snotty attitude, and I'll tell you what, you're sober enough to be a snot, you're sober enough to get a job."

So, the next day, with my youth and my Post Punk Detox good looks on my side, I get myself a job at a cardboard box factory.

I stand at the end of a conveyor belt, catching and folding flaps of cardboard. My fellow cardboard workers are two speedfreak Skinhead guys who take pleasure in feeding boxes into the machine so fast the flaps fly into my face, I lose control of the cardboard, fall backwards and get cardboard dust stuck in my mohawk.

By the end of the day I stink of cardboard and I need a drink. I trudge home to rehab. I sit in the communal lounge area picking at the Welfare Office's generous donation of a big hunk of cheesefood. Then I notice this new rehab inmate. He's sloshed. He's slumped down in the orange chair, mumbling to himself. He's drunk, he's beautiful, he's not a day over 17. He looks up and smiles at me drunkenly: "Hi, I'm Robbie."

I smile at him soberly. Then Michelle the Counselor appears, whisks Robbie away and sends me off to a self-help meeting at the Salvation Army.

The self-help meeting is mostly compulsive gambler guys in trenchcoats and racetrack faces. A few housefraus with hairspray habits. I sit in the back and manage to get this one strand from the front of my mohawk down to lip level so I can suck on it.

Then I notice this other girl around my age. She's what you call a "big girl." She's got pale blue overalls and army boots and her face is like a connect the dots painting. I'm trying to figure out just what you'd end up with if you did get around to connecting the dots of her zits. Then the meeting's over. They clap and pray and touch each other. I go up to the big girl.

"Hi, I'm Maggie."

"Hi, I'm Hilda," she says in a gravely voice.

Turns out Hilda's detoxing from a valium habit. She's also legally schizophrenic. But she's stabilizing. And she's looking for work.

So the next day I get Hilda a job at the box factory too. We're a dreamteam me and her. She feeds the machine, she's graceful, fluid, she's a box goddess. I catch and fold the flaps, seamless, smooth, orchestrated.

Mr Peets, the box factory manager, looks on, pleased at our productivity.

At lunch break we go sit in Hilda's blue Nova in the parking lot. We're listening to the Stones *Sucking in the 70s*.

"Come on, Hilda, can't we listen to the Sex Pistols, please." I've got my ubiquitous copy of *Never Mind the Bullocks* tucked into my pants.

But Hilda's quick to deny me this most basic of pleasures: "No way, get away from me with the Sex Pistols stuff, my therapist says Punk Rock makes me do downers."

"Oh."

We eat lunch. Hilda whips out a salami, Cheez Doodles, a big bag of M&M's and 32 ozs of Diet Coke. Then she whips out a joint of killer pot. Clearly this is no novice weed, my nose hairs are preening, my mouth is watering, my whole being is aching to get zonked. But then I imagine Michelle the Counselor finding suspicious pot smells on my person and booting me out of rehab. I don't have anywhere else to go, all I've got to my name is my bad self and my mohawk that stinks of cardboard.

But Hilda's taunting me: "Oooh, come on, Maggie, it's gonna feel soooo nice, you're gonna get so fucked up, you're gonna get so fucked up you're gonna get so fucked up . . ."

"Okay okay okay okay," I give in, "if we can listen to the Sex Pistols, I'll get stoned with you."

Hilda agrees. As *God Save the Queen* thunders through the crackly speakers of Hilda's Nova, we light up. Just two tokes and the shit zooms to my head. I'm feeling good, really good. But then, just as quickly, my head starts spinning, pot paranoia sets in and Hilda, apparently possessed by the gods of weed, suddenly yanks me to her and starts to lick my mouth.

Now, I'm your basic hetero girl. But my last boyfriend was almost a year back, Robbie the Teenage alcoholic is locked into another ward of the rehab, and, you know, Hilda, she's kinda sweet.

So I go for it, I mush my hand into her huge thigh, lick the Cheez Doodle crumbs from her lips and heave an enormous sigh.

Then, as the last chords of *God Save the Queen* fade out, as Hilda's tongue travels at Warp Nine from the tip of my chin down the modest cleavage of my Iggy T-shirt, just then, Mr Peets, Box Factory Manager, presses his face against the steamed-up car window.

And what a sight it must be: Two red-eyed same-gendered cardboard workers humping through a cloud of pot smoke.

Mr Peets' face turns beet red. He makes "o" shapes with his mouth but no sounds come out. He slowly backs away from the car.

Me and Hilda stop humping, straighten out our frumped-up clothing and return to our work stations. No one at the factory says a word to us.

The next morning we find pink slips in our pay envelopes. This sends Hilda into a fit of low self-esteem and I can see her zit population quadrupling as we stand there, pink slips in hand.

But I'm resilient now. Within two days I get myself hired on for the graveyard shift at a screw factory. Well, they didn't actually manufacture screws, I don't even know what the hell they manufactured, but my job was to use this tiny screwdiver and screw tiny crews into little metal plates.

One night Hilda comes to visit me on my 3am lunch break. We go out back by the toxic pond. We're sitting on a tree stump. It's cold and quiet and smelly. Just as a big metal pipe belches waste materials into the pond, I put my hand on Hilda's thigh. But Hilda's starts to cry, huge Hilda tears stream down her face.

"Hilda, Hilda, what's wrong?"

"Well I . . . Snarf . . . I stopped taking my medication and now I'm all moody and stuff and I . . . Snarf . . . Don't take it personal or anything but I don't have any sex drive left and . . . PLEASE DON'T TOUCH ME."

Well fine then.

I take my hand off her thigh and help her back to her car. I return to my work station and furiously screw the screws into the little metal plates.

7am, time to go home to rehab. I trudge through the door, tired, defeated, smelly and horny. But before I have time to get in the bathroom and masturbate, Michelle intercepts me, hands me some toilet tools and orders me to do 6 toilets before going to sleep.

I go up to the dim little bathroom next to the ancient Electric Shock Therapy room. I'm so lonely and filled with sexual tension that I start to cry. I cry and scrub and cry and scrub. And then, a miracle. They're always telling you to pray in these places, I'm already down on my knees so I just start mumbling: Dear Universe, please let me have sex and I will do anything.

Then the bathroom door opens. A crescent of brightness shines onto the filthy bathroom floor and there, his face made radiant by the fluorescent hallway light, there stands Robbie the Teenage Alcoholic.

"Michelle said to bring you this," he drawls deliciously as he hands me the blue shit for the toilet bowl.

"Thank you," I say softly.

As I reach for the blue shit, our fingers entwine around the bottle and we both start to squeeze real hard. My breath catches in my throat. Robbie's heartbeat pumps through the thin fabric of his Metallica T-shirt As he presses his mouth to mine we both squeeze the bottle so hard the top pops off and the blue shit oozes out and puddles on the floor. But I don't care, I grab at Robbie's ass so fiercely I lose my balance and slide onto the floor.

Robbie falls on top of me and starts humping my thigh. We rip off our clothes and go at it til our pubic patches are smeared with blue shit and we both come in one blinding instant.

Turns out this was both me and Robbie's "Spiritual Awakening." Falling in love by the toilet bowl kept us both off booze.

Eventually, Robbie was sent home to his parents.

Hilda stayed off valium and her schizophrenia stabilized. She still sends Christmas cards.

I moved to Colorado and became a dishwasher.

The Whiny Generation

David Martin's Anti-Rant

for Newsweek

This angry essay from Newsweek demonstrates the all-too-common boomer inability to perceive anything but complaints in GenX literature. Feeling he is being blamed for the GenX predicament, this forty-three-year-old lawyer rails against the busters, dubbing us the "whiners." What makes this piece appear so arrogant and insensitive to busters is its condescending, humorless insensitivity as well as its refusal to acknowledge that Generation X has taken responsibility for its own fate. This diatribe shows, by example and in its content, how some boomers understand the rant.

Ever since the publication of Douglas Coupland's book *Generation X,* we've been subjected to a barrage of essays, op-ed pieces and feature articles blaming us baby boomers for the sad face of the twentysomething generation: the boomers took all the good jobs; the boomers are destroying the planet, the media is boomer-dominated and boomer-obsessed. The litany is never-ending. If you believe the Generation X essayists, all the troubles of the world can be traced to us fortysomethings.

Well, enough is enough. As a baby boomer, I'm fed up with the ceaseless carping of a handful of spoiled, self-indulgent, overgrown adolescents. Generation Xers may like to call themselves the "Why Me?" generation, but they should be called the "Whiny" generation. If these pusillanimous purveyors of pseudo-angst would put as much effort into getting a life as they do into writing about their horrible fate, we'd be spared the weekly diatribes that pass for reasoned argument in newspapers and magazines.

Let's examine for a moment the horrible fate visited on Generation X. This is a generation that was raised with the highest standard of living in the history of the world. By the time they arrived on the scene, their parents were comfortably established in the middle class and could afford to satisfy their offsprings' every whim. And they did, in spades.

Growing up in the '70s and '80s, the twentysomethings were indulged with every toy, game and electronic device available. They didn't even have to learn how to amuse themselves since Mom and Dad were always there to ferry them from one organized activity to another. If we baby boomers were spoiled, the Whiny Generation was left out to rot. They had it all.

That's the essence of the Generation X problem. We have a generation (or at least part of a generation) whose every need has been catered to since birth. Now, when they finally face adulthood, they expect the gift-giving to continue. I'm 28 and I'll never own a house, whines the Generation Xer. I'm 25 and I don't have a high-paying job, says another.

Are these realistic expectations? Of course not. It's the rare individual in the last 40 years who had a high-paying job and owned a home prior to his or her 30th birthday. But the Whiners want everything now. A generation raised on the principle of instant satisfaction simply can't understand the concepts of long-term planning and deferred gratification. What's their reaction when they don't get what they want? That's right—they throw a tantrum.

The Whiners' most common complaint is that they've been relegated to what Mr. Coupland calls McJobs—low-paying, low-end positions in the service industry. I don't doubt that many Whiners are stuck in such jobs. But whose fault is that? Here's a generation that had enormous educational opportunities. But many Whiners squandered those chances figuring that a good job was a right not a privilege.

My parents' generation provided a better shot at post-secondary education for their boomer children than they themselves had enjoyed. And we took advantage of that situation in droves as the number of college and university graduates soared. The Whiners were afforded even greater scope for educational success but many of them failed to maximize their opportunities. They had the chance to reach higher but often chose not to or chose foolishly or unwisely.

Those who pursued a liberal-arts degree with a view to obtaining a job were either wealthy or naive. Those who thought that fine arts or film studies would yield more than a subsistence living were only fooling themselves. And those who entered law school will find sympathy hard to come by. More lawyers is one thing we definitely don't need.

The twentysomethings who planned their education wisely and spent the required years specializing in the technologies of the '90s now have the inside track in the job market. Those who chose to slide through high school to achieve semiliteracy are understandably unemployed or underemployed. Their cries of anguish do not now ring true. In fact, the youth unemployment rate is lower today than it was during the baby-boom recession of the early '80s. And despite the current recession, there are still plenty of positions available for highly skilled workers who exhibited the foresight and determination to achieve the necessary abilities.

The Whiners decry the lack of entry-level professional positions in the marketplace. Granted, during this current recession there are fewer such jobs. But that was also true in the early '80s. Instead of blaming everyone for this state of affairs, the Whiners should acquire more skills, education and specialized knowledge for the careers of the 21st century that will be awaiting those who have prepared themselves. Forget a career in law; start thinking about computers, telecommunications and health care.

Positions of power

As for the Whiners' complaint about the media being boomer-dominated and boomer-obsessed, that's nothing new. Once a generation has worked long and hard enough, it's only natural that some of its members become ensconced in positions of power. And once in power, it's not that surprising that they reflect the views, taste and concerns of their contemporaries. Why should the media revolve around the lives of 25-year-olds? Remember, this is the generation whose biggest achievement to date is something called grunge rock. Once they've accomplished more, they'll get the media coverage.

So, I invite the Whiners to put aside their TV-generation values and accept cold, hard reality. Interesting, high-paying jobs and rich lifestyles are not automatic; they're not even commonplace. Most people live ordinary lives of quiet desperation stuck in uninteresting jobs that they're afraid to lose. If you want more than that, move out of your parents' houses, start working, and for heaven's sake, stop whining.

CHAPTER 7

RAVING

Raving

The GenX dependence on and admiration for technology has given us unique insights into the direction of our culture. Taking our cue from cyberpunk authors such as William Gibson and Rudy Rucker, we whole-heartedly reject the linear reasoning and straight-edged reality handed down to us by our parents and teachers and instead look to chaos math, science fiction, and pagan spirituality for new sorts of answers.

However frighteningly random postmodern civilization may look to adults, GenXers understand the complexities of nonlinear reality and use new models such as the fractal to comprehend the swirl.

Admittedly, we do this with varying degrees of success. While some GenXers are hard at work in the lab or on their computers, experimenting with new equations, tiny particles, and cognitive-enhancing chemicals, others accept their discoveries and insights as they trickle down through fringe magazines, House music recordings, or word of mouth. The place to find out about and even experience these ideas is the rave.

Many GenXers look down on the rave phenomenon; soft, squishy, and touchy-feely, all-night technotronic psychedelic festivals have been seized upon by the media as evidence of our generation's gullibility and drug abuse. But the well-produced rave can also be an educational experience. Ravers were the first members of the general public directly exposed to fractals, virtual reality, brain machines, and "smart nutrients" as well as the concept of morphogenesis, Bohm's physics theories, and new interpretations of ancient calendrical systems. While all members of the rave subculture may not be able to articulate or even understand everything in *Wired* magazine, they exude an optimism about the future of the human race and its ability to transcend any obstacle through positive thought.

Breakthrough science and technology also find their way down to popular culture through GenX cyberliterature, which blurs the line between science fiction and science fact. The wildest speculations of these writers often turn out to be true, making this branch of fiction a rich source of ideas for computer research and development professionals.

Rave On!

Jody Radzik in Raygun

As promoter for many of northern and southern California's most success-
ful raves, Jody Radzik has a lot to share with would-be ravers about how
to get it all together. A Renaissance man, Radzik has worked as a clothing
designer, advertising executive, and art director of the magazine Morph's
Outpost on the Digital Frontier. *Central to Radzik's vision is the notion that*
marketing and spirituality need not be mutually exclusive. He sees it as his
mission to turn the marketing machine on itself; he popularizes the high-
est spiritual ideals by making them trendy.

When you party for unity and they play house music, it's called a rave. According to popular legend, house music was born in Chicago, migrated to Detroit and landed in London, where the term rave was first used.

Back then, these illegal, all-night warehouse parties fused a contemporary form of spirituality with technology into a poly-cultural organism. Admittedly that sounds like a mouthful, but the mix is essential if a group consciousness which the individual can lose him or herself in is to be generated.

As with any good party, the key is in the mix. Imagine bringing together over 8,000 shamanic citizens, all dancing their hineys off. If 7,000 of them pay $20 apiece for the pleasure—and that's just to get in—imagine what you have to work with. Not just in terms of money, but in terms of awareness. When you bring that many people together and give them some common reference point, such as the music, scene and vibe, you have the makings of quite the family affair.

So go ahead. Throw your own rave. Become a promoter. It's easier than you think.

All a promoter needs is three things: a staff, access to the necessary hardware and location and lots of spending money to pay for everything. While not necessary, good intentions don't hurt. Being connected with the established rave community doesn't hurt either. Without them, you can get shut-down, shut-out and shut up, particularly in an area like Los Angeles, where promoter wars can be fierce and ugly.

But don't let that stop you. Now that you're a promoter, pick a name and a date for the rave. Don't worry about the location yet. You have until the night of the party to take care of that. Besides, a good name can make or break a rave, so you have to choose this one carefully.

You could get a catchy, now, wow term like "Magical Mickey's Holy Water Adventure" that ignites the fever to frenzy; or you could name it after a friend, as in "A Rave Called Sharon." You could communicate a message of hope, a la "The Future," or go cyberpunk with a name like "Armageddon." Tap into a Dionysian theme along the lines of "Aphrodite's Temple," or a biospiritual trip such as "Osmosis." You can even try techno-cartoon vibes like "Toon Town" or "Clown Alley."

Whatever you do, however, don't call it Ecstasy, or any words that begin with "X." This is a sure sign of promotional incompetence. And once your core market thinks you are incompetent, you might as well give away your cash, because no one who is anyone will come.

The date is equally important. And this is where connections in the scene are vitally important. You absolutely do not—repeat do not—want to throw your rave on a night when there are two or three or more big ones.

You might resort to diplomatic prowess to convince your competition that the scene benefits from sharing the market (thus allowing you to make all the money that night). Or you can agree to copromote a single event. By slicing the pie in various sized slices, you thereby borrow their name, reputation and connections.

If you don't come to some agreement, beware. Picking the wrong date can easily escalate into a promoter's war, during which lovers and friends instantly turn into enemies. There have even been rumors of foul play in the particularly fierce L.A. promoter wars, although they have been hushed up for the good of the scene.

Once you get a name and a date, you have to print a flyer. Because this is one of your big drawing cards, spare no expense on it. You might also want to follow the trend and hand out posters and brochures in the latest Mac-generated emissions.

Whatever you produce need not say much except where and how many who's will be there. You also might want to stir the masses towards modern multi-cultural globalism by including semi-inspired spiritualisms on it.

If you're in California, you have the benefit of choosing between nine or ten established flyer designers. They produce most of the authentic rave-scene art, so they will at least insure that your flyer look authentic (always important in California).

They, like most other Mac pundits, work best with loose design parameters, so give them a creative free-for-all. In addition to talent, look for an artist with an inside line on printing, because that can save you time, money and headaches.

So the flyer can be impressive, make contact with as many rave-wear designers as you can. Offer them a short guest list in exchange for their support.

Don't worry about there not being enough of these to go around, either. Every day some entrepreneurial kid coaxes a few thousand out of his dad to start a new ravewear company. These manifestors of mass-produced originality may not be around next week but for now they are "faces," and you want as many "faces" there as possible. Of course, a movie or rock star or two won't hurt, either.

As the flyer is being designed, you can be assembling your promotional team. If you won the cooperation of other promoters, you can borrow their sub-promoters (people who promote the rave but don't have their name on the flyer). The more you get of these, the better you'll be, especially if they work for a short guest list in lieu of cash.

Give them at least two (in places like San Francisco) to four (in places like L.A.) weeks to pass out flyers. In the meantime, make sure you yourself hit all the big raves and pass out flyers yourself. Be as visible as possible. Leave stacks of them in all the "in" stores, in all the "in" spots right up to the day of the event. It creates the buzz you need.

You might want to contact the media, and tell them how massive it's going to be. The savviest promoters hold press parties the day before the event. Get MTV if you can. Use the media to manipulate the commercial plane and generate anticipation. This might turn off a few of the hardcore, but if there's nothing else going on that night, they'll come anyway.

As the excitement builds, hire the "in" contractors so you can back up all your claims. Good sound is critical, so you might hire your lower frequencies from "The Shredder." The kids will thus be able to enter into a trance, and worship a bass sound which literally pulses through each cell of their bodies. Lasers and intellebeams create the "lesser acid test" effect, as do computer animation and Madelbrot set videos. It is customary to pay these vendors up front, in cash.

(Note: In the meccas, people rent specifically for the rave market. Outside these, your best bet for both sound and lighting is a rental company specializing in theater and concert set-ups.)

Most importantly, you'll need dj's, the cyber-shamanic rock stars of tomorrow. Everyone in the scene knows who they are; some fans even collect their autographs. Try to get the best, and be prepared to be generous, as they will probably have dozens of offers on any given day.

Entice them by giving them the space to create. The best use the mood of the crowd as a kind of canvas upon which they can paint a beautiful picture of spiritual and social harmony. Some can drive the crowd into a frenzy of freedom. Sometimes you can see the Goddess Herself dancing in the bodies of those who have been set free. It is a most impressive sight.

Play into this festival atmosphere by attracting concessionaires. Get at least one "smart bar." If anything, the placebo effect will carry the crowd into the night. Let some of the small ravewear concerns set up stands. Sometimes, you can even charge them for the privilege. Finally, set up your own stand, and sell your own commemorative posters and T-shirts. Do your job right, and they'll turn up in the books that will chronicle the rave scene several years down the line.

Above all, remember that whether you're into the money, fame or social implications, your rave will affect a lot of people. A positive experience for them will mean positive results for you. Especially when it comes to your next rave which, in the best Hollywood fashion, will be the sequel.

Sounds like a conclusion. But you're right. We've forgotten to tell you about the location. Find a beat-up building, parking lot or out-of-the-way field. We're not going to say anymore on the subject. After all, you're the promoter. Act like it.

Earth Girl

This Is the Dawning

Earth Girl is one of the highest-profile personalities on the rave scene. As bartendress for cyberculture's first smart bar, she became House culture's media emblem and was featured on network news shows and books and periodicals ranging from Rolling Stone *to the* Los Angeles Times. *Beautiful, witty, outrageous, and sometimes outlandish, Earth Girl embodies the House sentiment in all its frailty, optimism, glamour, and innocence. We sent her a fax with some questions; she faxed us back with these answers.*

What is happening to the planet right now?

A Giant Globe-All Quake Up call. Change, change, change and more change. Adding up to a different sort of sense. It's a pair-O-dime shift. Healing the rift. We're breaking free from gravitease restriction. Moving from fear-filled fact to fun-filled fiction. Giving up reason for rhyme-loaded diction. History has ended our Big Time addiction. We are now experiencing The Great Galaxious Youniversall Growing Upgrade Tour de Source.

What does the generation born in the late 60's early 70's have to do with it?

We are the Children of the Evolution. Building the Future House Solution.

How is this generation different from the one before?

We're the Cabbage Patch Kids from Sesame Street living on this big Blue Marble. We went from mother's milk to moving picture elicksure. Thanks to the afterschool special our life is just a field trip. Media magic has afforded us the luxury of being aware of all inhabitants on Planet 3. Mass realization of the soul 'O' world-planet-people vibe. Connecting the dot matrix of the multi-colored rainbow love tribe. We are all the same family, phylum, class, genus, species. No longer isolated individuals on distant continents, floating anonymously through space. On this Planetary Universe-city, in our ever unique diversity, we are a race of ONE. And we've only just begun, to have sum fun.

We have House music. We have more to work with, more to sample from. More choice. More freedom. More responsibility. More knowledge, more understanding, more depth. More . . . to explore as we go through the door. We are the information saturation generation kicking off the imagination celebration of our glorious House nation.

What is the responsibility of this generation in ushering in mankind's future?

It is our full response ability to answer the phone home call to activation. It is our job to turn on our heart lights now. It is up to us to travel through the spirals of antiquity into the polished future of positivity. To part E heart E. It is our response ability to wake up, trip in and groove on into the light of tomorrowlands magical miracles of majesty. To be set free. To recognize our divinity and re-affiliate our affinity with the highest good of Planet E. We are the Map Makers. We are the Reality Creators. We are the Dreamers of the Dream. Here to receive the rainbow cotton candy kiss of transcendental bliss.

Pop culture?

Snap. Crackle. Pop goes the weasel. Fad Factor E. Everyone worships eMpTy V. Praise to the new. Wave in the stadium. Jive talking. Moon Walking. P.Y.T. Flashdancing and romancing the stoned and immaculate conception of the virgin whore mother Mary Magdalene Madonna does McDonald's. Girls just wanna have fun. Bubble fresh fantastic. Chewy pink elastic. Like candy covered plastic. Getting into the groove wishing on that lucky star to take you on a holiday somewhere far into the teen theme dream of the coked up Pepsi scene. Inquiring minds want to know. Jiffy pop in fresh dough. Add water and mix to get your fix of super lame insta-fame. We make 'em to break 'em. Glitter glitz and glam. Wham Bam. Thank you ma'am. Wonder bread and hot pink Spam. Turn off the program. Nonsense stimulation. Media manipulation. Prime timed to their function, the art of sweet seduction. Mind control and thought suction. Racial riots. Starvation diets. Gotta brain they can fry it. Go on down and try it. Buy it all now. They'll show you how. Don't you sweat it. Get it on credit. Become indebted. There is no rest in the quest for MOREGASM.

Politics?

Growing up in an ever expanding rubber banding monotonous monopoly board of dichotomy. Left vs. right. black against white. Roe vs. Wade. Made in the shade. Pie in the sky. Vote for that guy. With the teeth smiling. Money stock piling. Our Planet defiling. It's all so theoretical. It's simply Hype pathetical. Voting as a chic, trendy, turned-on, coffee crunching, out to lunching, young sophisticate motif. Suspending all belief. Hail to the chief? Good Grief! Overcoming the Great Divide and Conquer theme show, come on kids, Just Say Know.

We the people, in order out of chaos, to form a more perfect communion through the participation emancipation proclamation, establish the way forward with the everGreen party of major positive action on the Globe-All front tier.

Technology?

Nintendo. Sega. Apple. Ford. Lexus. Kinko's. Boeing on board. ATM. CNN. ATT. MTV. ABC. 123. KFC technology. Genetic engineering, corporate profiteering. Leaving behind this earthly race, blasting off into hyperspace. Giving tools a brand new face, making the world a better place. (Or, in the old way of thinking. . . . the patriarchs with something so new, can only create more violence for you.) Microwave-Techno rave. Isolation-Communication. Pacification-Elevation. Unchartered galaxies of all possible access-able imagination-all dream-E-scapes. Positively user-friendly; illuminates, educates, masturbates, hallucinates, roller skates. Laser beams and Disco dreams carry you through moonlit streams of consciousness in the whole-E-graphic house of sampled bits and bytes of tomorrow today. We live in an age of alchemy, where what you get is not what you see. Nothing is as it appears to be in this fractal based reality. Turning sand into silicon, ideas to acts, plastic to purchase, cattle to Big Macs. "Get Smart Inspector Gadget, 007's got the fax; the trance mission is clear. The future is here."

Earth Girl wishes to give "extra credit" to M.C. Love Bunny for assistin' her with this project.

URB Magazine

"I, Ambient" by Meredith Chinn and Todd C. Roberts

As rave culture progressed, so did its ambitions and 'zine production. By 1990, almost every major U.S. city had its own "rave" publication. Los Angeles based URB *magazine ("paper, ink, and soul") distinguished itself from the pack in two important ways: The magazine's editors, Raymond Leon Roker and Todd C. Roberts, chose to cover not only the mostly white, techno-acid house scene, but also the black hip-hop house movement. Even better, by combining these two camps, they were making a social statement for harmony, or "synergy," between them.*

The formula worked, and URB *has lasted into its fourth year. Entrusted with embodying the house spirit in journalistic form,* URB *manages to wed rave optimism with fairly hard journalism. Here, Todd C. Roberts and guest contributor Meredith Chinn report on the new direction for rave culture—an introspective, heady club experience called Ambient, which hopes to create a space for our increasingly frenzied global culture to chill out.*

Down a dark alley, a faceless warehouse stands alone but for a few souls fidgeting in the San Francisco cold. A faint thump rolls along the concrete walls. Inside through a long hallway, colored lights and projections fill the walls. The music is charged with the funky bells of disco and house. Only a smattering of dancers populate the area near the DJ, more fill the small room at the back glowing with candles and lit cigarettes. Beyond is a slow rumble of bass.

Downstairs through the black curtain strewn over the narrow, rickety staircase, the rumble thickens. Descending the stairs, the bass builds and at the bottom the bass echoes out, phasing into the slow moan of deeply-layered dub. The DJ nods in time to the slow dub, his face is only lit by a small row of candles and burning incense. A mass audience fills the floor atop bean bags and pillows, squatted in corners, resting against the walls. Small groups of beaded imitation B-boys wander through the spaces between—they groove unconsciously to the bubbles of sound. Baggy be-decked hippies roam looking for a good seat.

On the floor, a liquid chrome voice floats in amongst the violins. "Space out," it says in the tiniest of voices, echoes and then repeats. I close my eyes and breathe deeply, the sound of waterfall cascade over me. A lush roar of jungle noises pans into frame; the giggle of exotic birds and creatures. Water drips from the thick foliage. Butterflies the size of birds wander by amidst the deep green backdrop. If I weren't awake I'd think I was dreaming. As I look around the rest of the room, eyes gaze intently on the ambient shaman. A phasing whale noise crashes through the air fading slowly into an echoed vocal fragment which transforms into a baby's cry. It's a complex and powerful force—the audience is listening.

Trying to describe "ambient" is like describing a marshmallow to someone who has never seen or eaten one. The task then of defining ambient music is a difficult one—and without limits, probably suicidal. Webster's Dictionary defines the word "ambient" as: that which encompasses on all sides; surrounding; encircling. The prefix "ambi" comes from the Latin *ambo*, meaning a combining or both, (as in ambidextrous). Then ambient is the harmonizing of disparately separate entities—the blending of different sounds to create one. Ambient culture is the synthesis of one from many. Ambience is a consonance of life's noise—an accord between the ego and the psyche. A symbiotic resonance of spirit. Sounds a bit "Zen" like inner peace bullshit, but the point of ambient may be simply for its own sake.

Ambient music is all musics. Ever since cavemen began banging on rocks or the church music of the 14th century, music was a device of wordless communication. Mozart tried to translate humor through his Opera Buffa and Gustav Mahler emulated the color of trees through his composition.. Throughout the ages composers have worked to create music that evokes life and nature. French composer Eric Satie, in 1889, started the idea of "furniture music" with his "Trois Gymnopedies," three classical piano pieces that are commercially used, and almost over-used, by TV and commercial producers to instantly evoke the appropriate mood of a situation with its unlimited tonal color. It's through Satie's free compositional style that modern ambient music was realized. It was also through his ideas that ambient's impetus was formed. His gospel was: music is art. Since then, ambient music has gone through different seasonal changes with the advent of prog-rock, techno, various types of experimental, and progressive house, etc. Ambient music's omnipresence is found in the various compartments of established pop culture.

Modern ambient sound is a culmination of technology and spiritual upheaval. The psychedelia and enhanced awareness of the '60s and early '70s fuse with the technology and digitalization of today's young primitives. Relaxed Hip-hop beats, perhaps an ode to the ambient music's cultural weaving, create the backbone for many tracks. Along with the infectious 808 drum, echoing reggae dub melodies build a tonal texture while sampled operatic voices and the natural fabric of jungle and aquatic sounds float in via audible crevices.

The name that eventually arrives into every discussion of ambient is Brian Eno. No doubt, who some people dub the creator of modern electronic music, was responsible for the focus of early experimental ambient work on albums like *Before and After Science, Music for Airports* and various collaborations with his brother Roger, pianist Harold Budd and David Byrne. His stark, minimalistic style was initially considered part of the avant-garde art scene but eventually landed him a "new age" title though his work continued to be more challenging than most of the genre. Eno's work continues to be a huge influence for a large component of modern ambient music.

The '70s was amassed by pioneers of the synthesizer, Tangerine Dream, creating melodic music with subtle percussion to be used on film-soundtracks and mood music. With the arrival of the '80s, the ambient genre becomes troublesome. Some arrived under the auspices of what now seems more like bad art-rock or minimalist avant garde. Groups like Gong fronted by guitarist Steve Hillage were deemed sedentary—stuck in the hippy ethics of psychedelic rock. Though his past has been exonerated by his recruitment of various techno/house musicians like The Orb's Alex Patterson and

Youth, the group at that time went largely criticized or ignored. Other ambient types took the form of "new age"—a stain on the fabric of ambient's neat fabric. It had gone pop. Playing to a generation of listeners ready to retire to the armchair, Andreas Vollenvieder and Vangelis both had successful "conceptual" careers in the "new age" genre. Since then, the bulk of music created has ended up in the trade-in bins and swap meets everywhere.

Two years ago, KLF released *Last Train to Trancentral*, the first of many ambient albums to be distributed on a major domestic label but was largely ignored beyond the quirkier dance tracks like "Justified and Ancient." Around the same time, The Orb released their domestic *Adventures Beyond the Ultraworld*, a grab bag of dub-laden ambient dance music. With their head games of sound and silence, techno would never be the same. Meat Beat Manifesto broke ranks from their hardcore industrial scene to create tracks like "Pot Sounds" that saw them in a new ambient light. Last year, Ultramarine released *Everyman and Woman is a Star* and the subsequent EP *Nightfall in Sweetleaf* redefining the ambient dance music genre with lots of folk influenced rock. This year the flavor is decidedly dub. Bottom heavy tunes with a rootsy influence, the steady roll of reggae bass and head-nodding percussion. Groups like Original Rockers, One Dove and Voices of Kwan have set the stage for a new phase of music called ambient dub.

Dub was the natural mate to electronic atmospheres (see next page). Originally used for the instrumental of vocal tracks to be used live, dub techniques, found in most of ambient's catalog, revolutionized the mixing of multiple track recordings worldwide. The heavy use of echo and reverb took reggae to a new landscape—outer space. Engineers like King Tubby and Lee "Scratch" Perry took risks with early "version," dropping drum or guitar tracks from the mix, slipping in vocal bites and adding echo only to phase the tracks selectively back in. Dub is the psychedelic side of reggae. As Luke Ehrlich writes in *Reggae International*, "If reggae is Africa in the New World, dub must be Africa on the moon; it's the psychedelic music I expected to hear in the '60s and didn't." Much like ambient, dub uses each instrumental track as raw element combining them in an artist embrace of vast space and sound. The greatest thing ambient shares with dub is it's love of experimentation that in turn effects its capacity for change.

The growth and popularity of ambient during '93 has been staggering.

The number of compilations and new signings has brought about the current need for discussion. Most musicians and DJs see it as a logical step in its maturation. The ambient phase of techno is more accessible than its hardcore cousin. Now the audience includes the scope from Rastas to new age hippies. Ambient can contain all of the influences that exist in our brain's sound palette, more than sometimes imaginable. The strength of the ambient palette is that it can hold many different sounds and still make sense. Groups like Irresistible Force, the Rising High Collective and William Orbit have been known to envelope a wide array of sounds and textures. Future Sound of London with its anthem "Papua New Ginea" involved for the first time in modern music the aboriginal didjerido as well as a 14th century choral singer. English artist Electra's "Destiny" includes a Pink Floyd sample. Ambient Dream's "Shine On You Crazy Diamond" simply remade the Floyd classic of the same name, beginning with a slow swirling synth worked into a guitar track that takes off into a rocketing solo. A big favorite of ambient experts is "O Je Suis Seul" by the West India Co. (remixed by the Orb and Sabre's of Paradise's Andy Weatherall), which includes a subtle Indian feel with a muted Indian female singer. Ambient, similar to traditional techno, takes chances at every turn.

Kim Cascone, producer for San Francisco's Silent Records offers that ambient music is "atmospheric music with balls, with an attitude. It has an edge." He goes on to describe the departure it has taken from background music—"Muzak"—and the realization it's taken from popular music. It serves a purpose for the new edge. Recently, a new generation has found a niche in applying different influences to what's been called everything from "new electronic music" to "armchair techno." It applies the same faceless delivery that most dance musics possess yet with a departure into quietude. Ambient, like its cousin techno, takes on popular culture with its DIY attitude—it's a bedroom DJ sport. It reinvents itself at every turn. Although, sometimes it works and other times it falls into background music mode—a long track of boring, uninspired noise.

A bit nebulous by definition, ambient is like a wet ball of gum, picking up whatever it comes in contact with, taking a new shape with each move. With the arrival of sampling and digital simulation, ambient has been built largely by technology. Yet, modern ambient music has increasingly embraced the sounds of other primitive cultures. Nick Phillip of San

Francisco's Chill Core Collective believes that "technology affects consciousness." Nick is responsible for various "ambient parties" throughout California, travelling as a DJ and promoter of the culture. A firm believer in the power of ambient culture, he says that with technology we are able to reprogram sensibilities in our awareness. There is a dissolution of boundaries, of cultural differences. He uses the idea of the ambient chill-out room, a side room for dancers to relax, socialize and come down, as an example. He says it reflects what is happening in society today. "Its like a micro of that macro. The boundaries are blurred—between people, between songs. In that setting all our reference points are gone." This is the reason, he says, for the increased attention to ancient or primitive cultures. "We're looking back to the ancients, to primitive civilizations for information. Modern culture is rediscovering what primitive culture already knew. Gaian, or pagan beliefs are becoming more important."

Ambient music's ability to transfer information to large audiences may be its greatest strength. Like most music, ambient is communication in layers—melody, concept and language. Nick likens it to computer-based communication. "Ambient is like 16-bit music," translating a variety of information. He says, "Madonna would be considered 4-bit (a narrow band width of information being transmitted). Ambient music transmits on a lot of deeper levels. It transmits experience, feelings and intentions." The depth of the music is defined by the performer, or the programmer in this case.

Other DJs and musicians believe in the power of ambient is its essence—nature. Largely the sample list or chart of influences for most ambient music, from Eno to know, would stem from sounds found in nature. Either through culmination of life's accidents or through computerized simulation, the backdrop to the sparse tones of ambient are splashes of rainforests, rain, whales, waterfalls and bird cadences. Cascone says, "Ambient music was created by the ocean." Adam Douglas of Earth Rise defines ambient music as a constant. "Birds, winds, cars, people—a rhythm of random, natural sounds perpetually performed: the concert of life," read the liner notes of his *Deeper Than Space* album. The intervention of technology is only an afterthought. "It's a human response to nature, like remixing nature," says Charlie, and ambient DJ and designer for San Francisco based clothing and consciousness company Anarchic Adjustment.

However, Ambient has as much to do with silence as it does with sound. The delays between heartbeats are as much part of the organism as the pulse. It is a balance between the two. Ambient music is surrounded by the potential for sound as well as the absence of sound. In fact, sometimes ambience is the space between sounds. Ambient may come to be the bridge between musical movements we are traversing today. The silence may be where the element is void—inside that tiny gap is the reason for existence—when the machine shuts off. For purists, percussion is meaningless and vocals are dubious. Is it ambient or is it techno. The fine line is blurred by the lack of any real definition of ambient.

Many acts create ambient music that in any other context would be considered just dance music. Techno has driven a large part of the attention to the new form of electronic music. Yet the antagonism is present in the continually dividing scope of this music. Some techno purists see it as boring and slow, others simply see it as a reaction for those who can't keep up. Ambient fans and DJs are adamant about ambient's ability to push the envelope, travel new territory. Mike Barnett of Beyond Records, the label that produced the three classic Ambient Dub compilations, proudly responds, "We're on a mission to kill swing beat."

Sven Vath and Matthias Gruen of Germany's Recycle or Die records regard both techno and ambient very closely. They refer to ambient and techno, as the New Electronic Music. They believe it to be autonomous from culture's contextual restraints. "It's the first music that doesn't primarily react on what society's doing," they say. "Of course, it's a result of society's development, but New Electronic Music does not want to change anything on a public level. It's the singular person this music wants to reach."

Still, with ambient the individual occasionally seems to be the missing component. But as Eno states in a recent issue of England's *I-D* magazine, People are an integral part of the ambient process. He tries to reach "an ethereal network of people trying to connect the edges of our culture with science, philosophy and thinking in general." Though machines make the sounds available, it is the organization of those sounds that create the landscape. Ambient is about shaping the future with human hands. As Pete Namlook DJ/musician on England's Fax records relates, "ambient music is the sound of one man's soul talking to another man's soul." It's the transfer of unquantified emotion and intention.

Chill-out rooms have provided the context for ambient music among the niche of rave culture. They sprang up in response to the energy expelled from raving and drug use. Alex Patterson of The Orb has been documented as one of the true pioneers in the chill room timeline. Over two years ago, pre-Orb, one could find Alex in the small room, upstairs at a popular London club called Heaven. Serving as the ambient compliment to DJ Paul Oakenfold's mainroom madness, after a short stint, Alex Patterson's idea became an intense alternative to dancing. The music of Mr. Eno was always squeezed in at least a dozen times during Patterson's sheaths of sound patterns with current ambient dance tracks, and different part of songs that together knitted a warm scarf for the chilly clubbers. Patterson's sonic ability to produce the awe-inspiring force of four different DJs at once, it's no surprise that he's where he is today. And the ambient scene as it is today, couldn't have progressed as rapidly without Alex.

Chill out rooms may be the place where the individual comes in. "People really needed it because it could get so intense in the other room," Jonah Sharp of San Francisco based Space Time Continuum explains. Clubs started to hire ambient music DJs to soothe the sweaty dancers' minds and give their feet a rest. "It's a place where people communicate orally, not just physically by dancing; the music in those rooms are not just about whale noises, it's about an awareness of style with no rules attached. As Charlie Ambiento says, "It's not about keeping time, it's about being aware."

Ambient music tends to fall into a psychedelic framework—alluding to the spacey, hallucinogenic qualities of being stoned or under the influence of drugs. The music lends itself to this categorization through various techniques like echo and reverb. The deep meditative tones simulate the anodyne qualities of most popular drugs. However, according to most fans of ambient music, drug use is a personal choice. And for those involved with this kind of music that don't delve into drugs, they probably become tiresome of the stereotyping. Justin Fletcher from the U.S. based group Seefeel speaks for the band on the subject of drugs, "None of the band regularly takes drugs. The music is not a result of drugs. When we're in the studio we don't take any drugs whatsoever. We keep our music clean. Like our veins."

Others, like Charlie Ambiento claim drugs to be part of the inspiration of their music. Charlie says of ambient techno, "It's like trying to recreate the sounds you hear on DMT." He sees ambient music as the simulation of what it is to be high. He equates the psychological effects with those attributed to mushrooms, peyote and LSD." Ambient music is a trans-sensory experience, teaching us to see without ears, listen with our heart and feel with our minds." Still many more believe that the question is irrelevant. Drugs are not an essential part of the ambient experience but rather spirituality provides the euphoria. Kim Cascone says that ambient is about the awareness of sound. "Anywhere in the world you have spiritual awareness, you have awareness of sound," he says. He goes on to tell me about Gil, a friend who is an ambient DJ in Goa, India, sort of the mecca for ambient chill out sessions (3-30 days). The land itself relates back to the sufis and whirling dervishes that were very aware of sound in their religious pursuits. Still, Kim believes that in reality drugs are an impetus for the genesis of chill out rooms. He says, "In chill rooms, they play music in a womb-like environment, to bring people down to normal heart rate and breathing patterns."

According to Nick from C3, "Ambient music is more spiritual than drugs, which by that definition is a bit hedonistic. The music sort of takes you to those levels, beyond the body." Although drugs can not be denied as a force in today's ambient scene, the musical allusions to drug use is tenuous. "Its the metaphor not the actual place; the map not the territory." Still, the greatest revelation this generation has made through ambient is the possibilities of the future and of space travel. The space between your ears. Like the '60s generation, the new edge has embraced the cognitive frontier of psychedelia and a new culture of communal thought and harmony. "The rave scene has this underpinning of a generation raised by hippies," says Cascone. He believes that the music, the context and the attitude have grown into a culture. DJ Simon of Effective records agrees, "Quality and care is essential. Ambient music is for the mind and spirit."

The general consensus for all ambient DJs is that there are no rules. Charlie from Anarchic and Jonah Sharp of Space Time Continuum are both part of the growing ambient scene in San Francisco, as DJs and promoters. "Ambient sound gardeners" are the door keepers to the ambient experience. However, the normal limits of dance music are gone. As a DJ, Nick doesn't follow the traditional methods of dance music. "I don't play much dance music anymore, in fact, practically none. It offers sort of a rigid structure for playing music with the narrow slipstream of beats. Ambient music opens many more possibilities."

Now with the rapid growth technology, things such as virtual reality, mind machines, CD-ROM, home-recording CD players, and all the interactive gidgets and gadgets that are making their way into the market, electronic music will potentially gain from the new mediums. Greg Scanavino, the Young American Primitive, thinks that the advancement of technology will help promote our ambient future. "Technology advancement will only help promote electronic music, and give it a positive means to develop."

As the attention to ambient electronic music continues to grow here in the U.S. there are already changes in the definition of the sound. Various groups have been dubbed next year's "post-ambient" sound in the U.K. As the revolution just begins for American audiences, the *evolution* keeps rolling. The amount of music available now is undeniably large. With releases out in multitudes, a revival of sorts is happening in attitude and spirit among the ranks of ravers and every other imaginable lifestyle. New agers, rockers, house-head and even hip-hoppers have found something appealing about the ambient genre. The potential for a large audience with ambient is limitless. As Nick from C3 says, "That's the great thing about ambient; the doors are wide open."

The Night Before Jesus Woke up

A Transmission from 3393

The computer networks, in addition to carrying E-mail, permitting confer-encing, and allowing document retrieval, serve as a conduit for what might best be described as digital graffiti. Like a message in a bottle, this particular transmission appeared on bulletin boards and mail servers in key locations throughout the Internet. The author, who identifies himself with a numerological sequence connoting transformational energy, relates his experience of a rave from a Judeo-Christian–hip-hop perspective. Good luck.

It wasn't the biggest rave I'd been to. But what it lacked in size it more than made up for in other ways. Not that it wasn't big. It was. It was cleanly massive. Not the messy massive that had been on at other raves. A big clean space (a shrine of sorts) with big clean security, big clean promoters, big clean Dj's, concessions, atmosphere, little girl ravers, little boy ravers, little alien ravers. The vibe was right for everyone. All the dudes were hard but down for unity that night. The spirit of the event had captured them with love. All the chicks were down with the Mother that night. Mini goddesses all and they were working it (the dudes were lovin' it). It was a massive mind orgy, a huge love quake measuring 9.3. All those children were one with the Earth but reaching for the stars. It was if they were pulling the whole planet out into the Milky Way (or at least to the Moon). The comfort-ably frenzied dancing went on to the end, and then we went on our ways, all of our ways.

And in the morning at dawn, Jesus woke up. The dude had been dead for

THREE days. Went and got hisself killed on Good Friday. Seems more like 2000 years to me but it was actually THREE days. And when he woke up it was if he had never ever left. And the reason I know that is cause Jesus is DOWN. You know what I'm saying, Jesus is DOWN.

Jesus is down with everything. Jesus is down with a Sunday morning drive down the coast highway. He's down with Del Taco breakfast burritos. He's down with Macintosh and he's down with IBM. He's down with deep and he's down with techno. He's down with peace and he's down with love.

And LA became the blessed place that it really is deep down underneath all the wonderfully treacherous commerciality. Mother Maya's Magical Mansion of Mad, Manic Mirth. And Jesus and I started talkin 'bout how crazy our Mother was. How she just gets herself into the most convoluted, tweaky contortions that a mind can (can't) even fathom. Neither of us can understand her. We both agreed to that and we both agreed that we should never even try.

But Jesus said to me that you always got to accept her. And I already knew that cuz I read it in the yoga books. But my heart wasn't ever really, really in to it. Not until I heard it from Jesus. When he told me it made sense. And I knew he was right cuz Jesus is down with everything that's up.

Suddenly everything was OK. Jesus just woke up. The light was on. Jesus said don't worry cuz he was down with the raves. He was quite the hardcore raver in his day. Wouldn't have it any other way. Dudes in power put him on trial for it. Maybe dudes in power gonna put us on trial for it. Don't know about that but if it does happen we just gotta do what Jesus did, be ourselves and stand up for our hearts.

And Jesus told me not to worry, cuz it was our crazy Mother doin' the whole thing for her pleasure anyway. It was her trip and there weren't nobody gonna take it away from her. And this I thought I knew as well, only this time I felt it good.

So there you have it. Jesus is awake in LA. I don't think he'll be goin anywhere. He's still got a lot of work to do bein down with everything that's up. And I know that things are gonna get good. Good and crazy. A little healthy madness for the masses. Bout time they got to know their Mother.

Probability
Pipeline

Marc Laidlaw
and Rudy Rucker

Marc Laidlaw, author of Dad's Nuke *and* Neon Lotus, *collaborated with cyberpunk theorist Rudy Rucker, author of* Software *and* Wetware, *for this rip-roaring surf adventure into hyperspace. No matter how scientifically complex or physically dangerous things get, the characters maintain a perfectly relaxed slacker mind-set. This story demonstrates the cyberlit genre at its best and depicts in its characters the kinds of quirks and qualities GenX reveres.*

The trouble started in Surf City, and it ended in another dimension.

Delbert was loud and spidery, Zep was tall and absent and a year older. Being in different grades, they didn't see each other much in the winters, but in the summers they were best friends on and off the beach. When Zep graduated, he spent a year at UC Santa Cruz before drugging out—he said he'd overfed his head. Delbert didn't like drugs, so when he graduated he didn't bother going to college at all. Now it was summer all year long.

It was November in Surf City and the pipeline was coming in steady. For the last few weeks they'd been without a surfboard, though these days the word was *stick*, not *board*, meaning Del and Zep were stickless. The way this particular bummer had come down was that Del had been bragging about his escape from a great white shark, and no one had believed him, so maximum Zep had cut a big shark-bite shape out of the dinged longboard he and Delbert shared, and still no one had believed. Basically Zep had thrashed the board for nothing, but at least Delbert was able to sell it to the Pup-Tent, a surfer snack shop where his girl Jen worked—not that Jen was really Delbert's *girl* in any intense physical sense of the word, and not that the Pup-Tent had actually *paid* anything for the shark-bit board that Delbert had mounted on the wall over the cash register. But it looked rad up there.

Often, in the mid-morning, when things were slow at the Pup-Tent, Jen would grill Zep and Delbert some burgers, and the three of them would sit on the bench out in front of the Pup-Tent, staring through their shades at the bright, perfect sky, or at the cars and people going by, or across the street at the cliffs and the beach and the endlessly various Pacific ocean, dotted with wet-suited surfers. Zep sat on the left, Jen on the right, and Delbert in the middle; Delbert usually talking, either rapping off what he saw or telling one of his long, bogus stories, like about the time when he'd been flying a kite on the beach and a Coast Guard plane had swooped down low enough to suck his kite into its jet and he'd been pulled out to sea about half a mile, dangling twenty feet above the water until he'd flashed to let loose of the string.

One particular day that November, Delbert was telling Jen about a book on hypnotism he'd read the day before, and how last night he'd tried to activate Zep's thrashed genius by putting Zep in a trance and telling him he was a great scientist and asking him to invent invisibility.

"He did that, Zep?" asked Jen, briefly interested. "Did it work?"

"I, uh, I . . . thought of peroxide," said Zep. Peroxide was a big thing with Zep; he'd stripped his hair so often that its color was faintly ultraviolet. When Zep felt like somebody might understand him, he'd talk a lot about the weird science stuff he'd learned at Santa Cruz, but just now he wasn't quite on.

"We put seven coats of it on a sheet of paper," said Delbert, "and for a second we thought it was working, but it was really just the paper falling apart."

"Oxo wow," said Jen, suddenly pointing out at the horizon. "Outsider." That was the traditional word for a big wave. "Far outsider . . . and ohmigod! . . . like . . ." Jen often ended her sentences that way, with a "like" and a gesture. This time it was her Vanna White move: both hands held out to the left side of her body, left hand high and right hand low, both hands palms up. She was watching one of the Stoke Pilgrims out there carve the outsider.

It was Lex Loach—Delbert could recognize him from the red-and-white checkerboard pattern on his wet suit. Loach executed a last nifty vertical snap, shot up off the face of the ripped outsider, and flew through the air, his wing squash turbo board glued to his feet by the suction cups on his neo-prene booties.

Jen sighed and slowly turned her hands palms down. The Vanna White move, if done with the hands palms down, was known as Egyptian Style. Jen gave Delbert a sarcastic little neck-chop with her stiff left hand. "I wish you could ride, Delbert. I wish you had a stick."

"This surf's mush, Jen. Dig it, I saw a tidal wave when I was a kid. I was with my dad on Hawaii, and this volcano blew up, and the next minute all the water went out to sea and formed a gigantic—" He held out his arms as if to embrace a weather balloon.

"You saw that in a movie," said Zep.

"Did not!" yelled Delbert. He was always yelling, and consequently he was always hoarse.

"Yo, dude. *Krakatoa East of Java.*"

"I never saw that movie, it really happened! We got stranded on the edge of the volcano and they had to come get us in a hot air balloon. Listen up, dude, my dad—"

Delbert jabbered on, trying to distract Jen from Lex Loach's awesomely stoked breakouts. By the time a customer showed up, she seemed glad to go inside.

"Do you think she likes me?" Delbert asked Zep.

"No. You should have gone to college." Zep's voice was slow and even.

"What about you, brain-death?" challenged Del.

"I'm doing my detox, dude." Zep got a tense, distant look when people questioned his sanity. But his voice stayed calm and disengaged. "The pro-grams are in place, dude. All I need is run time. Chaos, fractals, dynamics, cellular automata. I did ten years' research in two weeks last spring, dude. It's just a matter of working out the applications."

"Like to what?"

"You name it, bro."

"Waves," said Del. "Surfing. The new stick I need to bang Jen."

Zep stared out at the horizon so long that Delbert thought he was lost in a flashback. But suddenly Zep's voice was running tight and fast.

"Dig it, Del, I'm not going to say this twice. The ocean is a chaotic dy-namical system with sensitive dependence on initial conditions. Macro info keeps being folded in while micro info keeps being excavated. In terms of the phase-space, it works by a kneading process, continually doubling the size of a region and folding it over on itself like saltwater taffy with the ribbony layers of color all shot through. Big waves disappear in the chop and the right small ripple can amp on up to make an outsider. If you do the right thing to the ocean, it'll do whatever you want back. The thing about a chaotic system is that the slightest change in initial conditions produces a big effect—and I mean right away. Like on a pool table, dude, after ten bounces the position of the ball has been affected by the gravity from a pebble in a ring of Saturn. There's a whole space of dynamic states, and the places where the system settles down are called chaotic attractors. We do right, and the ocean'll do right by us."

Del was like: "Chaos attractor? How do we control it?"

"There's no formula because the computation is irreducibly complex. The only way to predict the ocean is to simulate it faster than real-time. Could be done on a gigahertz CA. By the right head. The ocean ... Delbert, the ocean's state is a point in ten-trillion-dimensional surfspace."

"Surfspace?" Delbert grinned over at his long blond friend with the dark, wandering eyes. When Zep got into one of his head trips he tended to let his cool, slow surfer pose slide. He'd been a punk before a surfer, and a science nerd before that.

"You gotta relate, babe," enunciated Zep, as he tore on into the rest of his riff. "The wave pattern at any time is a fractal. Waves upon waves upon waves. Like a mountain range, and an ant thinks he's at the top of a hill, but he's only at the top of a bump on rock on an outcrop on a peak on the range on the planet. And there's a cracky crack between his six legs. For our present purposes, it's probably enough to take ten levels of waves into account."

"Ten levels of waves?"

"Sure man, like put your nose near the water and there's shivers on the ripples. The shivers have got kind of sketchy foam on them too. So sketchy foam, shivers, ripples, wads, and slidy sheets, now we bet getting some meat to carve, uh, actual waves, peaks—those choppy peaks that look like Mr. Frostee's head, you wave—steamers and hollow surf, mongo mothers, outsiders and number ten the tide. So the wave pattern at any given spot is a ten-dimensional quality, and the wave patterns at a trillion different spots make a point in ten-trillion-dimensional surfspace."

"What's all the trillions for?" Out on the sea, Lex Loach and four other Stoke Pilgrims were riding in from the break. Loach, Mr. Scrote, Shrimp Chips, Squid Puppy, and Floathead, same as usual. They usually came up to the Pup-Tent for lunch. Delbert and Zep usually left before the Pilgrims got there. "Talk faster, Zep."

"I'm telling you, dude. Say I'm interested in predicting or influencing the waves over the next few minutes. Waves don't move all that fast, so anything that can influence the surf here in the next few minutes is going to depend on the surfspace values within a neighboring area of, say, one square kilometer. I'm only going to fine-grain down to the millimeter level, you wave, so we're looking at, uh, one trillion sample points. Million squared. Don't interrupt again, Delbert, or I won't build you the chaotic attractor."

"You're going to build me a new stick?"

"I got the idea when you hypnotized me last night. Only I'd forgotten till just now. Ten fractal surf levels at a trillion sample points. We model that with an imipolex CA, we use a nerve-patch modem outset unit to send the rider's surfest desires down a co-ax inside the leash, the CA does a chaotic back simulation of the fractal inset, the board does a jiggly doo, and . . ."

"TSUUUNAMIIIIII!" screamed Delbert, leaping up on the bench and striking a boss surfer pose.

Just then Lex Loach and the Stoke Pilgrims appeared, up from the beach. Lex looked at Delbert with the usual contempt. "*Ride* that bench, gnarly geek. Been puffing some of Zep's KJ?"

Lex Loach had been boss of Surf City as long as Delbert could remember. He lived here all year long, except when he went to snow-board at Big Bear in short pants and no shirt. Delbert thought he looked like a carrot. He was tall and thin like a carrot, narrow at the bottom and very wide at the shoulders; and like a carrot, his torso was ribbed and downy.

Loach's aging sidekick, Mr. Scrote, darted forward and made a vicious grab for Delbert's balls. Mr. Scrote was wrinkled and mean. He had bloodshot eyes and was half deaf from surfer's ear, and all his jokes had to do with genital pain. Delbert fended him off with a kick that missed. "Couldn't help myself," said Mr. Scrote to the other Pilgrims as he danced back out of reach. "Dude looks soooo killer on his new stick."

"I *am* getting a new stick," cried Delbert furiously. "Chaos Attractor. Zep's building it."

"What does a junkie know about surf?" put in Shrimp Chips, a burly young guy with bleached hair. "Zep can't even stand to take a bath."

"Zep's clean," said Delbert loyally. "And he knows all about surf just from sitting here and watching."

"Same way you know about girls, right, weenie?" said Loach. "Want to watch me and Jen get it on?"

Delbert leaped off the bench and butted his head right into the middle of that carroty washboard of an abdomen. Loach fell over backward, and suddenly there were kids everywhere, screaming, "It's a fight!"

Zep pulled Delbert back before Loach could pulverize him. The Stoke Pilgrims lined up around their chief carrot, ready to charge.

"Wait a minute," Delbert yelped, holding out his hand. "Let's handle this like real men. Lex, we challenge you to a duel. Zep'll have my new gun ready by tomorrow. If you and your boys can close us out, it's yours. And if we win, you give me your wing squash turbo."

Loach shook his head and Mr. Scrote spoke up for him, widening his bloodshot eyes. "I doubt Lex'd want any piece of trash you'd ride. No, Delbert, if you lose, you suck a sea anemone and tell Jen you're a fag." The Stoke Pilgrims' laughter was like the barking of seals. Delbert's tongue prickled.

"Tomorrow by the San Diablo N-plant where the surf's the gnarliest," said Lex Loach, heading into the Pup-Tent. "Slack tide, dudes. Be there or we'll find you."

Up on the cliff, the N-plant looked like a gray golf ball sinking into a sand trap. The cliff was overgrown with yellow ice plant whose succulent, radiation-warmed leaves were fat as drowned men's fingers. A colonic loop of cooling pipe jagged down the cliff, out into the sea, and back up the cliff to the reactor. The beach was littered with fish killed by the reactor's thermal pollution. Closer to the sea, the tide's full moon low had exposed great beds of oversize sea anemones that were bright, mutated warm-water sports. Having your face pushed into one of them would be no joke.

"Trust me, bro," said Zep. He was greasy and jittery. "You'll sluice roosters in Loach's face. No prob. And after this we stalk the big tournament moola."

"The surf is mush, Zep. I know it's a drag, bro, but be objective. Look the hell at the zon." The horizon was indeed flat. Closer to shore were long rows of small, parallel lines where the dead sea's ripples came limping in. Delbert was secretly glad that the contest might well be called off.

"No way," shouted Zep, angrily brandishing the nylon case that held the new board. "All you gotta do is plug in your leash and put Chaos Attractor in the water. The surf will definitely rise, little dude."

"It's mush."

"Only because *you* are. Dig it!" Zep grabbed his friend by the front of his brand-new paisley wet suit and shook him. "You haven't looked at my new stick!" Zep dropped to his knees and unzipped Chaos Attractor's case. He drew out a long, grayish, misshapen board. Most of it seemed actually transparent, though there were some dark, right-angled shapes embedded in the thing's center.

Delbert jerked back in horror. For this he'd given Zep two hundred dollars? All his savings for what looked like a dime-store Styrofoam toy surfboard that a slushed druggie had doused in epoxy?

"It . . . it's transparent?" said Delbert after a time. In the dull day's light you could see Zep's scalp through his no-color hair. Del had trusted Zep and Zep had blown it. It was sad.

"Does that embarrass you?" snarled Zep, sensing Delbert's pity. "Is there something wrong with transparency? And screw your two hundred bucks cause this stick didn't cost me nothing. I spent your money on crank, mofo, on clean Hell's Angels blow. What else, Delbert, who do you think I am? Yeah! Touch the board!"

Delbert stroked the surface of the board uncertainly. "It's rough," he said finally.

"Yeah!" Zep wanted to get the whole story out, how he'd immediately spent the money on crank, and how then in the first comedown's guilt he'd laid meth on Cowboy Bob, a dope-starved biker who hung around the meth dealer's. Zep had fed Cowboy Bob's head so Bob'd take him out breaking and entering: First they hit the KZ Kustom Zurf-Shop for a primo transparent surfboard blank, then they barreled Bob's chopped hog up to Oakland to liberate imipolex from the I.G. Farben research labs in the wake of a diversionary firebomb, and then they'd done the rest of the speed and shot over the Bay Bridge to dynamite open the door of System Concepts and score a Cellular Automaton Machine, the CAM8, right, and by 3:00 A.M. Zep had scored the goods and spent the rest of the night wiring the CAM board into the imipolex-wrapped blank's honeyheart with tiny wires connecting to the stick's surface all over, and then finally at dawn Zep had gone in through the back window of a butcher shop and wedged the board into the huge vacuum meat packer there to vacuum-sputter the new stick's finish up into as weird a fractal as a snowflake Koch curve or a rucked Sierpinski carpet. And now lame little Delbert is all worried and:

"Why's it so rough?"

Zep took a deep breath and concentrated on slowing down his heartbeat. Another breath. "This stick, Del, it uses its fractal surface for a real time surfspace simulation. The board's surface is a fractal CA model of the sea, you wave?"

"Zep, what's that gray thing in the middle like a shark's skeleton? Loach is going to laugh at us."

"Shut up about Loach," snarled Zep, losing all patience once again. "Lex Loach is like a poisonous mutant warty sculpin choked by a plastic tampon insert at the mouth of an offshore toxic-waste pipe, man, thrashing around and stinging everybody in his spastic nowhere death throes."

"He's standing right behind you."

Zep spun around and saw that Delbert was more or less correct, given his tendency toward exaggeration. Loach was striding down the beach toward them, along with the four other Stoke Pilgrims. They were carrying lean, tapering sticks with sharp noses and foiled rails. Loach and Mr. Scrote wore lurid wet suits. The younger three had painted their bodies with Day-Glo thermopaints.

"Gonna shred you suckers!" yelled Loach.

"Stupid clones!" whooped Zep, lifting Chaos Attractor high overhead. "Freestyle rules!"

"What kind of weird joke is this?" asked Loach, eyeing the new stick.

"Care to try it out?"

"Maybe. I'm gonna win it anyway, right?"

Zep nodded, calm and scientistlike now that the action had finally begun. It was good to have real flesh-and-blood enemies to deal with. "Let me show you where to plug it in. This might sting a bit at first."

He knelt down and began to brush sand from Loach's ankle.

"What're you doing?" Loach asked, jumping back when he saw Zep coming at him with a wire terminating in sharp pins.

"You need this special leash to ride the board," Zep said. "Without human input, the board would go out of control. The thing is, the fractal surface writhes in a data-simulation altered by the leash input. These fang things are a parallel nerve-port, wave? It feeds into the CAM8 along with the fractal wave analyses, so the board knows what to do."

Mr. Scrote gave Zep a sharp kick in the ribs. "You're gonna stick that thing in his ankle, you junkie, and give him AIDS?"

Zep bared his teeth in a confused grin. "Just hold still, Lex. It doesn't hurt. I'd like to see what you can do with it."

Loach stepped well back. "You're whacked, dude. You been over the falls one too many times. Your brain is whitewater. Yo, Delbert! See you out at the break. It's flat now, but there'll be peaks once the tide starts in—believe it!" Loach and the Stoke Pilgrims hit the mushy warm water and began paddling out.

Zep was still crouched over Chaos Attractor. He glanced slyly up at Delbert. "You ready?"

"No."

"Look, Del, you and my stick have to go out there and show the guys how to carve."

"No way."

"Get rad. Be an adventurist. You'll be part of the system, man. Don't you remember how I explained about waves?"

"I don't care about waves," said little Delbert. "I want to go home. It's stupid to think I would ever be a major surfer. Who talked me into this anyway? Was it you?"

Zep stared out at the zon. Loach and the Stoke Pilgrims were bobbing on the mucky water, waiting for a set. Suddenly he frowned. "You know, Del, maybe it's not such a great idea for you to use this board."

"What do you mean? It's my stick isn't it? I gave you two hundred dollars."

"You still don't have the big picture. At any moment, the relevant sea-configuration is ten trillion bits of analog info, right? Which folds up to one point in the ten-trillion-dimensional surfspace. As the ocean dynamically evolves, the point traces out a trajectory. But Del! The *mind*, Del, the *mind* is meanwhile and always jamming in the infinite-dimensional *mindscape*. Mindscape being larger than surfspace, you wave. My good tool Chaos Attractor picks up what you're looking for and sends tiny ripples out into the ocean, pulsing them just right, so that they cause interference way out there and bounce back what you want. The coupled system of board and rider in the mindscape are riding the surfspace. You sketch yourself into your own picture."

"So why can't I ride the board?"

"Because, Delbert, because ..." Zep gave a long, shuddery sigh and clamped the leash's fangs into his own ankle. "Because you have a bad attitude and you'll deal a mess and thrash the board before it gets burnt in. Because it's mine. Because right now I'm plugged in and you're not. Because ..." Zep paused and smiled oddly. "I don't like to say the word for what you are."

"What word?"

"Ho-dad."

Delbert's tense frame sagged. "That's really depressing, Zep." In the distance a car had begun insistently to honk. At a loss for words, Delbert craned up the cliff at the N-plant parking lot. There was a girl up there, standing next to a car and waving and reaching in through the car window to honk. It was Jen! Delbert turned his back to Zep and waved both arms at Jen. "Come on down, baby," he screamed. "Zep's gonna break the board in for me and then I'll shut down this beach for true!" Jen began slowly to pick her way down the steep cliff path. Delbert turned back to Zep, all smiles. "Be careful, my man. The Pilgrims'll probably try to ram you."

"I'm not afraid of Loach," said Zep softly. "He's a clone surfer. No sense of freestyle. We're both 'dads, man, but we're *still* avant-garde. And you, man, you go and put some heavy physical moves on Jen while she's standing here."

Zep padded down to the water's edge, avoiding the lurid, overgrown anemones. Clams squirted dark brown water from their holes. Sand crabs hid with only their antennae showing, dredging the slack warm water for the luminous plankton indigenous to the San Diablo break.

The N-plant made for an empty beach. There was plenty of room in the water, even with the five Stoke Pilgrims out there in a lineup. Floathead and Shrimp Chips were playing tic-tac-toe in the body paints on each other's chests, and Squid Puppy was fiddling with a wristwatch video game.

Chaos Attractor lit up the instant it hit the water. Zep found himself looking into a percolating, turbulent lens. The board was a window into surfspace. Zep could see the swirling high-dimensional probability fluid, tiny torsion curls composed of tinier curls composed of tinier torsions. It made him almost high on life. Zep flopped belly-down on the board and began paddling out through the wavelets that lapped the shore.

"Hang ten trillion!" called Delbert.

Ripples spread away from Zep's stick, expanding and crossing paths as they rushed toward the open sea. The water was laced with slimy indigo kelp. Zep thought of jellyfish. In this quap water, they'd be mongo. He kept paddling. The sun looked like the ghost of a silver dollar. He sploshed through some parallel lines of number-three wavies. Stroke followed stroke, and finally he was far enough out. He let himself drift, riding up and down on the humping wave embryos. Chaos Attractor was sending out ripples all the time and now things were beginning to . . .

"Check the zon!" shouted Squid Puppy.

Zep sat up. Row upon row of waves were coming in from the zon, each wave bigger than the one before. The sea was starting to look like a staircase. Remain calm, carver. Nothing too big and nasty. A few even test waves would do nicely. Something with a long, lean lip and a smoothed-under ledge.

"Curl or crawl," Loach called, glancing sidelong at Zep with a confident sneer.

Zep could feel the power between his legs. The surface of Chaos Attractor was flexing and rippling now, a faithful model of the sea's surface. Looking down, Zep could see moving bands of color that matched the approaching waves. Wouldn't it be great if . . .

The leash fed Zep's thought to the CAM8. The CAM8 jived the imipolex. The imipolex fed a shudder to the sea. The surface band-pattern changed and . . .

"Mexican beach break!" screamed Zep.

The huge blue wall came out of nowhere and crashed onto Loach and his glittering board—all in the space of an exclamation point.

Zep aimed into the churning stampede of white foam, endured a moment of watery rage, and shot effortlessly out into calm tides. The real wave-set was marching in now. Zep decided to catch the seventh.

Loach surfaced a few meters off, all uptight. "Carve him, Pilgrims!"

Zep grinned. Not likely.

As the war-painted sea dogs huffed and puffed against the current, he calmly bent his will toward shaping that perfect seventh wave. The Stoke Pilgrims yelled in glee, catching waves from the set. Squid Puppy and Shrimp Chips came after Zep, dogsledding it in zigzags over the curl and down the hollow. Near miss. Here was Zep's wave. He took his time getting to his feet after a slow takeoff, and looked back to see the prune-faced Mr. Scrote snaking after him, befouling the wave in his eagerness to slyve Zep.

It was time to hang ten.

Zep took a ginger step toward the nose and watched the gliding water rise up. Perfect, perfect . . . aaauuuuummmm. A shadow fell over Zep. He leaned farther out over the nose, and the shadow grew—like an ever-thicker cloud closing over the sun.

Zep looked back, and he saw that the sky was green and alive with foam, a shivering vault of water. Floating amid that enormous green curved world, which looked like some fathomless cavern made from bottle glass, was a lurid, red-eyed giant—a Macy's Parade Mr. Scrote.

Zep flicked around, banked back toward the behemoth, and cruised up the slick green tube until he was at Scrote's eye level. The sight of the bulging capillaries sickened him, and he stretched his arms straight out ahead of him, gripping the very tip of the board with his naked toes. He had all the time in the world. The wave didn't seem to be breaking anymore.

The green expanse spread out around him. The curve above flowed like melting wax, drawing him into it. Rationally, he knew he was upside down, but it felt more like he was sliding down one side of a vast, translucent bowl. Under the board he could see a shimmering disk of white light, like a fire in the water: Was that the sun? He stepped back to the middle of Chaos Attractor, tilting the board up for greater speed, plunging ever deeper in the maelstrom spiral of the tube. He was nearing the heart of pure foam: the calm, still center of the ever-receding void.

Suddenly, a huge stain came steaming toward him out of the vortex. Gelatin, nausea, quaking purple spots, a glutinous leviathan with purple organs the size of aircraft carriers. Mile upon mile of slithery stinging tendrils drifted behind the thing, stretching clear back to the singular center that had been Zep's goal.

It was a jellyfish, and . . . Zep was less than a centimeter tall. It figured, Zep thought, realizing what was up—it figured that he'd shrink. That's what he'd always wanted from the drugs he couldn't quite kick: annihilation, cessation of pain, the deep inattention of the zero. The jellyfish steamed closer, lurid as a bad trip, urgently quaking.

Zep sighed and dug in his stick's back rail. Water shot up, and Zep grew. The jellyfish zoom-lensed back down to size. Chaos Attractor shot up out of the tube, and Zep fell down into the warm gray-and-green sea.

He surfaced into the raging chop and reeled Chaos Attractor in by the leash. Mr. Scrote was behind a crest somewhere, screaming at Loach. "He disappeared, Lex! I swear to God, dude—I had him, and he shrunk to nothing. Flat out disappeared!"

Zep got back on Chaos Attractor and rode some whitewater toward shore. There were Del and Jen, waving and making gestures. Del had his arm around her waist. Off to the right was the stupid N-plant cooling pipe. Zep glared up at the plant, feeling a hot, angry flash of righteous ecological rage. The nuke-pigs said no N-plant could ever explode, but it would be so rad if like this one went up, just to show the pigs that . . .

Ripples sped over the cooling pipe, and suddenly Zep noticed a cloud of steam or smoke in the air over the N-plant. Had that been there before? And was that rumbling noise thunder? Had to be thunder. Or a jet. Or maybe not. What was that he'd been thinking about an explosion? Forget it! Think pro-nuke, Zep baby!

When Zep was near shore, Delbert gave Jen a big kiss, dived in, and came stroking out, buoyed by his wet suit. He ducked a breaker or two and then he was holding onto the side of Chaos Attractor, totally stoked.

"I saw that, Zep! It was awesome! It does everything you said it does. It made great waves—and you shrank right up like you were surfing into a zero."

"Yeah, Del, but listen—"

"Let me try now, Zep. I think I can do it."

Zep back-paddled, gripping the board between his thighs. "I don't think that's such a hot idea."

Delbert reddened. "Yeah? You know, Zep, you're a real wipe sometimes. What is this, huh? You get me to fork over all my savings so you can go and build a board that didn't cost you a cent in the first place—and now you act like it's yours! You took my money for a board you would have made anyway!"

"It's not that, Del. It's just that—it's more powerful than I thought. We maybe shouldn't be using it around here. Look at the nuke."

"Oh, yeah, try to distract me. What a bunch of crap! Give me that board, Zep. Come on, and the leash, too."

"Del, look—"

Another spurt of steam went up from the plant. Zep gave thanks that the wind wasn't blowing their way.

"You two dudes are maka sushi!" yelled Loach.

"The Stoke Pilgrims cried out in unison, "Shred 'em!"

Zep looked away from the board just long enough for Del to grab it away from him. Delbert got up on the board and pushed Zep under, holding him down with his feet and reeling in on the leash. Zep's foot surfaced, and Delbert ripped the leash fangs out of his ankle. By the time Zep got his head back in the air, Delbert had installed the leash on himself and was paddling away, triumph in his eyes.

"It's my stick, dude," called Del.

"Oh, no, Delbert. Please, I swear I'm not goofing. If you do it, you'd better stay really, really cool. Go for the little waves. And don't look at the N-plant. And if you do look, just remember that it can't possibly explode. No fancy tricks, dude."

"Bull!" screamed Delbert, shooting over a small peak. "This gun was built for tricks, Zep, and you know it. That's the thrill, man! *Anything* can happen! That's what this is all about!"

Delbert was belly to the board, stroking for the horizon. Back on the beach, Jen had noticed the N-plant's activity, and she was making gestures of distress. Zep dog-paddled, wondering what to do. Suddenly four of the surf punks surrounded him.

"He looks kind of helpless down there, don't he," said Floathead.

"Watch him close," said Mr. Scrote. "He's slippery."

"Let's use his head for water polo," suggested Squid Puppy, darting the sharp end of his board at Zep.

Zep dove to the bottom and resurfaced, only to find the Stoke Pilgrims' boards nosed in around him like an asterisk with his head at the center. "Mess with my mind, I don't care," said Zep. "But just don't put Delbert uptight."

"We won't bother bufu Delbert," said Mr. Scrote. "He's Lex's now."

"I know this is going to sound weird," Zep began. "But . . ."

"Holy righteous mother of God," interrupted Floathead. "Check out the zon, bros."

All the Pilgrims craned westward. And moaned.

"Far, far, faaar outsider," someone whispered. The horizon looked bent in the middle, and it took an effort of will to realize that the great smooth bell-curve was an actual wave of actual water. It swelled up and up like a droplet on a faucet, swelled so big that you half expected it to break free of the sea and fly upward into great chaotic spheres. It was far enough off that there still might have been time to reach the safety of the cliffs . . . but that's not what the surfers did. They broke formation and raced farther out to sea, out to where they guessed the monster wave would break.

Zep power-stroked out after the others, out toward where Loach and Delbert were waiting, Delbert bobbing up and down with a dismayed expression as Loach kept shouting at him. Just as Zep got there, Loach reached over and smacked Delbert in the face.

Delbert screamed in anger, his face going redder every second. "I'm gonna kill you, Loach!"

"Hoo-hoo-hoo!" cried the Stoke Pilgrims, forming their lineup. "Delbert is a ho-dad!"

"You can't always bully me, Loach," continued Delbert. "If you get near me one more time—if you snake in while I'm riding this super wave, *my* wave—it's all over for you."

"Oh, I'm shaking," Loach said, slapping the water as he laughed. "Come on, paddle boy. Do your worst—and I do mean *mega*worst." Loach grinned past Del at the other Stoke Pilgrims. "Contest's over, guys! Let's take this dip's board right now!"

Zep watched Delbert's face run through some fast changes, from helpless to terrified to grim to enraged to psychotic. It was as if some vicious bug had erupted from shy caterpillar Delbert. Some kind of catastrophic transition took place, and Delbert was a death's head moth. All the while Chaos Attractor was churning out a moireed blur of weird ripples, making the oncoming wave grow yet more monstrous.

Zep felt himself sucked up into the breast of a mountainous wall of water, a blackish green fortress whose surface rippled and coiled until it formed an immense, godlike face glaring down on all of them. Zep had never seen such cold eyes: The black depths of space had been drawn into them by the chaotic attractor. Sky had bent down to earth, drawing the sea up to see. Del and the Pilgrims and Zep all went rushing up toward a foamy green hell, while below . . .

Below was the rumbling, and now a ferocious cracking, accompanied by gouts of radioactive steam. Sirens and hooters. High up on the godwave, Zep looked down and saw the N-plant rocking in its bed, as if nudged from beneath by a gigantic mole. Blue luminescence pulsed upward through the failing N-plant's shimmering veils of deadly mist, blending into the green savagery of the spray trailing down from their wave. Frantic Jen had flung herself into the surf and was thrashing there, goggling up at the twin catastrophes of N-plant and Neptune's wave.

Looking up, Zep saw Delbert streaking down the long beaked nose of Neptune while Loach and the Pilgrims skidded down the cheeks, thrown from their boards, eating it.

Zep felt proud. *Delbert, I didn't know you had it in you. Shut the beach DOWN!*

Cracks crazed the surface of the N-plant. It was ready to blow. Way down there was Jen, screaming, "Save me!" like Olive Oyl. Del carved the pure surfspace, sending up a rooster tail of probability spray, jamming as if he'd been born on silvery, shadowy Chaos Attractor. He looked like he'd been to the edge of the universe and back already. He raved down deep to snatch up his Jen and set her in the board's center; and then he snapped up the wall to wrap a tight spiral around floundering Zep.

"Latch on, dude!"

Zep clamped onto Chaos Attractor's back rail and pulled himself aboard. The stick reared like a horse and sent them scudding up over the lip of the tsunami, out over the arching neck of the slow-breaking wave. Del glanced back through the falls and saw the filtered light of the San Diablo Nuclear Plant's explosion, saw the light and the chunks of concrete and steel tumbling outward, borne on the shock-wave's A-bomb energy.

The two waves intermingled in a chaotic mindscape abstraction. Up and up they flew, the fin scraping sparks from the edges of the unknown. Zep saw stars swimming under them, a great spiral of stars.

Everything was still, so still.

And then Del's hand shot out. Across the galactic wheel a gleaming figure shared their space. It was coming straight at them. Rider of the tides of night, carver of blackhole beaches and neutron tubes. Bent low on his luminous board—graceful, poised, inhuman.

"Stoked," said Jen. "God's a surfer!"

G E

C
H
A
P
T
E
R
8

GENXPLOITATION

N X

GenXploitation

Whether or not we will ever be acknowledged for our literary achievements, GenX has been quickly seized upon for its demographic value. As if it weren't enough that we were deluged with media backwash as children, now our own fledgling, self-created identity is to be sold back to us by marketeers. For money.

We haven't fallen for it, further enraging our critics. We understand the tools of marketing and consumer pandering better than anyone else and see through these crude attempts at milking from us the few dollars we have left. Because we won't buy in, they tell us we've sold out.

The outside world, so far, has only two ways of looking at busters: as a lost generation or as a new market segment. This chapter of outsiders' explanations of the GenX phenomenon (and a couple of insiders' responses) has been saved for last so that readers will understand, as busters do, just how pathetic the mainstream media's efforts at understanding us have been and how ravenous profiteering is the greatest enemy to the continuance of a sustainable American economy.

Generalization X

Nathaniel Wice

Soon to be publisher of his own GenX magazine, buster journalist Nathaniel Wice attended the first GenX marketing conference, which promised to teach participants how to create "profitable and targeted marketing programs for the twentysomething generation." Most fascinatingly, he comes to the conclusion that as far as these nostalgic marketing experts are concerned, GenX does not represent a real population or social movement but a reflection of their own boomer identity in flux.

> *"Dear Executive: The twentysomething generation has stepped out of baby boomers' shadow as today's trendsetters and tomorrow's chief consumers. Call them buster or cynics or slackers, but don't call them dispassionate shoppers."*
> —introduction to the brochure promoting the
> recent "Generation X" marketing conference
> at the Marriot Marquis, Times Square.

As Ann Glover, Strategy Manager for Mountain Dew at Pepsico, makes points in her speech, they come up on a slide screen one by one for the hundred-plus attendees of the first-ever marketing conference devoted to the newly discovered demographic bulge of 46 million Americans born between 1963 and 1974. The screen beside her spells out UNDER-RATED BRAND MEETS UNDER-RATED GENERATION.

Unfamiliar with marketing presentations, I was impressed at first by all the slides and video clips. But as the lights dimmed for this, the morning's third speech, I realize that a slide carousel is no guarantee of an enlightening exposition.

Glover is straining to connect her product with a very desirable market.

Over the last year, the first significant generation gap since the sixties has been declared, not atop student barricades, but in a flood of soft news features about "Generation X," "twentysomethings," and "baby busters." And in the media trade press young adults have emerged as the "hot" target audience.

Companies as diverse as Taco Bell, Ford Motor, and Bugle Boy Jeans have come to this Generation X conference to get a fix on kids today. ("A $125 Billion Market" shouts the conference brochure. It's sponsored by the Institute for International Research, a market research group specializing in conferences.) Presenters share their experiences marketing to this elusive generation, and at the same time promote their own products or services. Everyone in attendance hopes a little Generation X excitement will rub off on them.

The Mountain Dew presentation, called "Getting Busters to 'Do Diet Dew'," is one of the heavy-handed ones. Glover argues that Mountain Dew and Gen X—as it is referred to at the conference—have a lot in common. Not only do they stand for similar values—"Xers prioritize physical self-improvement" and Mountain Dew advertising features "Lots of physical activity"—they are each badly misunderstood. Gen X is unfairly labelled dumb, hopeless, and angry, while Mountain Dew is mistakenly regarded as a small regional brand with a miniscule advertising budget. Let the facts show, though, click, chunk goes the projector, that Mountain Dew is the sixth most popular soft drink brand in the country, and that its ad budgets are comparable to those of Sprite and Gatorade.

Every speaker has his or her own particular use for Gen X. They often contradict. Even the parameters for the astrological reasoning—date of birth determining consciousness—are fuzzy. One speaker includes older teenagers, but not people in their early thirties; another interprets twentysomething literally, excluding both border groups: in the formulation of at least one presenter there is even a chance to be counted born baby boomer and baby buster, if you were born in 1963 or 1964. Being twenty-five years old, though, my X'er credentials are impeccable. I have my own commercial designs on the current crop of young adults—a magazine proposal that a partnership has been shopping around—but I am not a marketer. At this conference, I am a celebrity. Isn't it nice, I think, that all these people are interested in me? About as nice as being a bear at a hunting convention.

* * *

At the Conference are representatives of the youth bloc of the mass media, including MTV and *Rolling Stone*, and many of their advertisers, from Coke to Coors and Sprint to Sony. These are the people who buy and sell ads, who commission them and who try to measure their effectiveness, not the *Thirtysomething* creative types who get to sit around, their feet up on the desk, throwing crumpled paper through wastepaper hoops and thinking the ads up.

Karen Ritchie is the folksy fiftysomething director of media services at the Detroit office of MacCann-Erickson ad agency, and she handles many General Motors accounts. She was repeatedly credited at the conference for having "delivered a wake-up call" to marketers about the new generation. At a magazine publisher's convention in Bermuda last October, she delivered a speech entitled "Farewell Boomers, Hello Generation X." She took the term from the title of 29-year-old Douglas Coupland's 1991 novel.

(Coupland did not coin the phrase, contrary to the assumption of many at the conference. Generation X was the name of Billy Idol's age-irrelevant early eighties glam-punk band. Also irrelevant in the vast majority of Generation X talk is another association, Malcolm X.)

Ritchie's speech was further disseminated in *Advertising Age*: "When I look at my little brother the Baby Boomer, I see a 45-year-old man with a pot belly, a bald spot, and his own corporation. Yet I still hear media presentations every week from your sales staffs that talk about reaching the younger Baby Boomer audience. What younger Baby Boomer audience? Face it. Boomers are getting old."

This morning Ritchie begins her remarks—which turn out to be an encore of the seven-month-old address—talking about the mail she got from young people in response to her speech. Many of the writers were looking for jobs (no small part of any understanding of young adult worldviews) but others were fans, expressing their gratitude for her generational advocacy. She summarized, "To be 25 years old in America today is to be invisible. And that is the theme expressed over and over again."

As the conference goes on, I find myself learning less about my age cohort and more about the marketers'. For all their talk of "Generation X" and "twentysomethings," many of these marketers are obviously still perplexed by the idea of a new generation that leaves them—most in their late thirties and forties—on the wrong side of a divide by which they once defined themselves. The most interesting projections aren't beaming from the slide carousels, they're coming out of the baby boomers' sense of themselves. Confronted with their juniors, they seem to feel, well, guilty.

Scott Kauffman, the emcee of the conference and the head of marketing at *Entertainment Weekly*, affects a twelve-step confession in his opening remarks: "There's something I have to say. It's not something I'm particularly proud of, but there's no shying away from it. I . . . I am a boomer. And as I look out at you, I see a room full of boomers."

These boomers' guilt is over having ignored the busters as a generation. And the guilty feelings are reinforced by a statistic several speakers cite, that about half of all Gen X individuals experienced the divorce of their parents. Another speaker, *Details* magazine publisher Mitchell Fox, quotes a Gen X specimen: " 'I feel my voice mute in a world increasingly target marketed for people who need spray on hair.' "

At times the speakers, in their advocacy for better aimed advertisements and outlets for those ads, adopt the tone of social reformers. Ritchie's use of Ralph Ellison's existential language was only the most bathetic example. For her, "invisibility" refers not to the lack of government services for young people, but a paucity of twentysomething ad campaigns.

Marilyn Adler, the founder of a marketing firm aimed at young adults and called Creative Targets, leads a panel discussion at the end of the first day of the two day conference in which real live twentysomethings "speak out." But when audience question time begins, the rap session soon narrows from generational ideology to focus group research. Enough about environmental neglect and the viability of the social security trust fund in 2033, the most disturbing moment for the audience was when one of the six happy-to-please subjects said how much she liked the Energizer bunny commercials. "It's funny and ironic. It's for Duracell, right?" Later Adler quotes a survey in which 26 percent of all people in their twenties were found to throw out junk mail unopened, and the audience gasps audibly.

But at other points in the conference much is made of the media savviness of Gen X. Several speakers discussed it with awe. Many repeat variations of the theme, "They change channels as soon as they sense the sell." Lest this be confused with the idealism of a generation ago, advertising and commercialism are accepted by Gen X as facts of life, part of the programming—or so the line goes. In the consumption-friendly construct of Gen X, youth prides itself on being hip to advertising and holding it to high standards.

Another focus-group researcher to speak at the conference, Marian Salzman, strives to help the middle-aged marketers *understand*. Still in her early thirties, Salzman is the founder of her own marketing firm BKG Youth. She is the sensible older sister, trying to explain her younger sibling to her parents. It is one of the more careful presentations, interpreting Gen X's reputation for apathy and cynicism—especially as regards advertisers—as fidelity to traditional values like honesty and quality. Her recommendations for crafting ad campaigns turn the contradictions of Gen X hype—and they are innumerable—into guidelines for advertisers. Craving simplicity, Gen X supposedly responds well to outdoors imagery: with commitments such as home ownership out of reach, they "feather their nests with electronic luxuries recast as 'essentials.' "

Gen X, another speaker explains, "demands to be entertained." Wieden & Kennedy, responsible for some of Nike's best ad campaigns, is ridiculed by conference speakers for an overzealous Subaru ad which they executed. In this spot, a young man who looks like a cross between Corey Feldman and Christian Slater compares the Subaru to punk rock. Hopelessly unhip. Much more popular is a Converse ad that the sneaker company showcases at the conference: A street punk unleashes a Dennis Leary-like diatribe against the tyranny of beautiful people pictured in ads. The spot, called "Ugly," ends with the tagline, "I don't want to live in a beer commercial." It is currently running on MTV.

On the second day of the conference MTV gives its own confident presentation, and takes on the task of naming the generation. No one brand name has been settled on for the population cohort, in part because the members themselves seem stubbornly unwilling to identify themselves as one group. Of the many attempts, there are baby busters, an Oedipal play on baby boomers; boomerangs, a comment on the fact that more than a third of us live at home; the lost generation, with no apologies to Gertrude Stein; and slackers, the title of Richard Linklater's 1992 film and an honorofic for those frustrated by "McJobs."

So what is MTV's suggestion? What else: the MTV Generation. This illusion is made on screen with political posturing—"vote, it's good for you," "racism is bad"—and incessant self-congratulatory talk of a "music revolution" in spite of the fact that MTV's programming mainly consists of corporate record company-produced video promotions.

During the breaks in conference action, people file out for coffee and phone calls. Nobody talks on the phone, but lines form anyway because everyone is listening in turn to their voice mail. A woman who's with me on line tells me that she is an account supervisor at a San Francisco ad agency. Age-wise, I'd peg her as a tailend Boomer. Her primary clients are Levi's and Taco Bell. As soon as I tell her I am writing a piece about the conference, her language becomes extremely stiff—she speaks as a flack for corporate strategy and "core values." Taco Bell is the "fast food place for kids to be themselves," unlike McDonald's "where you go with your parents." She nervously calls *New York* the next week to explain that she cannot be quoted without first clearing her answers through the company's press office.

Throughout the conference the same boomer-buster cycle plays itself out over and over: the middle-aged marketers take generational resentment and turn it into corporate sales fuel. Real conflict—like the fact that older people have the good jobs and real estate—is not addressed. In its place the marketers celebrate the savvy, idealism, and hipness of the young. They even laugh at themselves in the process. One speaker says: "The last thing this group wants is us sitting around thinking about them, and here we are, all of us boomers, trying to figure out how we are going to get these people."

But the middle-aged media planners are not simply analysing this generation, they are creating it. Generation X is a market not an identity, owing more to advertising than social movements. As conceptualized at the conference, Generation X is not a new demographic, it is another manifestation of the boomer identity in flux. Nostalgic for the youth cohesion that promised so much twenty-five years ago, the new improved, more understanding parents talk about audiences as if they were communities.

Only a few speakers are willing to be candid about where "Generation X" came from and what it really means. Scott Kauffman called his opening speech "Anatomy of a Marketing Phenomenon," and he did not speak about a generation growing up under Reagan, *Wayne's World*, Bart Simpson, the simultaneous resurgence and splintering of white youth culture evidenced in the spread of homemade magazines and neo-garage rock, or anything else like that. Instead, Kauffman began with *Time*'s July, 1990, "Twentysomething" cover. "Proceeding with Caution: The Twentysomething Generation Is Balking At Work, Marriage and Baby-Boomer Values. Why Are Today's Young Adults So Skeptical?" Kauffman astutely commented on the peculiar emphasis of the article, "so much of which spoke to marketers." One section on "Shopping: Less Passion for Prestige" concluded that "a twentysomething adult picks a Hershey's bar over Godiva chocolates."

Another marketing text was the Douglas Coupland novel, *Generation X*, which became a surprise success in 1991. Coupland liberally employed arid marketing terms and neologisms, often as marginalia that he laid out himself on his Macintosh, to tell the stories of three twentysomething characters sharing in-jokes as they drift from sterile offices and uncommunicative middle-class families to TV land and back. One chapter title was "I am not a target market."

The aging baby boomer story suddenly had an interesting new angle when the baby buster emerged in magazine cover stories last winter. *BusinessWeek* announced, "Move Over Boomers: The Busters are Here—And They're Angry." Grunge, a term that had already been devalued by rock critics and appropriated by high fashion designers, was defined in large type in the article: "GRUNGE n: a fashion that celebrates the ill-kempt, lumberjack look."

The founder of *Spin* magazine, Bob Guccione, Jr., put the hype in perspective, when quoted in "The Media Wakes Up to Generation X" an *Advertising Age* February cover story: "Waking up to the discovery of 46 million people is like all of a sudden noticing France."

Call it discovery or invention, the generational generalizations serve the interests of many at the conference. MTV and the handful of magazines present at the conference are thrilled with the idea that their readerships are vital, well defined, and difficult to reach through other means. They would be crazy not to position themselves as Generation X's institutions.

Since all of these magazines depend on advertisers more than readers for revenue, the magazines contribute in their own way to the marketing of distinct youth sensibilities. When the magazines go selling, they are pitching their readership.

The publisher of *Mademoiselle*, Julie Lewit-Nirenberg, spoke most frankly about the need for new media kits and other sales tools, joking that the function of fancy studies like the 'Twentysomething Report," that she commissioned from the Roper Organization for the recent refocussing of

Mademoiselle, "is to sprinkle holy water on the market and legitimize it." The key task left to do is to remake the supposedly cynical, fickle, and churlish generation into a bunch of lovable spendthrifts who splurge lavishly in key advertiser categories.

Lewit is a small-framed dynamo with an Eastern European accent, and a charming manner even when she loses her place in the middle of her pre-pared speech and calls impatiently to her twentysomething assistant for help. According to Roper's research, these women "love to shop" Lewit says. They are "fun loving" and into "product experimentation," but they are also not unfaithful. The same generation that is supposed to have "less passion for prestige" is known affectionately by *Mademoiselle,* as "little snobs" who "believe brands are a reflection not only of quality, but of themselves." The celebration of the generation is a way to move ad pages.

At lunch the second day, with nine of the eleven presentations over, the younger people at the conference finally found each other casually self-segregated at a version of the kid's table. I sit down near Amy, a 26-year-old from MTV's research department in Chicago who had the quiet look of someone who does not expect much from her job; Patty, a 27-year-old im-peccably dressed in a white blouse and long black skirt for a ride in the el-evator at Conde Nast, where it turns out she works writing twentysomething promotional brochures for *Mademoiselle,* and Tim, a big friendly 27-year-old advertising account manager from Austin, who apologetically explains that his division's main client is Coors.

Everyone's been taking copious notes—or so they claim—but my fellow age bracketers seem too weary to take offense at the conference or savor its ironies. People light up only as I stop asking questions, and the conversation shifts to Beavis and Butt-head, MTV's answer to Bart Simpson, Under-achiever. The show centers around two badly animated suburban heavy-metal fans who are so ignorant and alienated that they make *Wayne's World* look like MacNeil Lehrer. They mainly make erection jokes while watching music videos, and the cartoon is contagiously funny. The conversation bub-bles along until it abruptly stops with the announcement that it's time to go back for "A Cosmepak Case Study: Moving the Retail Market," the story of the low-priced beauty organizers for young women that they said wouldn't sell. No one complains or even comments as the giggling stops and we file back to work. I think to myself, these are my people.

The X Factor

Debra Goldman

in Adweek

While her article infuriated members of the WELL's GenX Conference, Debra Goldman here demonstrates a healthy respect for the twentysomething market segment. Although she relies on examples from the media with which true GenXers would prefer not to be associated, she seems to be aware that these television efforts fall far short of correctly representing the buster movement. Adweek, for the time being, will have to content itself with accepting us as a mystery.

Angry, disillusioned and media-savvy, the newly discovered twentysomething generation is shaping up as a very tough sell.

Early in *Generation X*, the 1991 novel set in the McJob underworld where baby busters subsist on low pay and irony, one character confronts his boomer boss, an ex-hippie sellout with a salt-and-pepper ponytail. "Do you really think," he sneers with a victim's superiority, "we enjoy hearing about your brand new million-dollar *home*, when we can barely afford to eat Kraft Dinner sandwiches in our own grimy little shoe boxes and we're pushing *thirty*? . . . You'd last about 10 minutes if you were my age, Martin."

That's you he's talking to: Martin is an ad exec, and as such, the perfect villain for the twentysomethings—a label that is, like so much in the culture of today's young adults, a hand-me-down. In fact, the heroes of *Generation X* are more like twentynothings for whom demography is destiny. Too late for the gravy train, their portion is the detritus of an inexhaustible pop culture machine. A target market all their lives, they are at the same time invisible. And they're angry about it. Every American counterculture has had it out for advertising since advertising became a cultural power, but this generation of young malcontents is taking it personally.

In typical boomerish fashion, I haven't paid much attention to this group. Yet even the most self-absorbed boomer, head buried in a best-seller about menopause, can't help but notice this summer that twentynothings have two TV shows of their own—or at least to share with teens, whose growing numbers have goosed TV's interest in the youth audience. In these dog days of the television season, Fox's *Melrose Place* and MTV's *The Real World*—and the youth oriented shows that will follow—have created a buzz.

The rush, after all these years, to define and cash in on the "something-dom" of this largely mute sector is especially intriguing because marketers want to know what makes this group tick. Twentynothings are the ultimate example of the old marketing conundrum that says the more successful marketing is, the faster its object of desire retreats and the harder that object becomes to find, read and reach. At worst, the twentynothings hate us. At best, they're a mystery. Notes Peter Moore, a corporate consultant and partner at Inferential Focus in New York, "Marketers don't have a clue who these kids are, so they're throwing anything and everything at them."

Although they're light-years from the terminally disaffected characters of *Generation X*, I don't find either the Reagan Kids who inhabit *Melrose Place* or the post-Warhol instant celebs of *The Real World* particularly reassuring. Last week on the Fox soap, the young wife responded to a fight with her husband by popping over to the neighborhood bar, slipping her wedding ring into her pocket and sampling the male "merchandise." If young marrieds resonate to this, I doubt the 50 percent divorce rate will decline anytime soon.

The Real World, meanwhile, is a misnamed contrivance that gathered seven MTVers, aged 19 to 25, in a Manhattan loft-cum-studio and taped their interaction for three months. Unlike 1973's *An American Family* (the original venture into video voyeurism, to which the current series is wrongly compared), *The Real World* is full of incidents: brief, stillborn romances; telegenic pranks; and a Jerry Brown rally. Mostly, there are performances, since almost all the inhabitants of *The Real World* are performers. But nothing actually happens, except that the participants get to be the stars of their own lives. As *American Family* star Lance Loud sniffed to the *Wall Street Journal*, "Reality isn't what it used to be."

In the *real* real world, consultant Moore recently had dinner with a dozen young management-track employees from a major financial institution. These were MBAs, with degrees from business schools that only a few years ago guaranteed a fast ride to the top. Moore asked them what they expected to be doing in 20 years. "If I'd asked that question five or six years ago, several would have said, 'I'll be the CEO of this company.' But *not one* of this group saw themselves ever playing that role."

This certainty didn't depress them, he noticed. They were reasonably confident there was some path to success. But they would have to figure it out by themselves, because, as Moore observes, "they reach out for the rungs of the ladder and there's nothing there." On its own, the group has banded together to discuss business issues; no management mentor is present at these meetings.

It's here that these Best and Brightest intersect with their fictional counterparts. By historical necessity, the twentynothings are the front line of resourcefulness in an age where life calls for more resourcefulness every day. *Generation X* is right: We boomers probably wouldn't last 10 minutes if we were their age these days. How twentynothings manage to do it, marketers will probably be the last to know.

The New Generation Gap

Neil Howe and

William Strauss

for The Atlantic

This article was probably most responsible for putting the GenX phenomenon—what Howe and Strauss call the "Thirteenth Generation"—on the mainstream cultural map. Backed by much more economic and historical evidence than most journalists who have attempted to tackle the twentysomething issue, their report amused GenXers, who in many ways appreciated being treated as a socioeconomic reality rather than a self-aggrandized illusion. Still, with its depiction of our world view as an evolutionary inevitability rather than an original and inventive life strategy, the piece makes us feel a bit more like laboratory specimens than human beings.

THIRTEENERS

As they shield their eyes with Ray-Ban wayfarer sunglasses, and their ears with Model TCD-D3 Sony Walkmen, today's teens and twentysomethings present to Boomer eyes a splintered image of brassy looks and smooth manner, of kids growing up too tough to be cute, of kids more comfortable shopping or playing than working or studying. Ads target them as beasts of pleasure and pain who have trouble understanding words longer than one syllable, sentences longer than three words. Pop music on their Top 40 stations—heavy metal, alternative rock, rap—strikes many a Boomer ear as a rock-and-roll end game of harsh sounds, goin'-nowhere melodies, and clumsy poetry. News clips document a young-adult wasteland of academic nonperformance, political apathy, suicide pacts, date-rape trials, wilding, and hate crimes.

Who are they, and what are they up to? On the job, Thirteeners are the reckless bicycle messengers, pizza drivers, yard workers, Wal-Mart shelf-stockers, health-care trainees, and miscellaneous scavengers, hustlers, and McJobbers in the low-wage/low-benefit service economy. They're the wandering nomads of the temp world, directionless slackers, habitual nonvoters. In school they're a group of staggering diversity—not just in ethnicity but also in attitude, performance, and rewards. After graduation they're the ones with big loans who were supposed to graduate into jobs and move out of the house but didn't, and who seem to get poorer the longer they've been away from home—unlike their parents at that age, who seemed to get richer.

In inner cities Thirteeners are the unmarried teen mothers and unconcerned teen fathers, the Crips and Bloods, the innocent hip-hoppers grown weary of watching white Boomers cross the street to avoid them. In suburbs they're the kids at the mall, kids buying family groceries for busy moms and dads, kids in mutual-protection circles of friends, girding against an adolescent world far more dangerous than anything their parents knew, kids struggling to unlink sex from disease and death.

In them lies much of the doubt, distress, and endangered dream of late-twentieth-century America. As a group they aren't what older people ever wanted but rather what they themselves know they need to be: pragmatic, quick, sharp-eyed, able to step outside themselves and understand how the world really works. From the Thirteener vantage point, America's greatest need these days is to clear out the underbrush of name-calling and ideology so that simple things can work again. Others don't yet see it, but today's young people are beginning to realize that their upbringing has endowed them with a street sense and pragmatism their elders lack. Many admit they *are* a bad generation—but so, too, do they suspect that they are a *necessary* generation for a society in dire need of survival lessons.

When they look into the future, they see a much bleaker vision than any of today's older generations ever saw in their own youth. Polls show that

Thirteeners believe it will be much harder for them to get ahead than it was for their parents—and that they are overwhelmingly pessimistic about the long-term fate of their generation and nation. They sense that they're the clean-up crew, that their role in history will be sacrificial—that whatever comeuppance America has to face, they'll bear more than their share of the burden. It's a new twist, and not a happy one, on the American Dream.

Trace the life cycle to date of Americans born in 1961. They were among the first babies people took pills not to have. During the 1967 Summer of Love they were the kindergartners who paid the price for America's new divorce epidemic. In 1970 they were fourth-graders trying to learn arithmetic amid the chaos of open classrooms and New Math curricula. In 1973 they were the bell-bottomed sixth-graders who got their first real-life civics lesson watching the Watergate hearings on TV. Through the late 1970s they were the teenage mall-hoppers who spawned the Valley Girls and other flagrantly non-Boomer youth trends. In 1979 they were the graduating seniors of Carter-era malaise who registered record-low SAT scores and record-high crime and drug-abuse rates.

In 1980 they cast their first votes, mostly for Reagan, became the high-quality nineteen-year-old enlistees who began surging into the military, and arrived on campus as the smooth, get-it-done freshmen who evidenced a sudden turnaround from the intellectual arrogance and social immaturity of Boomer students. They were the college class of 1983, whose graduation coincided with the ballyhooed *A Nation at Risk* report, which warned that education was beset by "a rising tide of mediocrity." In 1985 they were the MBA grads who launched the meteoric rise in job applications to Wall Street. And in 1991 they hit age thirty just when turning "thirtysomething" (a big deal for yuppies in the 1980s) became a tired subject—and when the pretentious TV serial with that title was yanked off the air.

Like any generation, Thirteeners grew up with parents who are distributed in roughly equal measure between the two prior generations (Silent and Boom). But also like any generation, they were decisively influenced by the senior parental cohort. Much as GIs shaped the *Sputnik* 1950s for Boomers, the Silent Generation provided the media producers, community leaders, influential educators, and rising politicians during the R-rated 1970s, the decade that most Thirteeners still regard as their childhood home.

And what did Thirteeners absorb from that generation and that era? Mostly they learned to be cynical about adults whom they perceived to be sensitive yet powerless, better at talking about issues than solving problems. For the Silent Generation, then hitting midlife, the cultural upheaval of the 1970s meant liberation from youthful conformism, a now-or-never passage away from marriages made too young and careers chosen too early. But for Thirteeners just growing up, the 1970s meant something very different: an adult world that expressed moral ambivalence where children sought clear answers, that expected children to cope with real-world problems, that hesitated to impose structure on children's behavior, and that demonstrated an amazing (even stupefying) tolerance for the rising torrent of pathology and negativism that engulfed children's daily life.

When they were small, the nation was riding high. When they reached adolescence, national confidence weakened, and community and family life splintered. Older people focused less on the future, planned less for it, and invested less in it. A Consciousness Revolution that seemed euphoric to young adults was to Thirteeners the beginning of a ride on a down escalator. The public debacles of their youth fostered the view that adults were not especially virtuous or competent—that kids couldn't count on adults to protect them from danger.

From Boom to Thirteenth, America's children went from a family culture of *My Three Sons* to one of *My Two Dads*. As millions of mothers flocked into the work force, the proportion of preschoolers cared for in their own homes fell by half. For the first time, adults ranked automobiles ahead of children as necessary for "the good life." The cost of raising a child, never very worrisome when Boomers were little, suddenly became a fraught issue. Adults of fertile age doubled their rate of surgical sterilization. The legal-abortion rate grew to the point where one out of every three pregnancies was terminated. Back in 1962 half of all adults agreed that parents in bad marriages should stay together for the sake of the children. By 1980 less than a fifth agreed. America's divorce rate doubled from 1965 to 1975, just as first-born Thirteeners passed through middle childhood.

The pop culture conveyed to little kids and (by 1980) teenagers a recurring message from the adult world: that they weren't wanted, and weren't even liked, by the grown-ups around them. Polls and social statistics showed a sharp shift in public attitudes toward (and treatment of) children. Taxpayers revolted against school funding, and landlords and neighborhoods that had once smiled on young Boomers started banning children. The Zero Population Growth movement declared the creation of each additional infant to be a bad thing, and the moviegoing public showed an unquenchable thirst for a new cinematic genre: the devil-child horror film. The same year Boomers were blissing out at Woodstock, the baby that riveted America's attention had a mother named Rosemary (*Please* don't have this baby, millions of viewers whispered to themselves).

From the late 1960s until the early 1980s America's pre-adolescents grasped what nurture they could through the most virulently anti-child period in modern American history. Ugly new phrases ("latchkey child," "throwaway child," and "boomerang child") joined the sad new lexicon of youth. America's priorities lay elsewhere, as millions of kids sank into poverty, schools deteriorated, and a congeries of elected politicians set a new and distinctly child-hostile course of national overconsumption. Then, when Thirteeners were ready to enter the adult labor force, the politicians pushed every policy lever conceivable—tax codes, entitlements, public debt, unfunded liabilities, labor laws, hiring practices—to tilt the economic playing field away from the young and toward the old. The results were predictable.

Since the early 1970s the overall stagnation in American economic progress has masked some vastly unequal changes in living standards by phase of life. Older people have prospered, Boomers have barely held their own, and Thirteeners have fallen off a cliff. The columnist Robert Kuttner describes Thirteeners as victims of a "remarkable generational economic distress. . . . a depression of the young," which makes them feel "uniquely thirsty in a sea of affluence." Ever since the first Thirteeners reached their teens, the inflation-adjusted income of all adult men under age thirty-five has sunk—dropping by more than 20 percent since as recently as 1979. Twenty years ago a typical thirty-year-old male made six percent more than a typical sixty-year-old male; today he makes 14 percent less. The same widening age gap can be observed in poverty rates, public benefits, home ownership, union membership, health insurance, and pension participation. Along the way, this is becoming a generation of betrayed expectations. Polls show that most teenagers (of both sexes) expect to be earning $30,000 or more by age thirty, but in 1990 the U.S. Census Bureau reported that among Americans aged twenty-five to twenty-nine there were eight with total annual incomes of under $30,000 for every one making more than $30,000.

Welcome, Thirteeners, to contemporary American life: While older age brackets are getting richer, yours is getting poorer. Where earlier twentieth-century generations could comfortably look forward to outpacing Mom and

Dad, you probably won't even be able to keep up. If, when you leave home, you have a high school degree or better, there's a 40 percent chance you'll "boomerang" back to live with your parents at least once. (Today more young adults are living with their parents than at any other time since the Great Depression.) When you marry, you and your spouse will both work—not for Boomerish self-fulfillment but because you need to just to make ends meet. If you want children, you'll have to defy statistics showing that since 1973 the median real income has fallen by 30 percent for families with children which are headed by persons under thirty. And you'd better not slip up. Over the past twenty years the poverty rate among under-thirty families has more than doubled. Your generation, in fact, has a weaker middle class than any other generation born in this century—which means that the distance is widening between those of you who are beating the average and those who are sinking beneath it.

Everywhere they look, Thirteeners see the workplace system rigged against them. As they view it, the families, schools, and training programs that could have prepared them for worthwhile careers have been allowed to rot, but the institutions that safeguard the occupational livelihood of mature workers have been maintained with full vigor. Trade quotas protect decaying industries. Immigration quotas protect dinosaur unions. Two-tier wage scales discriminate against young workers. Federal labor regulations protect outmoded skills. State credential laws protect overpriced professions. Huge FICA taxes take away Thirteener money that, polls show, most Thirteeners expect never to see again. And every year another incomprehensible twelve-digit number gets added to the national debt, which Thirteeners know will someday get dumped on them. Whatever may happen to the meek, they know it's not their generation that's about to inherit the earth.

Like warriors on the eve of battle, Thirteeners face their future with a mixture of bravado and fatalism. Squared off competitively against one another, this mélange of scared city kids, suburban slackers, hungry immigrants, desperate grads, and shameless hustlers is collectively coming to realize that America rewards only a select set of winners with its Dream—and that America cares little about its anonymous losers. Sizing up the odds, each Thirteener finds himself or herself essentially alone, to an extent that most elders would have difficulty comprehending. Between his own relative poverty and the affluence he desires, the Thirteener sees no intermediary signposts, no sure, step-by-step path along which society will help him, urge him, congratulate him. Instead, all he sees is an enormous obstacle, with him on one side and everything he wants on the other.

And what's the obstacle? Those damn Boomers.

The Slacker Factor

Andrew Hultkrans

for Mondo 2000

As a columnist for fringe culture's Mondo 2000 *magazine, twentysome-thing Andrew Hultkrans may be the foremost inside expert on the slacker phenomenon and its relationship to our culture's religion of consumerism. "Pimping the Reality Principle" captures the essence of life in the market-ing simulacra. "GenXploitation" is a self-referential tour de force, teaching busters how to get paid for marketing GenX aesthetics back to ourselves.*

But enough of these forewords, already. Hultkrans can speak for him-self, and for the rest of us, too.

PIMPING THE REALITY PRINCIPLE

"Angry, disillusioned and media-savvy, the newly discovered twentysomething generation is shaping up as a very hard sell."

—Debra Goldman, *Adweek*

"Belief in advertising is not like breathing. It doesn't come naturally; it must be taught."

—Edwin L. Artzt, Proctor & Gamble CEO

"It's got to be real."

—Levi's 501 jeans advertisement

Hard sell, indeed. Did you expect the generation weaned on Watergate, raised on Reagan, and schooled on the S & L bailout to fall for a straight pitch? I mean, *really*, as children we witnessed captialism's finest hour as our parents happily lined up to buy us our very own "Pet Rocks." We were so goddamn media-savvy that the phrase "The Medium is the Message" has for us the cozy familiarity of a nursery rhyme. Hence, sez Ms. Goldman, we're the ultimate example of the old marketing conundrum that says "the more successful marketing is, the faster its object of desire retreats and the harder that object becomes to find, read, and reach." Read these Nikes, Debra.

The Boomers, by contrast, *invented* psychographics and elevated consumerism to a high art form. Luxuriating in their media-reflected self-image, Boomers assume those qualities apply to the elusive GenX market as well. Their Narcissus-like fascination with their own canons of taste and style provided fodder for marketing analysts for over a decade. But now Generation X is proving immune, vaccinated with precocious cynicism. Boomer ad execs are crying in their Chardonnay. *Entrepreneur* magazine vainly reassures them that their targets are *just like them* in at least one respect: "Both groups are looking for authenticity." Boomer ad execs and TV producers are therefore repackaging "authenticity"—"real" products and programs for "real" people. Boomer trendmonger Faith Popcorn (doesn't that say it all?) characterizes the 90's as a decade when the enlightened consumer will "look for what is real, what is honest, what is quality."

Television has cashed in on this craving for the "real": the camcorder revolution has littered the networks with eyewitness "true crime" shows that set new standards for bogosity. For a generation unwilling—or unable—to suspend disbelief, there are now dramatizations, simulations, and faux documentaries to flirt with our jaded sensibilities. "Is it a crotch patch . . . or is it for real?" is a question that carries a special *frisson* in this age of video voyeurism. A generation anaesthetized to the gory shock value of B splatter films begs to be bludgeoned. Our adolescence welcomed the emergence of the ultimate subgenre of twisted voyeurism—the *Faces of Death* series and underground "snuff" films. A new demand has been placed on "authenticity" by the desensitized organism. Boomer media jockeys have banked on this hunger for true grit with a proliferation of "real life" advertising and programming targeted directly at GenX.

Take Levi's. After years of being squeezed out of the denim market by

The Gap, Levi's has bounced back with a mega-campaign aimed at the slack generation. Setting a new benchmark in the unrelatedness of ad to product, the spots offer quickcut images of mostly male twentynothings, clad in denim, sublimely inarticulate and gloriously unemployed. With a jingle celebrating the notion that a product (or lifestyle) has "got to be real" to pass our sophisticated bullshit detectors, the new Levi's 501 jeans campaign (currently saturating MTV) is the first major corporate attempt at "slice-of-life" images of GenXers.

In a related attempt to create "authentic" media images of GenX, this year's *Real World*—an MTV update of the 1950's televised "social experiment" *An American Family* (whose ruinous impact on the monitored Loud family caused father Lance Loud to reflect sadly "Reality isn't what it used to be")—dropped seven Xers into the well-appointed Lower Manhattan petri dish and recorded their interactions. Despite the grand simulation of the whole setup, and the scripted nature of each installment (focusing on one or two participants' problems per show), *Real World*'s veneer of authenticity scored big with the show's target audience. Less grittily real but with a similar strategy, the latest installment of Aaron Spelling's Youth for Racial Cleansing project (begun with the mega-popular *Beverly Hills 90210*), *Melrose Place* is an L.A. bungalow apartment playground for squeaky clean neo-Reagan youth to go through GenX post-college tribulations without the rough edges, nicotine, or black clothing.

Oppositional voices also aggressively sell the "real" to GenXers, albeit from a dramatically different perspective: gangsta rappers of the South Central school wage "authenticity" wars against one another. Justifying the raw scenarios of 1989's seminal *Straight Outta Compton*, Eazy-E of N.W.A. called gangsta rap street-level reportage on the trials of inner city life, or "kicking reality." Two years later, however, in the wake of countless imitators, N.W.A. released the musically powerful but lyrically insecure *Efil4zaggin*—its entire first side a defensive reassurance of the group's "street" credibility.

With songs like "Real Niggaz," "Niggaz 4 Life," and "Real Niggaz Don't Die," the listener is battered repeatedly with reminders that N.W.A. are "real niggaz" and that the recorded product in hand is an "authentic" document of the perils of the 'hood. "False niggaz," "House niggaz" and other inauthentic sellouts are dissed with venom usually reserved for the LAPD and other manifestations of white authority. What may have passed with *Straight*

Outta Compton is revealed as simulation by the curious defensiveness of *Efil4zaggin*. Behind the gangsta posturing we find that Eazy-E was the only member of the group to have ever been an active gangbanger; Dr. Dre and DJ Yella wore makeup and Prince-esque frills in their mid-80's group the World Class Wrecking Cru; and Ice Cube—with whom the group has been jockeying for authenticity—attended technical college in Tucson, Arizona. Although Ice Cube, as a matter of principle, still maintains a residence in South Central L.A., the other members of N.W.A. allegedly moved to the affluent precincts of Riverside. No matter though, for despite our wariness of Establishment marketing, GenXers gladly suspend disbelief for the voice of the Other—making *Efil4zaggin* #1 on the *Billboard* charts within its first week of release, with no radio airplay.

IT'S THE HYPERREAL THING

Frederic Jameson calls postmodernism "the cultural logic of late capitalism," and given the economic signals of the past year, it may be *too late* for capitalism, period. Yet the stewards of its rhetoric—advertising execs and their braintrust—have, in many cases, adopted a more sophisticated self-referential strategy that verges on the parodic. The ad industry's late-breaking comprehension of the pomo condition has led to its inevitable end: the deconstruction of artifice and the emergence of a long-buried truth—*the commodity is the only real thing in this society of simulacra.*

From the Coca-Cola Company, the original purveyors of "the Real Thing," the new Sprite ad with MacCaulay Culkin exemplifies this wink, wink "Hey, we know" strategy. In the TV ad, chicken porn refugee Culkin sits in front of a house with his prepube paramour, who is leaning over to kiss him. With a "silly rabbit" smile, he reveals "I'm not really your boyfriend, I'm an actor. And this house isn't real, it's a set." He pushes over the facade, revealing a cluttered soundstage. Persisting in the deconstruction, Culkin says "And these aren't your parents, they're just extras" as the girl's "parents" are shown at their backstage makeup mirrors. He offers her a Sprite from a conveniently placed cooler as consolation for her punctured reality. "The only things that aren't fake are you, me, and Sprite," he says comfortingly. Then, in a final sinister twist that confirms the primacy of advertising, the girl morphs into a cardboard simulation and is whisked away by a stagehand, leaving the sempiternal Sprite as the only remnant of reality.

There may still be hope. As pomo Jeremiad slanger Jean Baudrillard maintains in his otherwise bleak vision of a society that has lost all connection to the "real," "Irony preserves what little reality the world has." And, as we all know, irony is the Xer's true birthright.

I'd like to give a shout out to all the folx in the Generation X Conference on The WELL, hosted by your friendly neighborhood irony mongers Jeffrey McManus and Cynsa "heh" Bonorris. Type "go genx" at the OK prompt (genx@well.sf.ca.us). Thanks to Adbusters *magazine for the tasty Proctor & Gamble CEO quote. Sporadically published but perfect fare for Mondoids,* Adbusters *deconstructs images and slogans and delightfully skewers the American advertising machine.*

GENXPLOITATION

When you get quoted in *Sassy*, and your Boomer Editor-in-Chief gets interviewed as an "expert on twentysomethings," it's time to do some direct marketing. According to several recent articles in business trade journals, GenXers are hungry for "money, power, and status." Who am I to argue? "What's in it for me?" Damn straight. I want it all. I'm going to milk this media virus for all the coke, limos, and airtime I can get my selfish little hands on.

Like the noble protagonist of Mark Leyner's *Et Tu Babe*, I want to command a guerrilla media machine, a crack team of Valvoline-smooth agents dedicated to the promotion and proliferation of my image as the ultimate GenXer. In a refurbished gymnasium designed to my specifications, I will keep representatives of the national media like a harem of parasites. Surrounded by 52″ RCA Home Projection Theatres pumping glorious Technicolor reels of my every action, they will genuflect and cluck—eagerly awaiting the next kernel of information issued from my Media War Room. I will charge exorbitant consulting fees for week-long seminars in which I school top advertising agencies in how to capture the slippery GenX consumer. Legions of sniveling Boomer yes-men will tail me as I tour my compound in a custom E-Z Boy golf cart, collecting the note cards on which I scribble new buzzwords and virus ideas.

In this information economy, airtime is power, viral disinformation is a Gold Card, and getting coverage is getting head. Quality is irrelevant—ask Madonna's accountant. Pressing the flesh has been replaced by fleshing the press. Bill Clinton's populism is a media virus, propagated by countless glad-handing photo ops and televised "town meetings." Ross Perot *is* a media virus. Their success is due to their ability to ride the mediasphere like a pliant lover. It's time for me to follow suit. Information may *want* to be free, but I want dead presidents up front for options on *my* information. Finally, Boomer media jockeys are pimping someone other than their own kind, but they're *clueless*. They'll buy every scrap of psychographic info you care to provide. Don't be a dork—righteous purism is a tired 60's conceit. Feed the piranhas . . . just make sure you get the royalties.

Face the muzak—it's impossible to retain integrity in the information economy. If you don't sell your "counterculture" image, someone else will. Within six months you'll find your cherished individual "lifestyle" plastered on billboards pushing blue jeans and wine coolers. Ever since the Situationists, we've known that the culture machine will eventually integrate even the most radical acts and slap a clearance sale price tag on it. Sure, you can move on—strive to "find the next edge" when Marky Mark cops a Prince Albert to improve his market share. But there's no scorched earth strategy in this war, d00d, they'll always be just a sitcom pilot away from your "hip scene." Stop bitching about the stacked deck that Boomers have left you, because they're beginning to play right into your hands. They want to know what makes you *tick*, so they can sell it back to you through ads, TV shows, movies, and manufactured entertainers. Of course, you won't *buy* any of the stuff, but *someone* will. There's always those mall-lemmings who made Vanilla Ice a platinum commodity. You'll just kick back and count your consulting fees.

You can't leave it to Beaver anymore. Already your straighter siblings are stealing the spotlight. *U.S. News & World Report* recently did a cover story on the "Twentysomething Rebellion." Dispelling the "apathy myth" by citing examples of several altruistic young go-getters, it proclaimed us the "Repair Generation." PUHLEEZE. These people are wannaboomers. Brimming with youthful idealism, they want to change the world by helping others. They probably hum "C'mon people now, smile on your brother . . ." as they strap on their liberation jumpsuits every morning. They don't even *whine*, ferchrissake. Gak! Pass the 40.

This same article begins by stating that "Twentysomethings are a generation in need of a press agent." Horse-puckies. We've already got plenty—witness the deluge of articles, ads, and TV shows vainly attempting to describe us. It's enough to make me wanna score a Beemer and start working on a cellular phone tumor. Problem is, we're letting opportunistic Boomers be our press agents, while we bitch and moan about unemployment and the violation of our precious "lifestyle." Wake up and smell the Starbucks.

This is our 15 minutes of fame. Sell out while you still have the chance. When the GenX media virus runs its course (as all do), you'll still be stuck in that McJob collecting interest on irony bonds. Graying Boomers will still be gathering cobwebs in middle management, preventing *you* from getting anywhere. After all, it's attention that we've wanted all along—approval from our elder siblings. Culture Inc. is finally bent over on the stretcher, eagerly accepting our penetration. Seize the media by the hips and take the plunge.

Grateful acknowledgment is made to Michael Krantz for additional research, and to the following for permission to reprint previously published material:

Chapter 1: Here We Are
Douglas Coupland—Interview in *Elle* Magazine
This article first appeared in the September 1993 issue of *Elle* Magazine. Copyright © *Elle* Magazine U.S.A.

Shampoo Planet—**Douglas Coupland**
Copyright © 1992 by Douglas Campbell Coupland. Reprinted by permission of Pocket Books, a division of Simon & Schuster, Inc.

Twentysomething—Jefferson Morley
Copyright © 1988 Jefferson Morley
First appeared in Washington *City Paper*, February 19–25, 1988.

Slacker—**Richard Linklater**
Slacker by Richard Linklater, copyright © 1992 by Richard Linklater. Reprinted by permission of St. Martin's Press, Inc. New York, NY.

Richard Linklater—Interview in *bOING! bOING!*
Richard Linklater interview by Carla Sinclair and Jon Lebkowski. Reprinted by permission of Carla Sinclair.

Whatever—Mark Saltveit
Copyright © 1994 by Mark Saltveit. All rights reserved.

Chapter 2: Legacy
Bradymania!—Elizabeth Moran in *Teenage Gang Debs*
Reprinted by permission of Elizabeth Moran.

Pagan Kennedy—My Religious Energy Crisis
From *Platforms* by Pagan Kennedy. Copyright © 1994 by Pagan Kennedy, St. Martin's Press, Inc., New York, NY.

Life in Hell—Matt Groening
From *Work is Hell* © 1986 by Matt Groening. All Rights Reserved. Reprinted by permission of Pantheon Books, a division of Random House, NY.

Classic Rock—Julian Dibble in *Details*
"Classic Rock" by Julian Dibbell. *Details*, July 1991. Reprinted by permission of Julian Dibbell.

Chapter 3: Truth, Justice, and the American Way
The End of Progress?—Eric Liu
Reprinted from *The Next Progressive*, Spring 1993. Copyright © The Next Progressive, 1993. Eric Liu is founding editor of *The Next Progressive*, a journal of opinion produced by men and women in their twenties.

Lead or Leave—Invest in the Future
Reprinted by permission of Lead or Leave.

Katie Roiphe—*The Morning After*
From *The Morning After* by Katie Roiphe, copyright © 1993 by Katherine Roiphe. Reprinted by permission of Little, Brown and Company.

Ice Cube—Cheo H. Coker for *The Source*
Copyright © Cheo H. Coker, 1994. "Down for Whatever" originally appeared in *The Source* magazine's February 1994 issue, and is reprinted by permission of *The Source*.

Strength through Apathy—Douglas Rushkoff
Copyright © 1990 Douglas Rushkoff.

Wiley Wiggins—*Happy!*
Reprinted by permission of Wiley Wiggins.

Chapter 4: The Dregs
Walter Kirn—Can't Get Started
Reprinted by permission of Walter Kirn.

Bruce Craven—*Fast Sofa*
Copyright © 1993 by Bruce Craven. Reprinted by permission of William Morrow and Co., Inc.

Darius James—*Negrophobia*
From *Negrophobia: An Urban Parable* by Darius James. Copyright © 1992 by Darius James. Published by arrangement with Carol Publishing Group. A Citadel Press Book.

Hate—**Peter Bagge**
"Whatever Happened to Babs Bradley" is copyright © 1994 Peter Bagge; from the *Hey, Buddy!* book collection, published by Fantagraphics Books.

Eightball—**Dan Clowes**
"The Party" is copyright © 1994 Daniel Clowes; from *Eightball* #11, published by Fantagraphics Books.

bOING! bOING!—**Mark Frauenfelder Reports from Toys "Я" Us**
"Toys 'Я' Us" by Mark Frauenfelder reprinted by permission of Mark Frauenfelder.

Chapter 5: Metamedia
***Ren & Stimpy*—Dan Persons Analyzes "Stimpy's Invention"**
Copyright © 1993 by Dan Persons.

Beavis and Butt-head—A *Rolling Stone* Interview by Charles M. Young
From "The Voice of a New Generation" by Charles M. Young from *Rolling Stone*, August 19, 1993. Copyright © by Straight Arrow Publishers, Inc. 1993. All Rights Reserved. Reprinted by Permission.

Seize the Media—The Immediast Underground
No copyright; 1992. Public Domain.

Mark Kriegel—Fear and Loathing in Atlanta
Copyright © *New York Daily News*. Reprinted by permission.

Seven Days and Seven Nights Alone with MTV—Hugh Gallagher's Experiment in Terror
Reprinted by permission of the William Morris Agency, Inc. on behalf of the Author. Copyright © Hugh Gallagher.

Chapter 6: Ranting
The GenX Computer Conference—People Try to Put Us Down
Responses reprinted by permission of the participants. The GenX Conference appears on the WELL, well@well.sf.ca.us.

The *I Hate Brenda Newsletter*—Slamming Shannen Doherty
Excerpts from the *I Hate Brenda Newsletter*, copyright © 1993 *Ben Is Dead* magazine.

R. U. Sirius—There's No Such Thing as An Original Debt: A Message of Hope to the So-called Generation X
Copyright © Ken Goffman, 1994.

Maggie Estep—Humping Hilda
Reprinted by permission of Maggie Estep

The Whiny Generation—David Martin's Anti-Rant for *Newsweek*
From David Martin's "My Turn" column in *Newsweek*, November 1, 1993. Copyright © 1993, Newsweek, Inc. All rights reserved. Reprinted by permission.

Chapter 7: Raving
Rave On!—Jody Radzik in *Raygun*
Reprinted by permission of Jody Radzik.

Earth Girl—This Is the Dawning
Earth Girl's responses are gratefully used by permission of Earth Girl.

***URB* Magazine—I, Ambient by Meredith Chinn and Todd C. Roberts**
"I, Ambient" by Todd C. Roberts and Meredith Chinn as appeared in *URB* magazine, December 1993, pp. 52–56.

The Night Before Jesus Woke Up—A Transmission from 3393
Reprinted by permission of the author.

***Probability Pipeline*—Marc Laidlaw and Rudy Rucker**
Copyright © 1988 by Rudy Rucker and Marc Laidlaw. First appeared in *Synergy 2*. Reprinted by permission of the authors.

Chapter 8: GenXploitation
Generalization X—Nathaniel Wice.
Reprinted by permission of Nathaniel Wice. Copyright © 1993 by Nathaniel Wice.

The X Factor—Debra Goldman in *Adweek*
Copyright © *Adweek* Magazine

The New Generation Gap—Neil Howe and William Strauss for *The Atlantic*
Excerpt from "The New Generation Gap" by Neil Howe and William Strauss reprinted from *The Atlantic*, December 1992. Howe and Strauss are the authors of *13th Gen*, Vintage Books, 1993.

The Slacker Factor—Andrew Hultkrans for *Mondo 2000*
By Andrew Hultkrans. Originally appeared in *Mondo 2000*, Issues #9 and #10, as "Genexploitation" and "Pumping the Reality Principle."

ABOUT THE AUTHOR

DOUGLAS RUSHKOFF is the first mainstream writer to cover topics like virtual reality, cyberpunks, the psychadelic revival, and rave culture. His articles have appeared in *GQ*, *Us*, *Vibe*, *The Miami Herald*, *The Wall Street Journal*, and *The Boston Globe*. He is the author of the forthcoming *Media Virus!: Hidden Agendas in Popular Culture* and *Cyberia: Life in the Trenches of Hyperspace*, and was Politics Editor of *Exposure* magazine in Los Angeles. He lives in New York City.